FROM PROHIBITED IMMIGRANTS TO CITIZENS

The origins of citizenship and nationality in South Africa

FROM PROHIBITED IMMIGRANTS TO CITIZENS

The origins of citizenship and nationality in South Africa

Jonathan Klaaren

From Prohibited Immigrants to Citizens:
The origins of citizenship and nationality in South Africa

First edition 2017

by UCT Press, an imprint of
Juta and Company (Pty) Ltd
PO Box 14373, Lansdowne 7779, Cape Town, South Africa
www.uctpress.co.za

© 2017 Jonathan Klaaren

ISBN 978 1 77582 209 7 (print)
ISBN 978 1 77582 228 8 (Web PDF)

All rights reserved. No part of this publication may be reproduced or transmitted in any form or by any means, electronic or mechanical, including photocopying, recording, or any information storage or retrieval system, without prior permission in writing from the publisher. Subject to any applicable licensing terms and conditions in the case of electronically supplied publications, a person may engage in fair dealing with a copy of this publication for his or her personal or private use, or his or her research or private study. See section 12(1)(a) of the Copyright Act 98 of 1978.

Project manager: Debbie Pienaar/Mmakasa Ramoshaba
Editor: Denise Fourie
Proofreader: Rae Dalton
Cover designer: Marius Roux
Cover image: Permission granted by Gandhi-Luthuli Documentation Centre
Typesetter: Purple Pocket Solutions
Indexer: Antoinette van Rooyen

Typeset in 11 pt on 14pt Minion Pro

The author and the publisher believe on the strength of due diligence exercised that this work does not contain any material that is the subject of copyright held by another person. In the alternative, they believe that any protected pre-existing material that may be comprised in it has been used with appropriate authority or has been used in circumstances that make such use permissible under the law.

This book has been independently peer-reviewed by academics who are experts in the field.

Contents

Acknowledgements	vii
List of legislation	ix
Glossary	xiii
Chapter 1: South African citizenship in context	1
Building a population	3
Migration and mobility studies	5
The development of South Africa's legal culture	8
The structure of this book	11
Chapter 2: Early practices of regulating mobility	14
Early mobility regimes directed at Asians: Population registration	16
Migration regulation of Indians in Natal	16
Migration regulation of Indians in the Transvaal	21
Migration regulation of Indians in the Orange Free State	27
The Cape Colony and regulation of the Chinese	28
Early mobility regimes directed at Africans: Pre-Union pass laws	30
Laws affecting African mobility in the Cape	32
Laws on African mobility in Natal	34
African mobility regulation in the Transvaal and Orange Free State	34
The Chinese mine-labour scheme	39
Conclusion	46
Chapter 3: The rise of borders	47
Immigration laws of the Cape	48
Laws pertaining to nationality in the Cape and Natal	51
Immigration and related legislation in the Transvaal	54
Citizenship and nationality in the Transvaal	60
Immigration and related legislation in the Orange Free State	60
Conclusion	62
Chapter 4: Union, the Act and the Registrar of Asiatics, 1907–1914	64
Economic and political unification	65
Union nationality and immigration laws	75

The Registrar of Asiatics and the Act 87
Conclusion 93

Chapter 5: Nationalisation of the immigration bureaucracy, 1914–1927. 95
The nationalisation of migration administration 96
The immigration bureaucracy and the development of the rule of law 101
The establishment of the Commissioner for Immigration and Asiatic
  Affairs 111
Conclusion 116

Chapter 6: African mobility and bureaucracy, 1911–1927 118
Two approaches for regulating extra-Union Africans 119
The rise of an internal boundary 129
Conclusion 134

Chapter 7: The Commissioner's population, 1927–1937 136
The restriction of mobility and a nationalised population 136
The 1933 repeal of the Chinese Exclusion Act 143
Conclusion 151

Chapter 8: One official South Africa 152
An official problem but differing solutions 153
An official solution 164
An official failure 172
Conclusion 183

Chapter 9: Enacting nationality, 1927–1937 185
The inauguration of Union nationality 188
The Acts of 1930–1931 and population regulation 194
The Acts of 1937 and population regulation 199
Conclusion 208

Chapter 10: South African citizenship and the way forward 210
Post-apartheid contestations of South African citizenship 212
Contemporary South African citizenship policy 219
Reflections on the new South African immigration politics: Towards
  Afropolitan denizenship? 222

Bibliography 229
Index 239

Acknowledgements

I have incurred a number of debts in the writing of this book. I am grateful for funding provided by the National Research Foundation and the Friedel Sellschop Award of the University of the Witwatersrand. Sandy Shepherd and her team of persons coordinated through UCT Press have been very facilitative, e-mail friendly and of great assistance in making this monograph better through the editing and production process. David Dickinson, many of my Law School colleagues and others at the University of the Witwatersrand have endured many friendly talks about this book for a long time. Many of my colleagues at WiSER have particularly influenced and assisted me – including Keith Breckenridge, Achille Mbembe and Debbie Posel. A special mention must be made of Isabel Hofmeyr, who has the prized ability to perceive the best in someone's work. My thanks to all. My primary debt is owed to Pippa Reyburn, who has given me the space, time and support to finish this book. Perhaps our children, Jessica and Rebecca, will one day read it.

This book is dedicated to my parents, Eugene and Mary Klaaren.

List of Legislation

South African (Union and Republic) legislation
Admission of Persons to the Union Regulation Amendment Act
   60 of 1961 2
Aliens Act 1 of 1937 .... 185, 195, 200, 203
Asiatics in the Northern Districts of Natal Act 33 of 1927 .... 139, 140
British Nationality in the Union and Naturalization and Status
   of Aliens Act 18 of 1926 .... 185, 189, 200
Constitution of the Republic of South Africa, Act 200 of 1993 ..... 209, 211
Constitution of the Republic of South Africa, 1996 .... 1, 2, 213, 214,
                                                                                        215, 217, 218, 219
Immigrants Regulation Act 22 of 1913 .... 2, 27, 47, 64 65, 76, 77, 80, 81,
Immigrants Restriction Act was another name for the Immigrants
   Regulation Act 22 of 1913 ... 82, 83, 87, 88, 96, 97, 98, 103, 119, 123, 127,
                           131, 135, 136, 138, 139, 141, 149, 150, 162, 173, 181,
                               182, 185, 193, 194, 195, 196, 197, 199, 203, 204
Immigration (Amendment) Act 15 of 1931 .... 19, 140, 141, 185, 197, 199
Immigration (Amendment) Act 19 of 1933 (Union) 30, 156, 187, 200
Immigration Act 13 of 2002 221
Immigration Amendment Act 27 of 1937 .... 185, 202, 203, 204
Immigration and Indian Relief (Further Provision) Act 37 of 1927 137,
                                                                                        138, 145, 147, 148
Immigration Quota Act 8 of 1930 .... 149, 185, 196
Indian Laws Amendment Act 68 of 1963 18
Indians Relief Act 22 of 1914 .... 79, 83, 84, 136, 145
Nationalization and Amnesty Act 14 of 1932 198
Native Labour Regulation Act 15 of 1911 .... 65, 87, 119, 120
Native Laws Amendment Act 46 of 1937 Act 186, 201, 205
Natives Act 31 of 1917 161
Natives Urban Areas Act 21 of 1923 .... 132, 134, 181, 185, 186, 201, 205
Naturalization of Aliens Act 4 of 1910 .... 64, 75
Refugees Act 130 of 1998 50

Social Assistance Act 59 of 1992 213
South Africa Act, 1909 .... 67, 71, 72, 73, 74, 75
South African Citizenship Act 44 of 1949 188
South African Citizenship Act 88 of 1995 221
South West Africa Naturalization of Aliens Act 30 of 1924 97
Union Nationality and Flags Act 40 of 1927 .... 185, 189, 191, 192, 204

Cape
Act 22 of 1867 (Cape) 174
Act 23 of 1879 (Cape) 32
Act 30 of 1895 (Cape) 33
Act 35 of 1889 (Cape) 51
Act 40 of 1902 (Cape) 33
Aliens Naturalisation Act 2 of 1883 (Cape) 51
Chinese Exclusion Act 37 of 1904 (Cape) 28, 29, 51, 143
Immigration Act 30 of 1906 (Cape) 48, 77
Immigration Act 47 of 1902 (Cape) 48

Natal
Act 17 of 1895 (Natal) 20, 84
Act 18 of 1905 (Natal) 54
Act 19 of 1898 (Natal) 20, 21
Act 2 of 1870 (Natal) 17
Act 2 of 1903 (Natal) 84
Act 28 of 1897 (Natal) 20, 139, 149
Act 39 of 1905 (Natal) 21, 84
Act 5 of 1906 29
Act 7 of 1904 (Natal) 42, 43
Coolie Law Consolidation Law of 1869 17
Immigrants Restriction Act 1 of 1897 (Natal) 11, 12, 51, 52
Immigration Law 1 of 1876 (Natal) 86
Immigration Restriction Act 30 of 1903 (Natal) 52, 53, 77
Indian Immigration Act 25 of 1891 (Natal) 17, 20, 99
Indian Immigration Law 25 of 1891 (Natal) 99
Natal Act of 1888 42
Law 8 of 1874 54
Proclamation 70 of 1904 43

List of Legislations

Orange Free State
A Law To Provide Against the Influx of Asiatics and for the Removal of White Criminals Entering This State from Elsewhere (1891) 27
Admission and Expulsion of Aliens To or From the Orange Free State Law 18 of 1899 (Free State) 60, 77
Immorality Ordinance 59
Indemnity and Peace Preservation Ordinance 25 of 1902 (High Commissioner) 62
Naturalization of Aliens (Amendment) Ordinance 10 of 1904 (High Commissioner) 60
Naturalization of Aliens Ordinance 1 of 1903 (High Commissioner) 62
Orange Free State Ordinance 28 of 1903 39

Transvaal
Act 18 of 1909 (Transvaal) 38
Act 9 of 1908 (Transvaal) 38
Asiatic Law Amendment Act 2 of 1907 (Transvaal) 24, 26, 27, 57, 58
Asiatics Registration Amendment Act 36 of 1908 (Transvaal) 26, 83, 138, 139
Gold Law 14 of 1894 (Transvaal) 35
Immigrants Restriction Act 15 of 1907 (Transvaal) 24, 27, 55, 57, 59, 60, 70, 77
Immorality Ordinance 59
Indentured Labour Laws (Temporary Continuance) Act of 1907 45
Indemnity and Peace Preservation Ordinance 25 of 1902 (High Commissioner) 62
Indemnity and Peace Preservation Ordinance 38 of 1902 55
Law 22 of 1895 (Transvaal) 35
Law 3 of 1872 (Transvaal) 34
Law 3 of 1885 (Transvaal) 21, 22, 23, 26, 27, 55, 60
Ordinance 28 of 1902 (High Commissioner) 38
Peace Preservation Ordinance 5 of 1903 (High Commissioner) 55
Proclamation 18 of 1903 38
Proclamation 19 of 1901 (High Commissioner) 38
Proclamation 35 of 1901 (High Commissioner) 38
Proclamation 37 of 1901 (High Commissioner) 38

Foreign Legislation
Trinidad Immigration Ordinance of 1893 42

South African Policy Documents
Department of Home Affairs on International Migration, March 2017
....210, 219, 220, 221, 222

Glossary

As a colleague of mine has noted, nomenclature is often difficult and complex. Many terms that were used historically may cause great offence in the present day. This may be especially so for terms, such as many of those in this book, which were used by people to identify themselves as well as for those terms which were used by others to identify groups of people. The terms for various political entities — such as a colony or a province — may also be complex and difficult. In this book, I have chosen to use terms in their historical context and do not generally use inverted commas to indicate that use. Where changes occured the change in the use of terms is often explained in the test. This glossary together with the text aims to assist in explaining the meaning of those terms. For the territorial terms, the glossary is based upon WPM Kennedy and HJ Schlosberg, *The Law and Custom of the South African Constitution: A Treatise on the Constitutional and Administrative Law of the Union of South Africa, the Mandated Territory of South-West Africa, and the South African Crown Territories* (London: Oxford University Press, 1935) and Martin Chanock, *Unconsummated Union: Britain, Rhodesia and South Africa, 1900-45* (Manchester University Press, 1977). For the identification terms, the glossary is based on John Dugard, *Human Rights and the South African Legal Order* (Princeton University Press, 1978) and Sally Peberdy, *Selecting Immigrants: National Identity and South Africa's Immigration Policies, 1910-2008* (Wits University Press, 2009) as well as AJ Christopher, 'Delineating the Nation: South African Censuses 1865–2007,' Political Geography 28, no. 2 (February 2009): 101–9.

Categories of people
African — black people whether born in South Africa, Africa or elsewhere; often referred to as 'natives' in South Africa legislation.
Asian — people born in Asia or of Asian descent in South Africa, including but not limited to Indian and Chinese people.

Asiatic — term often used in Natal and Union legislation to refer to Indian and to Asian people; often considered prerogative; used by the Minister of the Interior in 1913 in declaring 'every Asiatic person' to be a prohibited immigrant; popularly understood to refer to Asians of colour.

Chinese — people born in China or of Chinese descent in South Africa.

Coloured — people of mixed race born in South Africa.

European — white people whether born in South Africa, Africa or elsewhere.

Indian — from the second half of the 1800s, a term used in South African legislation to refer to all people immigrating to Natal from India in terms of legislation specifically regulating such immigration and to the descendants in Natal of such persons to Natal; later, a term that described the population of all people of Indian descent in South Africa, including those formerly described as Asiatics.

Territories

Barotseland-North-Western Rhodesia — a British territory, administered by the British South African Company from 1899, with the potential to join the Union of South Africa in terms of section 150 of the Union of South Africa Act, 1909, it formed part of Northern Rhodesia in 1911.

Basutoland — a British High Commission Territory annexed to the Cape Colony from 1871-1884, with the potential to join the Union of South Africa in terms of section 151 of the South Africa Act, 1909, it became the independent Kingdom of Lesotho in 1966.

Bechuanaland Protectorate — a British High Commission Territory from 1885 with clarification in 1891; a territory with the potential to join the Union of South Africa in terms of section 151 of the South Africa Act, 1909, it became the independent Republic of Botswana in 1966.

British South Africa — prior to 1910, a term used to refer to the High Commission Territories and the British South Africa Company Territories and after 1910 used to refer to the Union, the High Commission Territories and the British South Africa Company Territories.

Cape Colony — also called the Cape of Good Hope, a British colony, it was granted representative government in 1854; it became part of the Union of South Africa in 1910.

Natal Colony — a British territory annexed from 1843, it became a colony in 1847 and was granted representative government in 1856; it became part of the Union of South Africa in 1910.

North Eastern Rhodesia — a British territory, administered by the British South African Company from 1899, with the potential to join the Union of South Africa in terms of section 150 of the South Africa Act, 1909, it formed part of Northern Rhodesia in 1911.

Northern Rhodesia — a British territory, administered by the British South African Company, with the potential to join the Union of South Africa in terms of section 150 of the South Africa Act, 1909, composed of North Eastern Rhodesia and Barotse-North-Western Rhodesia; it became independent Zambia in 1964.

Nyasaland Protectorate — a British territory; it became became independent as Malawi in 1964.

Orange Free State (Oranje Vrij Staat/OFS) — briefly under British sovereignty from 1848, this territory was an independent Boer republic from 1854 to 1901 when it became the Orange River Colony.

Orange River Colony — proclaimed in 1901, formerly the independent Boer republic of Orange Free State, in 1910 it became part of the Union of South Africa.

Portuguese East Africa — a group of Portuguese colonies, some administered by companies, in the territory of the Republic of Mozambique, which became independent in 1975.

South African Republic (Zuid-Afrikaanse Republiek/ZAR) — an independent Boer republic formed from a number of smaller republics in 1858, it was annexed by the British Empire in 1877 with independence restored in 1881; in 1902, it became the Transvaal Colony.

South-West Africa — a German colony until the territory was handed over to the Union in terms of a mandate from the League of Nations; defined as part of Union by e.g. the Union Nationality and Flags Act, 1927.

Southern Rhodesia — a British Territory administered by the British South Africa Company from 1898, with the potential to join the

Union of South Africa in terms of section 150 of the South Africa Act, 1909; it became a colony with representative government in 1923 and the Republic of Zimbabwe in 1980.

Swaziland — a British High Commission Territory since 1906, with the potential to join the Union of South Africa in terms of section 151 of the South Africa Act, 1909, it became the independent Kingdom of Swaziland in 1968.

Transvaal Colony — proclaimed in 1902, formerly the South African Republic, in 1910 it became part of the Union of South Africa

Union of South Africa — formed in 1910 from the Cape Colony, Natal Colony, the Orange River Colony and the Transvaal Colony; it was composed of four provinces: Cape of Good Hope, Natal, Orange Free State and the Transvaal; it became the Republic of South Africa in 1961.

CHAPTER 1

South African citizenship in context

We, the people of South Africa ... believe that South Africa belongs to all who live within it, united in our diversity.

Preamble to the 1996 Constitution (South Africa)

This Bill of Rights is a cornerstone of democracy in South Africa. It enshrines the rights of all people in our country and affirms the democratic values of human dignity, equality and freedom.

Section 7(1) of the 1996 Constitution (South Africa)

INTRODUCTION

This book is about the past, but like all books it is written in the present. Twenty years ago, in 1996, the then-new Constitution of post-apartheid South Africa was viewed at home and worldwide as a wonderful achievement. At the time of this book being published, questions are being raised in the public sphere about the adequacy and fit of that Constitution to the current South African national order. Are all persons in South Africa truly treated as constitutional citizens and do they all enjoy and exercise their full rights, fulfilling the new Constitution's promise of equality? Is the constitutional project threatened by continued denial of these rights and the need to acknowledge the apartheid experience?[1] Is the Constitution itself irretrievably compromised?[2]

---

1 Klug, 2013.
2 Sibanda, 2011; 2017.

This book is not about those interesting questions — though the conclusion, 'South African citizenship and the way forward', will bring a historical perspective to bear on the present. Instead, this book goes back more than 100 years. It is about the making of an earlier South African constitutional citizenship — a citizenship with a racially unequal and substantively warped nature — in a process that was centrally concerned with regulating the movement of people within a defined territory. This process was concluded six decades before the post-apartheid Constitution. So, the questions that lie at the heart of the chapters that follow are when and how the South African population itself became constituted as something more than individuals living in a certain space, even if this constituted population was not yet a people. Where did South Africa's pre-constitutional citizenship — the one that apartheid ministers and bureaucrats from the mid to late twentieth century tried to warp and pervert but nonetheless around which they had to navigate — come from?

One of the tragedies of apartheid was its sustained and express attempt to make indigenous South African citizens foreigners in their own land.[3] The story of this book is the making of the citizenship of all South Africans in the first place. I argue that South African citizens were made from prohibited immigrants from 1897 to 1937 by the regulation of the mobility of three population groups — African, Asian and European — each faced with initially different and separate schemes of control over their mobility. Drawing on pre-existing provincial laws dating from as far back as 1897, the Immigrants Regulation Act 22 of 1913 declared certain categories of persons 'prohibited immigrants'. (It was not until 1961, in section 2 of the Admission of Persons to the Union Regulation Act 60 of 1961 that Parliament substituted the term 'prohibited persons' for 'prohibited immigrants' throughout the South African statute book.)

The story I tell starts in 1897 in pre-Union Natal with South Africa's first comprehensive immigration law — a law controlling the movement of black Africans, Asians and Europeans within one conceptual framework. It ends in 1937 with Parliament entrenching

---

3   Budlender, 1985.

a regime of control at South Africa's borders, subject to the right of permanent residence for all South African citizens (then termed 'Union nationals'). I also argue that the regulation and administration of the Asian population in the bureaucracy that is the direct predecessor of the current Department of Home Affairs provided the key platform for the conceptual elaboration and consolidation of the official vision of a unified although structurally unequal South African population.

BUILDING A POPULATION

How to tell an origins story? Especially in a study of the formation of citizenship, the identity and understanding of a political community cannot be assumed but must be explained. Focusing on the interaction between political elites and their publics, Rogers Smith explains citizenship laws by exploring what he terms 'the politics of people-building'.[4] According to Smith, the legal concept of citizenship assumes a collective political identity or a political peoplehood. To explain this political peoplehood, he proposes a theory of the politics of people-building, which identifies stories that inspire both trust and worth. Smith argues that 'enduring successful accounts of peoplehood inspire senses of trust and worth among the members of a people by weaving together economic [stories], political power [stories], and constitutive stories tailored to persuade a critical mass of constituents.'[5]

Smith describes people-building using rigorous social science. However, although his approach has been appreciated, he and others have been criticised by those who argue that it is a short step from such an account to a redemptive and teleological narrative, in which successively inclusive people-building becomes tightly identified with a national redemptive myth.[6] In explicit contrast to Smith, recent work on the history of citizenship has argued strongly for the worth of non-redemptive and indeed explicitly negative accounts of citizenship. Such an approach, employed by scholars such as Kunal Parker, focuses on the historical construction of the distinction between the citizen and the

---

4 Smith, 2001.
5 Ibid.
6 Parker, 2015.

immigrant,[7] arguing that it is an important corrective to the implicit redemptive narrative of inclusionary and people-building accounts of citizenship.[8] There is much to be said for such an avowedly neutral approach to the history of citizenship.

The school of African post-colonial studies emphasises the worth of examining the structures of domination critically and at historical depth. In his call for a re-examination and historicisation of European concepts such as 'civil society' (at least before their deployment in the African context), Achille Mbembe provides a view of boundaries and territoriality in Africa that highlights their historicity as well as their non-colonial aspects.[9] In a similar vein, Gary Wilder has given new texture to the idea of African citizenship by examining its relationship to imperial history.[10] For Wilder,[11]

> [r]ather than debate whether colonial citizenship entailed actual political rights or whether it was an empty ideological abstraction, I suggest we understand it, to use Marxian language, as a real abstraction. In other words, colonial citizenship may not have ensured liberty and equality for subject populations, but as a juridico-political status and object of struggle it opened a space from which colonial citizens could make historically significant claims on liberty and equality.

Generative as it is, the post-colonial school does not have an adequate concept of a 'population'. Deborah Posel provides a possible explanation for this lack in her work which describes the rise of the use of measurement data in modern South Africa.[12] Posel's study, which explores some of the scientific discourse that underpins the transition to apartheid, also discusses the concept of 'population' within the rise of modernity. She argues that the production and storage of social

---

7 Ibid.
8 Smith, 1997.
9 Mbembé, 2001.
10 Wilder, 1999.
11 Ibid.
12 Posel, 2000.

quanta (data) were increasingly routinised within the segregationist South African state, even though they were piecemeal and modest in comparison with later apartheid statistical work. Posel makes the significant argument that in South Africa the problematic of a 'population' did not succeed the problematic of a 'people' (as Foucault had argued was the case for Western society), but rather that these two problematics coexisted and intersected. My book fits within Posel's argument, linking the process and politics of building a people with the process and politics of building a population.[13] I present the historical context of South African citizenship and its role in the construction of the South African population.

MIGRATION AND MOBILITY STUDIES

By no means is this book an attempt to tell the history and founding myth of the South African nation. Instead, I present two arguments explaining the make-up of South African citizenship. First, I examine the regulation of people's mobility as a key practice in the formation of the South African population. The African pass laws, which restricted the movement of black South Africans, have long been recognised as a tool of apartheid, but control over human mobility was equally, if not more, significant in the formation of South Africa and South African citizenship. While migration status may have been (and often was) a tool or marker of oppression, it was often at the same time a marker of inclusion. To have a status was to be visible. Even to be an extra-Union 'native' or an 'Asiatic' (terms that today would be taboo) was to be given certain rights of legality in terms of official policy and were labels positively desired and actively sought by some.

This book fits within an area of scholarship known as mobility studies. The growing body of work that problematises the meaning of South Africa has not as yet directly grappled with migration regulation.[14] This study thus builds on and extends earlier Southern African studies around questions of mobility. Among those regarding the African

---

13   Smith, 2001.
14   Dubow, 2006.

population and prefiguring more contemporary work,[15] Patrick Harries's study of migrant labourers in Mozambique and South Africa from 1860 to 1910 argues that mobility was a useful resource available to these travelling labourers initially allowing them to negotiate with mine bosses on the Witwatersrand.[16] Indian migrants to South Africa have been extensively studied,[17] perhaps most prominently by Uma Dhupelia-Mesthrie, who has explored the kinds of employment Indian immigrants found in Cape Town and the severe effects of the permit system and immigration laws on their free mobility.[18] Sally Peberdy, in her excellent study, looks at immigration controls that were applied to immigrants who claimed to be European, from 1910 to post-apartheid days.[19]

While more celebrated for its theory than as a mobility study, Posel's groundbreaking work, *The making of apartheid*, on the development of apartheid policy from 1948 to 1961, covers the empirical nature of control over the movement of people. Posel makes her broader argument regarding the uneven character of the apartheid state on the basis of material in this area of state policy.[20] Studying the policy and practice of influx control in the early phase of apartheid, Posel argues that apartheid was not in origin a single, simple, coherent plan — capitalist interests too were fundamental in shaping apartheid — but full of contradictions, and provided an autonomous role for the state. My study, falling broadly within the theoretical paradigm of Posel's work, tackles the topic of the regulation of mobility as it unfolded in the decades prior to her work.

Scholarly interest and engagement with globalisation generally and specifically with questions around the rise of citizenships and borders have recently surged.[21] An example is the recent work of Adam McKeown, who traces the global history of regulating identification and practices of border control.[22] Neither concept is inherent in sovereignty.

---

15 Vigneswaran and Quirk, 2015.
16 Barnes, 1997; Harries, 1994; Hindson, 1987.
17 Bhana and Brain, 1990.
18 Dhupelia-Mesthrie, 2009.
19 Peberdy, 2009.
20 Posel, 1991.
21 Dauvergne, 2005; Klotz, 2016; Torpey, 2000.
22 Huttenback, 1976; McKeown, 2008.

Rather, they have, as McKeown shows, a particular history which stems from efforts by white settler nations, including Australia, Canada, South Africa and the United States, to regulate Asian migration. Indeed, McKeown's story has a major episode with a storyline that begins in South Africa. The development of discretionary literacy tests — starting with an English-language immigration test implemented by Natal and termed the 'Natal formula' — was an early example of the practice of border control, and an important precursor to the elaboration and diffusion of border controls across the world from 1907 to 1939.[23]

My second argument is that the regulation of the mobility of the Asian population in South Africa had at least as much influence on the development of the concept of citizenship as did the regulation of the European and African populations. While the force and effect of Asian migration on phenomena such as the rise of borders is increasingly acknowledged globally in the work of scholars such as McKeown,[24] its effect on South Africa in the reaction to the wave of migration from India in the 1880s, the struggle to enact the Immigrants Regulation Act of 1913 after Union, and the later acceptance by the Union of the permanent residence status of those of Indian origin staying in South Africa in the 1920s and 1930s, has not yet taken its rightful place in South African historiography.[25]

There are at least two exceptions, however. Martin Chanock's groundbreaking study of the legal culture of this period lays the foundation. He specifies the stratum of legal culture in South Africa at this time (discussed below) and points to the significant role played by Asians in the development of that culture.[26] As he pointed out, 'because Asians could not, like Africans, be relegated to a different legal regime, but had to be discriminated against within and by the ordinary law, they posed many of the most difficult problems to South African lawyers.' Without justifying the substance of such discrimination, he is pointing to the significance of its legal form. Audie Klotz uses an international

---

23   Op cit: 185–214.
24   Op cit.
25   Dhupelia-Mesthrie, 2009.
26   Chanock, 2001: 19.

relations perspective, explaining that the roots of contemporary South African xenophobia lie in its economic nationalism from pre-Union times and the weakness of its liberal coalition of advocates for markets and for rights. She foregrounds the role of Asians and the ambiguities of empire.[27]

Apart from these exceptions, the forging of South African citizenship — at the least a baseline for national identity — through the regulation of the mobility of the Asian as well as the European and African populations has not been adequately appreciated. In the formative and largely bureaucratic process covered in this book, the legal, colonial and demographic position of the Asian population has proved particularly significant to the development of South African citizenship.

THE DEVELOPMENT OF SOUTH AFRICA'S LEGAL CULTURE

As a legal academic work, this book undertakes a further task, one that has not been attempted in the current historiography on the formation of South Africa. It traces and provides the legal history of all the mobility-related laws for three constituent South African populations: European, Indian and African. It documents South African immigration legal history from 1897 to 1937. Given today's concerns around attention to mobility and imperial context, this theme of the book will be of significant value to other scholars as well as those wishing to understand the historical roots of South African immigration policy.

The starting place for my enquiry is the laws that regulate movement in South Africa. Any work on legal history in South Africa should begin with Martin Chanock's book, *The making of South African legal culture 1902–1936: Fear, favour and prejudice*. Chanock rightly states that the legal culture of South Africa established in the early decades of the 1900s was dominantly British, although it had, of course, its own particular inflection. His work on legal culture provides an envelope for this book's account of the development of South African citizenship as part of South Africa's legal culture.[28] Audie Klotz also helpfully defines 'legal culture' as 'essentially a set of assumptions that intersect discourse and practice

---

[27] Klotz, 2013.
[28] Chanock, 2001.

via administrative procedures'.[29] In the context of that legal culture, the object of the enquiry for this book — citizenship — is a legal cultural concept itself. In many ways, this concept is covered by the narrower and more doctrinal term 'nationality'. Still, I use the term 'citizenship' in order to recognise the socio-legal and non-doctrinal elements of the development related here. While I examine this development of South African citizenship, I also provide a doctrinal legal history of South African immigration and nationality law itself.[30]

Chanock noted the imperial context and origins of South African legal culture. The context of the British Empire and the comparative law of other British settler and non-settler colonies inheres in a great deal the development of the migration laws considered here.[31] To understand the development of South African citizenship, one must explore the comparative and transnational dimensions of legal culture and practices in the colonies of the British Empire. Indeed, there is a need to integrate historical scholarship on the metropole and the dominions.[32] In these terms, law in these colonies was a grand experiment.[33] This work can thus be seen as part of the move for a new South African colonial history.[34]

It is commonly accepted that South Africans are and have been strictly divided into citizens and subjects throughout the nation's history.[35] This book is a partial correction to that post-independence perspective. I argue that by 1937 there was more than mere legal formalism in the designation of all lawfully resident members of the population as members of a South African population.[36] In this sense, this book provides an account of how the 'South African population' came into existence. In Ivor Chipkin's use of the terms, this account is not about a 'people as datum' but about 'people as political subject'.[37]

---

29 Klotz, 2013: 53.
30 Salyer, 1995.
31 Kirkby and Coleborne, 2001: 230–274.
32 Gorman, 2006.
33 Foster, Berger and Buck, 2009.
34 Evans and Philips, 2001.
35 Mamdani, 1996.
36 Klotz, 2013: 28–29.
37 Chipkin, 2007: 2.

It is worth exploring Chipkin's terminology in a bit more depth and using it to be clear regarding this book's argument about what legal cultural concept is being formed from 1897 to 1937. The first term, 'the people as datum', refers to an empirical collection of individuals in a given geography; the second refers to a collectivity organised in pursuit of a political end.[38] The 'given geography' of the first case is what became by 1961, and remains today as, the Republic of South Africa. In 1897, there was a collection of individuals in that territory who could not be viewed as a collectivity or a political subject. Its disparity included the African, Asian, European, male, female, adult, child, Afrikaans-speaking, English-speaking, Tswana-speaking, Zulu-speaking, Xhosa-speaking, Gujarati-speaking, Khoi-speaking, Cape, Natal, Transvaal and Free State identities (to name a few). However, 40 years later, the individuals living in that given geography (some the same, just older, some new/born and some gone/died) can be seen as a collectivity — the South African population. The individuals living in that territory shared a common citizenship which was understood as being subject to the regulation of their mobility by the more or less joined-up components of the South African state.[39] The object of study here is thus beyond the 'people as datum' and is some essential form of the 'people as political subject'.

Finally, it is worth noting that the character of the South African citizenship that I explore is not necessarily tied to or determined by the right to vote. Nor is this a history of South African citizenship in that term's fullest sense. Other scholars have engaged in some of that work: there are studies of the existence of a public sphere on the mines and close examination of the extent of the identification of Africans with South Africa that existed at that time,[40] as well as the extent of the identification of the European population with the South African political community in the 1910s and the 1920s, the period directly prior to the formal establishment of South African citizenship (Union

[38] Ibid.
[39] Op cit: 2, 186. It is important to note that Chipkin uses the term 'population' in a sense different from mine. For him, population is a code for cultural characteristics: race, language, culture, etc.
[40] Breckenridge, 1998.

nationality) in 1927,[41] and, in a more literary mode, exploration of the cosmopolitan and complex identification of generations of Indians immigrants in South Africa.[42] These and other aspects of the rich and full social science concept of citizenship are of at least equal interest.

More narrowly conceived, citizenship in South Africa has often been investigated through the lens of apartheid concerns and thus in its political aspect (eg the franchise or its denial). The best and most rigorous of this work acknowledges that citizenship does not necessarily entail the right to vote.[43] Globally, this has been demonstrated by, for instance, the non-voting status of the citizenship enjoyed by many American women in the 1800s and into the 1900s, as well as by children and others in today's world.[44] While the right to vote often does construct and has significantly constructed citizenship in many parts of the world, these chapters focus on what can be understood as a different right, the freedom of movement and the influence of regulating mobility on the underlying legal cultural concept of South African citizenship.

THE STRUCTURE OF THIS BOOK

In the eight chapters that follow I structure my argument to track the development of South African citizenship: starting with the establishment of colonial borders; then by elaborating on national migration bureaucracies before and after Union, culminating in the establishment of the Commissioner for Immigration and Asiatic Affairs in 1927; and then ending with the Commissioner's efforts to co-ordinate the implementation of migration laws and the administration of the mobility of the national population.

The books begins in 1897 with the first comprehensive immigration law enacted in South Africa: the Immigrants Restriction Act 1 of 1897 (Natal). It covers the years from 1897 to 1907, when the comprehensive immigration laws of the polities (the Colonies of the Cape and Natal, and the former Republics of the Transvaal and Orange Free State) that would

---

41 Lambert, 2000, 2005.
42 Hassim, 2002.
43 Loveland, 1999.
44 Cott, 1998.

federate to form the Union of South Africa were constructed. Primarily providing a pre-1897 baseline for the chapters that follow, Chapter 2, 'Early practices of regulating mobility', surveys the sets of laws that specifically regulated Asian populations and established African pass controls. In order to provide context, Chapter 2 also details the short-lived population-specific regime that legalised the Chinese labour importation scheme from 1904 to 1907. Chapter 3, 'The rise of borders', outlines the development of comprehensive immigration laws in each of the four constituent territories from 1897 to 1907. Differing in significant respects of population coverage and method of enforcement, each of these colonial migration laws primarily responded to the same South African phenomenon — a new wave of migration from India beginning in the mid-1890s. Chapter 3 also traces the relationship of these laws to the nascent territorial laws of nationality, a story I pick up in Chapter 9. However, it begins in 1897 also with the first comprehensive immigration law enacted in South Africa: the Immigrants Restriction Act 1 of 1897 (Natal).

The next three chapters cover the years from 1907 to 1927 when the model of migration regulation developed in the Transvaal in respect of the Asian population was diffused and became dominant throughout the new Union including its application to the European and African populations in each of the four provinces. Chapter 4, 'Union, the Act and the Registrar of Asiatics, 1907–1914', examines the central place of the 1913 Immigration Regulation Act in the unification process. It also examines the development in the Transvaal of what came to be the joint office of the Registrar of Asiatics and the Principal Immigration Officer. How those Transvaal laws and structures spread and were themselves changed (particularly in Natal and the Cape) is the subject of Chapter 5, 'Nationalisation of the immigration bureaucracy, 1914–1927'. At the same time, Chapters 4 and 5, examine the migration regulation of the European and Asian populations. The national regulation of the mobility of the African population, which began in the Department of Native Affairs but which was aligned with the Commissioner of Indian and Asiatic Affairs, is the topic of Chapter 6, 'African mobility and bureaucracy, 1911–1927'. By 1927, the office of the Commissioner of Immigration and Asiatic Affairs (CIAA), the most direct organisational ancestor of the current Department of Home Affairs, had been established. This national structure had formal legal competence over the mobility of the European, Asian and African populations.

The book then moves on to the period directly following the establishment of the CIAA, 1927 to 1937. This demonstrates that it is in the administration and implementation of laws that they have their greatest impact.[45] Chapter 7, 'The Commissioner's population, 1927–1937', documents the paradoxical fashion in which migration regulation over Asians developed. On the one hand, the practice of interprovincial movement for persons who were termed 'Asiatics' became significantly restricted. On the other hand, Asians were increasingly treated as South African nationals. Simultaneously, as Chapter 8, 'One official South Africa,' details the lawful residence vision of citizenship inherent in the establishment of the Commissioner's office was bureaucratically consolidated in a fusion of migration regulation of all three populations. By 1931, South Africa had an official vision of co-ordinated migration regulation for all its population. Just as the Great Depression hit South Africa, the regulation of African mobility began to be officially conceived in terms analogous to the regulation of Asians and Europeans. Chapter 9, 'Enacting nationality, 1927–1937', details how Parliament exercised its legislative competence in the fields of migration and nationality to confirm the lawful residence character of South African citizenship.

---

45 Chanock, 2001.

CHAPTER 2

Early practices of regulating mobility

From the viewpoint of those living in 1897, it would be fair to say that the South Africa of 2016 or of 1996 and perhaps even that of 1961 or 1937 was nearly impossible to imagine. Yet the seed elements of the South African populations to come — the pre-Union mobility regimes discussed in this chapter — were already active and playing significant roles from this point. The year 1897 was also significant in that it was when South Africa's first facially neutral (that is, not specific with regard to race in the words of the statute) immigration legislation was enacted in Natal. Most accounts of this law have focused on its introduction to South Africa of the literacy clause (discussed in Chapter 3). However, its formal application to all persons entering the Natal Colony is equally significant.[1] This chapter covers the mobility regimes present in 1897 and their operation during the events leading up to Union in 1910, as well as the fertile ground of pre-1897 developments from which these elements were able to draw support. While starting points are always to some extent arbitrary, it is important to go back some years before Union in order to understand South Africa's citizenship history.[2]

The pre-Union regimes controlling mobility in what would later become the Union of South Africa functioned in three primary ways: by specifically regulating Asian populations; by establishing African pass laws; and by legalising a Chinese labour importation scheme. Read with the additional set of laws establishing the borders of the four colonies that would soon become provinces of the Union, these regimes constituted the legal context and ground from which the entangled legal concepts of prohibited immigrants and South African citizens would grow. In this legal world before generally applicable immigration

---

1   Klotz, 2013: 70.
2   Op cit: 18.

statutes (apart from the nascent Natal law), there were three relevant sets of population-specific migration regulation laws: those governing the population of Indians in the colonies of Natal and the Transvaal; those providing for the African pass law regime, and those encompassing the scheme for importing Chinese mine workers to the Transvaal. The operation of each of these elements informed and influenced the later developments around migration during Union.

First, prior to Union, each of the constituent territories had relatively long-standing laws directed specifically at Asian immigration and Asian affairs. Among the South African colonies, these laws differed significantly in historical origin, substantive policy and means of enforcement. Natal regulated Indian plantation workers and their descendants through a long-standing corporatist scheme. In the Transvaal, opposition to the influx of Asians particularly from Natal before the South African War led to the development of a registration system. In the post-War pre-Union period, the three-way political struggle between Asians, British and Afrikaners led to an intertwining of immigration and nationality concepts, with the clear distinction that legally resident Asians were to be registered in a territorial bureaucracy. The Cape had a short-lived policy directed specifically at gradually ousting the small Chinese community resident there.

Second, each of the constituent territories also had relatively long-standing laws directed particularly at African mobility, known as the pass laws. Industrial passes, urban passes and movement passes are all types of pass laws. The breakthrough to establishing relatively effective control over African mobility in South Africa occurred by combining all three. In the 1880s and 1890s, the mining industry of the Witwatersrand influenced state bureaucrats in the Transvaal and southern Mozambique (then Portuguese East Africa) to develop urban and movement passes respectively to coerce African mine workers into a pass law system that fed labour to the mines of the Rand. After the South African War of 1899–1902 this system was ratified and entrenched by the British High Commission.

Third, in a relatively less influential development, the mining industry in the Transvaal briefly but dramatically experimented with a scheme of imported Chinese labour in the years directly following the War. Conceived and executed within the structures of the British

Empire, the scheme itself was ended largely by domestic British politics just before the Transvaal was granted responsible government.

EARLY MOBILITY REGIMES DIRECTED AT ASIANS: POPULATION REGISTRATION

Migration regulation in pre-Union South Africa identified some persons in a population on the basis of nationality and some on the basis of race, as well as sometimes on a combination of the two concepts. This section thus distinguishes between facially neutral migration law such as the 1897 Natal immigration legislation and the population-specific migration laws discussed here. As we shall see, this distinction is itself a permeable and malleable one, but it is useful in describing the formal legal structure for the regulation of migration in the period immediately prior to the formation of the Union of South Africa in 1910. This section details the regulation of migration specific to Indians in Natal (1870, 1891), to Asians in the Transvaal and Orange Free State or Orange River Colony (1885, 1891 and 1906, 1907 and 1908 respectively) and to Chinese in the Cape (1904). Unlike the later comprehensive immigration laws, these laws were passed at various times responding to specific situations, and differed considerably among themselves in terms of legal form and practices as well as policies. One can differentiate these laws from those applicable to Africans, such as pass laws, not only by population, but also because the laws that specifically related to Asians addressed mobility across the borders of the pre-Union South African territory as well as mobility within the territory. The African pass laws discussed below applied only to movement within the territory. The laws relating to the Chinese mine workers in the Transvaal and in Natal cut across these distinctions and are discussed separately. In this chapter, developments in the Orange Free State or the Orange River Colony are discussed alongside those in the Transvaal.

Migration regulation of Indians in Natal

In Natal, a specific and detailed set of pre-Union laws was directed at the Indian population.[3] One set of Indian immigration laws in Natal begins

---

3   Bhana and Brain, 1990; Thompson, 1938.

in 1870 and ends in 1891. Even then, the first of these was a law amending and consolidating other earlier laws and their administrative structures. Act 2 of 1870 (Natal) was intended to 'amend and consolidate the Laws relating to the introduction of Coolie Immigrants into this Colony, and to the regulation and government of such Coolie Immigrants'. This 1870 statute, also known as the Coolie Law Consolidation Law of 1869, was itself amended and replaced by Act 25 of 1891 (Natal), the Indian Immigration Act.[4]

Importantly, the 1891 Indian Immigration Act (like its predecessors) applied only to the population of Indian immigrants in Natal. As defined in section 118, this meant

> *all Indians introduced from India to Natal under the provisions of the Laws regulating such introduction and those descendants of such Indians who may be resident in Natal. From the operation of this Law are excluded those persons who are usually described in this Colony as 'Asiatics', 'Arabs', or 'Arab traders', being persons who have not been introduced into this Colony under the Laws providing for the introduction of emigrants from India to Natal.*

As stated, the law purported to govern not only the first but also successive generations of Indians in Natal. For instance, the Protector of Indian Immigrants functioned as the Registrar of Births for any persons born into this population.[5]

The 1891 Indian Immigration Act perpetuated a crucial split with respect to the Indian population in Natal. It set up a distinction between Indian immigrants and other persons of Indian birth who had themselves not been part of the Indian migration scheme and who were also not descendants of the Indian immigrants. These non-indentured Indians — 'Asiatics', also known as 'passenger' Indians — were not

---

4   The long title of this law states its purpose, as with the 1870 Act: 'To amend and consolidate the Laws relating to the Introduction of Indian Immigrants into the Colony of Natal, and to the regulation and government of such Indian Immigrants'.

5   Sections 61 and 63.

covered by the 1891 Act. Ironically, this 1891 Act was finally repealed at the height of apartheid by Act 68 of 1963 (South Africa).

Instead, from 1897, passenger Indians were subject in Natal to the facially neutral Immigration Restriction Act. As Peberdy notes, various terms were used to describe and categorise the Indian population: 'indentured' not surprisingly referred to those who were still under contract; 'free' Indians were those people who had completed their indentures and remained in Natal; 'passenger' Indians were those who had arrived independently of the indentured scheme, usually with capital to start enterprises; and the terms 'colonial' and 'colonial born' were used to describe those who had been born in Natal. The 1897 Act would cover only passenger Indians and their colonial-born descendants.[6]

The 1891 Indian Immigration Act ran for 33 pages in the consolidated statute book. It was a comprehensive, exclusive and embracing administrative code dealing with many aspects of the life of Indian immigrants. In large part, the Act was a labour law. It regulated the requisition for Indian labour by Natal employers and the contracts that the immigrants themselves could sign. Deductions from wages and terms and conditions of service were covered. The Act covered the housing of Indian immigrants on the agricultural estates as well as their collection and transport by the employers from the arrival ports to the destination estates. Despite the nature of these functions, the legislation was essentially a private enabling charter. The primary implementation of the Indian Immigration Act was to be carried out by the officers of the Indian Immigration Trust Board, together with the employers of the immigrants.[7] In its operation, the Trust Board functioned as the agent of the large agricultural estates of Natal. For instance, the Trust Board's officers were not to be regarded as part of the civil service of the territory.[8]

Within the structure of the Indian Immigration Trust Board (and paid by the Board), the 1891 Act also set up the office of the Protector of Indian Immigrants. The Protector had a wide range of duties both in

---

[6] Peberdy, 2009.
[7] Section 7.
[8] Desai and Vahed, 2010: 95–99.

the operation and oversight of the employment of Indian immigrants.[9] The institution of the Protector itself had historical roots in the Indian Government's desire to protect its nationals in Mauritius.[10] The Trust Board Protector had duties assigned to him with respect to the administration of estates of Indian immigrants who had died as well as the registration of births, marriages and deaths.[11] This office also exercised operational powers regarding permission for marriages and granting of divorces. The Protector implemented these duties in part through a practice of central registration. He was required to keep a register containing the name and other details of each Indian immigrant,[12] and to assign each immigrant a unique number. Thus the Protector's numbering scheme differed from that used in the transportation of the immigrants from India to South Africa. (Each of the 152 184 Indian immigrants imported in 384 shiploads from 1860 to 1911 was assigned an individual number from 1 to 152 184).[13]

In 1910, the Indian Immigration Trust Board saw its mandate legislatively extended from Indian immigrants to Indians resident in Natal more generally.[14] This provision authorised the board to set up a bureau for the purpose of registering unemployed Indian labourers within Natal.

Another aspect of the Indian Immigration Act of 1891 was that it severely curtailed the freedom of movement of persons to whom it applied. Immigrants needed a licence to leave the colony and it took 10 years to obtain a licence. If found more than a mile from his or her place of employment, an immigrant could be brought forcibly back without a warrant, even by a private person. Section 31 allowed any police constable 'to stop any Indian Immigrant wherever he may find him'. The 1891 Act empowered the Indian Immigration Trust Board with the approval of the Governor in Council to make rules and regulations in this regard. These rules included facilitating 'the arrest of absconding

---

9   Bhana, 1991.
10 Ibid: 9.
11 Section 70 (registration of marriages).
12 Section 16.
13 Bhana, 1991: 2.
14 Section 2 of Law 19 of 1910 (Natal) (repealed by section 7 of Act 15 of 1931 (Union)).

Indians or Indians found at a distance from their employer's residence without passes or tickets of leave'.[15] An amendment to the 1891 Act in 1895 provided that an Indian immigrant at the end of his indenture who did not either return to India or become re-indentured was required to take out a pass to remain in Natal.[16] The provision applied to 'Colonial born' Indian immigrants as well as those of the first generation, but not to passenger Indians. The pass cost £3 and constituted a head tax. It engendered considerable community resistance. Since it applied to a specific population, this 1895 provision for a pass was not directly linked to an existing contract of employment.

Nonetheless, the consequences of the Indian Immigration Act of 1891 on freedom of movement went further than the category of Indian immigrants to whom it formally applied. Six years later this became clear in the enacting of Act 28 of 1897 (Natal) 'to protect uncovenanted Indians from arrest in mistake for absconding Indentured Indian Servants'. This law allowed Indians who were not and had not been indentured to apply for passes from a magistrate or from the Protector of Indian Immigrants. Section 2 of this 1897 Act provided: 'The possession and production of a pass under this Act shall be prima facie evidence of that status of the bearer of such pass, and of his exemption from liability to arrest under section 31 of Law No. 25, 1891.' These passes issued by the Protector or a magistrate were valid for a year. A schedule to the 1897 Act provided a model of the pass. The information retained by the issuer of the pass included the bearer's name, sex, place of origin (county and village), parents' names, caste, age, height, complexion, marks, if married to whom, status, residence and employment details.

For Indians, the risk of arbitrary arrest was high and, moreover, section 4 precluded any damages action for wrongful arrest. In response to the dissatisfaction voiced by the Indian community, some ameliorating effort was made in Act 19 of 1898 (Natal).[17] Facially

---

15 Section 116 of the Indian Immigration Act 25 of 1891 (Natal).
16 Section 6 of Act 17 of 1895 (Natal).
17 Section 4 of Act 28 of 1897 (Natal): 'If the Protector of Indian Immigrants, or any Magistrate, or Justice of the Peace, or any Police Constable, shall stop or arrest any Indian not carrying a pass granted under this Act, the Indian so stopped or arrested shall not be entitled to make any claim for wrongful arrest or detention merely on

optional, this 1897 law was an extension of jurisdiction over Indians not covered by the Indian Immigration Act, or at least over those not willing to run the risk of being arrested. In 1905, documentation regarding the Natal migration regulations became stricter. Section 2 of Act 39 of 1905 (Natal) prohibited any person from employing any Indian immigrant as a servant or an employee in any other capacity without producing a pass or licence.[18] It further provided for employer sanctions and made contracts contravening the terms of the Act invalid.[19]

Migration regulation of Indians in the Transvaal

The Transvaal had significant migration regulation specific to the Asian population dating from at least 1885. This regulation took at least four legal forms, starting with Law 3 of 1885 (Transvaal) and passing through a draft Ordinance in 1906, a voluntary registration law in 1907, and a mandatory Act in 1908.

To begin with, section 1 of Law 3 of 1885 (Transvaal) applied to 'the persons belonging to any of the native races of Asia, including the so-called Coolies, Arabs, Malays and Mohammedan subjects of the Turkish Dominion'.[20] Law 3 of 1885 contained four key provisions.[21] First, the persons to whom it applied could not naturalise in the Transvaal: 'They shall not be capable of obtaining burgher rights of the South African Republic.' Second, this Asiatic population needed to register with the Registrar of Asiatics.[22] Third, members of this population could not own

---

the ground that he was not an indentured Indian.' There was apparently at least some contestation of this policy. Act 19 of 1898 (Natal) inserts in this section the words 'under a bona fide belief or suspicion that he is an indentured Indian'.
18 Act 39 of 1905 (Natal).
19 Sections 3 and 4.
20 Law 3 of 1885 (Transvaal).
21 Section 2(a)–(d).
22 Section 2(c) provided in part: 'Those who settle in the Republic for the purpose of carrying on any trade or otherwise shall be bound to have their names entered in a register to be separately kept for the purpose by the Landdrosts of the various districts, in accordance with a form to be prescribed by the Government. On such registration, which shall be effected within eight days after arrival, a sum of 25 pounds sterling shall be paid.'

property. Fourth, such persons were subject to residential regulation.[23] In these last two aspects, Law 3 of 1885 linked migration status to economic citizenship, absolutely prohibiting property ownership and allowing for racial residential segregation.

However, upon protest from Britain and the presentation of an argument regarding how the London Convention preserved the rights of Indians who were British subjects, some aspects of the law were subsequently modified. According to Bradlow,[24] 'because of Article 14 of the London Convention, [the] entry [of Indians into the Transvaal from Natal] could not be legally prohibited'. The registration fee was reduced to £25 from £3 and Asians were allowed to buy property in locations.[25] Furthermore, subsection 2(c) was amended by Volksraad Resolution Article 1419 (12 August 1886) and Volksraad Resolution Article 128 (16 May 1890).

As migration regulation, Law 3 of 1885 had two significant features. First, its prohibition on naturalisation meant that, unless the law was repealed, no Asians could be citizens of the Transvaal, either then or in the future. Like the Chinese in the Cape, the Indians in the Transvaal had no prospects of provincial citizenship. Second, and perhaps more importantly, the requirement of population registration was the principal element of migration regulation in the Transvaal. Indeed, such registration was essentially the only basis of enforcement. In terms of Law 3 of 1885, there was no regulation of entry other than the requirement to register. Moreover, registration documents did not have to be produced on demand.

In tandem with the High Commissioner's 1903 Peace Preservation Ordinance, which was a facially neutral law, the registration provisions of Law 3 of 1885 initially continued to operate in the Transvaal after the South African War. Eager to reconstruct the territory, High Commissioner Alfred Milner aimed to reconcile British and Afrikaner interests rather than to protect those of Asians. Milner's colonial

---

23 Section 2(d): 'The Government shall have the right to point out certain streets, wards and locations for them to live in. This provision shall not apply to those who live with their employers.'
24 Bradlow, 1978: 13–14.
25 Yap and Man, 1996: 76.

administration thus assumed the function of the Registrar of Asiatics in terms of Law 3 of 1885 and used its provisions to issue registration certificates to Asians from 1902 to 1907. However, from the point of view of the Asian community, Law 3 of 1885 continued to be a source of tension, and the struggles pertaining to it during this period are well documented. Perhaps most notable is part of a deal proffered in 1904 by Gandhi. He drafted a law and proposed that Law 3 of 1885 be repealed, that trading licences be granted at the discretion of local authorities and that an immigration law be adopted on the same basis as the Australian immigration law, by which state officers could exclude any Asiatic or indeed any person at will. In a meeting with Colonial Secretary of the Transvaal, Patrick Duncan, Gandhi proposed a draft ordinance regarding the immigration bill, the content of which shows how consistent his thinking was with official thinking in using the categories of immigrants to address some of the incidents of citizenship, such as the franchise. In a note, Gandhi stated that the wishes of reasonable colonists were met by the prevention of 'immigration of all but Indians of a superior type'.[26]

From the British High Commission's point of view, the registration provisions for the Asiatic population were soon seen as inadequate and in need of strengthening, particularly given the difficulties of identification. As Bradlow points out, identification problems obstructed the implementation of the permit system under the 1903 Ordinance and led to the drafting of the Asiatic Law Amendment Ordinance 29 in 1906,

---

26 CIA 19, H40, vol 6. Gandhi's draft ordinance contained the following sections: '3. The immigration into the Transvaal of any person being, or appearing to be, of any of the classes defined by the following sub-sections is prohibited, namely: (a) Any person who, when asked to do so by any duly authorised officer, shall be unable through deficient education, to himself write out and sign in the characters of some European language an application to the satisfaction of any officer. (b) Any person without visible means of support or who is likely to become a pauper or a public charge, or any idiot or insane person or any person suffering from loathsome or dangerous contagious disease, etc. 4. A prohibited immigrant shall not be entitled to a licence to carry on any trade or calling, nor shall he be entitled to acquire land in leasehold, freehold or otherwise, or to exercise the franchise, or to be enrolled as a burgess of any borough, or to be on the roll of any township.'

Milner's attempt to strengthen the Transvaal's registration regime.[27] This draft law aimed to amend section 2(c) of Law 3 of 1885. Section 9 of the draft law would require Asiatics of 16 years and older to produce their certificate of registration upon demand by police or any other authorised official. In addition, the state's concerns regarding the difficulties of identification were to be addressed: each member of the Asiatic population had to provide personal particulars and also a means of identification (such as fingerprinting). Economic restrictions on Asiatics would also be tightened: section 13 of the 1906 Ordinance proposed prohibiting the issuing of trading licences to any Asiatics without certificates of registration. This proposed draft ordinance sparked great opposition and led to the renowned passive resistance campaign of the Indians led by Gandhi. In December 1906, the British Governor decided not to go ahead with this ordinance.

While all Asiatics in the Transvaal were subject to Law 3 from 1885 onwards, Chinese immigrants came in for additional specific regulation. In 1893, Chinese persons, most of them small traders and without the protection of British nationality, were singled out for a special yearly pass. By resolution on 8 September 1893, a £25 annual renewable residence pass was mandated. However, in the face of opposition by the British High Commissioner in Cape Town and shipping interests fearful of losing trade, the special Chinese pass was only sporadically enforced.[28]

The next legal form of specific population legislation with respect to Asians was soon to come. The Transvaal Colony had been granted responsible government by Britain by letters patent dated 6 December 1906 and at the first sitting of its legislature in February 1907 enacted the Asiatic Law Amendment Act 2 of 1907 (Transvaal), also known as 'the Black Act'. Effectively, Act 2 of 1907 was almost identical in content and form to the draft ordinance rejected by the British Governor the previous December. The provisions mandating the production of a registration certificate on demand, specifying a means of identification and prohibiting trading without a registration certificate were included.

---

27 Bradlow, 1978: 14.
28 Yap and Man, 1996: 79–80.

The new Transvaal government attempted to implement the Black Act from 1 July 1907 to 30 November 1907 along with the Immigrants Restriction Act 15 of 1907 (Transvaal). Bradlow correctly refers to these Acts as 'the twin bastions of Transvaal Asiatic policy to secure a register of every Asiatic lawfully in the country and attempting to close the doors to future immigration'.[29] Resistance and arrests followed. Migration authorities themselves played a significant role in the arrests related to the Black Act. Officials from all levels of the hierarchy engaged in surveillance, exclusion, detention and deportation, working at times uneasily with the police.[30] The success of the crackdown on those not complying with the 1907 Act was in part due to a sharp increase in the number of police officers appointed also as immigration officers.[31]

Fingerprinting was a particular point of contest. Calling for its abolition became an important dimension of opposition to the registration provisions, even though the practice was a key official demand. Nonetheless, the norm from 1907 was that all adult Indians and Chinese would be fingerprinted.[32] By 8 March 1907, the British Indian Association was reportedly objecting to full fingerprinting but not to

---

29   Bradlow, 1987: 15.
30   CIA 26, M2, vol 2: Secretary, SAC to All District Commanders, Transvaal (28 November 1907): 'You will note that the Registrar of Asiatics does not wish you to take any action at present re the non-registration of Asiatics, but he wishes to be informed of any cases of intimidation by Asiatics, acting as so called Pickets. This information the Inspector General approves of your sending direct to the Registrar of Asiatics, Colonial Secretary's Office, Pretoria, so as to save time, but a copy should be sent to this office for record. The Inspector General wishes me to inform you that it has not yet been decided if action will be taken as per the Registrar of Asiatics' letter forwarded to me under cover of my CR/33/306 dated 19:11:07, and I am to make it clear to you that you are to take no action re this matter without further instructions.'
31   CIA 26, M2, vol 2: Secretary, SAC to Registrar of Asiatics (9 December 1907). List of Members of the South African Constabulary for Authorisation by Colonial Secretary to call for Certificates of Registration of Asiatics (listing 154 SAC members at Inspector, Sergeant, Corporal, Lance Corporal and Constable grades); Acting Commissioner of Police to Registrar of Asiatics (10 December 1907) (list of sixty-six policemen in Deputy Commissioner, Inspector, Superintendent and Sergeant First Class grades). Just over a year earlier, the total number of persons authorised in both the police and the SAC was 22. CIA 26, M2, vol 1: Registrar to Chief Staff Officer, SAC (30 May 1906).
32   Breckenridge, 2014.

thumb impressions.³³ An apparent compromise was reached in January 1908 through a meeting of Gandhi and General Jan Smuts.³⁴ Registration would be voluntary and signatures rather than fingerprints would be allowed for educated persons. On the basis of this compromise, nearly all adult male Indians registered voluntarily. The Chinese community also registered voluntarily after being allowed to do so with two thumb prints rather than all 10 fingerprints.³⁵ Some further concessions were also made. On 12 May 1908, Montfort Chamney, the registrar of Asiatics, noted that 'it has been found necessary to accept the applications of a few educated and well-known Asiatics without the requirement on the Certificate of Registration of their thumb impression'.³⁶

Articulating the compromise purportedly reached with Smuts, Gandhi claimed also that the 1907 Act — with the produce-on-demand provision — would be repealed. Smuts, however, denied having made such a promise. Repudiating the claimed agreement, Smuts simply forged ahead, using state power to enact a law validating the voluntary registrations. The Asiatics Registration Amendment Act 36 of 1908 (Transvaal) was intended to 'validate the Voluntary Registration of certain Asiatics who failed to comply with the provisions of Act No. 2 of 1907 and to make further provision for the registration of Asiatics'. The 1907 Act with its voluntary registration provisions was not repealed, though it fell into disuse.

Smuts's 1908 Asiatic registration law replaced the registration provisions of Law 3 of 1885 (Transvaal) with a more restrictive migration regulation scheme. The 1908 Act dropped any explicit reference to the definition of Asiatic in Law 3 of 1885. Instead, an official, the Registrar of Asiatics, was to issue certificates and keep a register of Asiatics.³⁷ Those who were refused certificates of registration — a Transvaal Asiatic Registration Certificate — were entitled to appeal to a specially designated magistrate.³⁸ It might be appropriate to call this 1908

---

33   CIA 26, M2, vol 2: Registrar of Asiatics to Colonel Madoc (8 March 1907).
34   Yap and Man, 1996: 152.
35   Op cit: 152–153.
36   CIA 26, M2, vol 2: Registrar of Asiatics to Secretary, SAC (12 May 1908).
37   Section 1.
38   Section 6(2).

registration voluntary in that it was not compulsory. Nevertheless, certificates of registration were to be produced upon demand. The Governor could also issue permits to Asiatics to stay in the colony for a limited time only with the intention of having new arrivals apply for registration before entry.[39] Moreover, these certificates could be verified through identification including fingerprints.[40] Asiatics without certificates of registration could be ordered by resident magistrates to leave the territory in terms of the Immigrants Restriction Act 15 of 1907 (which provided for administrative detention and removal).[41] Furthermore, economic restrictions were maintained. Only Asiatics with certificates of registration, registered particulars and means of identification were allowed to receive trading licences.[42] Arguably, this Registrar of Asiatics is the forerunner of the contemporary Department of Home Affairs.

Gandhi's passive resistance campaign continued throughout this time. Its suspension was agreed upon only in May 1911, after Union and the promise to repeal Act 2 of 1907. Persons lawfully resident in terms of the 1908 Act would escape the effect of the section 4(1)(a) deeming order in terms of Act 22 of 1913 (Union).

Migration regulation of Indians in the Orange Free State

In the Orange Free State, as codified in 1891, Chapter XXXIII of the Free State Statutes contained a law entitled 'A Law To Provide Against the Influx of Asiatics and for the Removal of White Criminals Entering This State from Elsewhere'. Sections 1–6 of the chapter provided that 'No Arab, Chinaman, coolie, or other Asiatic coloured person' could reside in the state longer than two months without a permit.[43] The residence prohibition precluded naturalisation by Asiatics and they were also not allowed to hold property or become merchants or farmers.[44] The result was that Chapter XXXIII functioned in a similar manner to Law

---

39 Section 16; Bradlow, 1978: 16.
40 Section 9.
41 Section 6.
42 Section 14(1).
43 Section 12 exempted Cape Colony Malays from the operation of the Chapter.
44 Sections 7 and 8.

3 of 1885 (Transvaal): it kept Asians from naturalising as citizens in the territory and it linked their migration status to various economic exclusions. While Chapter XXXIII did not subject Asians to a system of centralised registration as in the Transvaal, its effect was such that there were very few Asians in that territory to put onto such a system.

The Cape Colony and regulation of the Chinese

In the Cape, soon after the South African War, the legislature passed the Chinese Exclusion Act 37 of 1904 (Cape). This Act provided no definition of its term of application, 'Chinaman', leaving the definition of this term to the discretion of officials and ultimately to the courts.[45] However, it effectively prohibited any new Chinese person from entering and residing in the Cape Colony.[46] It was a 'this far and no further' approach to Chinese immigration as its aim was to reduce and over time eliminate the Chinese population in the Cape.

The Cape Chinese Exclusion Act did not strip Chinese persons of their British nationality, but it made entry into or residence within the Cape for Chinese persons conditional on having a certificate of exemption. These certificates were granted to male children at 18 years of age and were to be renewed each year.[47] For Chinese persons not already resident in the Cape (eg immigrating to the Cape from either within or without the British Empire), these certificates were granted by the Governor upon proof of British subjecthood by birth or of a certificate of naturalisation in the Cape Colony.[48] Chinese persons already residing in the Cape would receive a Minister's certificate of exemption. Unlike the centralised registration of the Transvaal, the Cape Exclusion Act introduced a system of decentralised registration for its Chinese population. The Act required a Chinese person holding a certificate of exemption to report to the resident magistrate of the district where he or

---

45 Section 27 provided 'For the purposes of any prosecutions under this Act, the Court, Judge or Magistrate may decide upon their own view and judgment whether any person produced before them is a Chinaman.'
46 Section 3.
47 Section 9.
48 Section 3.

she wished to reside.[49] The magistrate was to enter the certificate into a register and the Minister was to compile one register for the colony.[50] The certificates of exemption thus constituted a comprehensive registration system for the Chinese population in the Cape.

Most legal rights and powers for the Chinese population depended directly on this registration status and not on the underlying status of nationality. For instance, licences to pursue an economic activity would be issued only to those Chinese persons with a certificate of exemption.[51] Temporary travel from one district to another required notifying both magistrates. Police officers were authorised to ask these persons to produce their certificates,[52] and failure to do so meant the person could be summarily dealt with by a magistrate and potentially be subject to arrest and trial proceedings.[53] Ultimate penalties for contravening the Chinese Exclusion Act included punishment and deportation.[54] A temporary detention centre was planned for Robben Island but the idea was later dropped.[55]

An amendment to the Exclusion Act two years later in 1906 modified the Cape migration control policy somewhat. The Chinese Exclusion Amendment Act allowed for holders of Minister's certificates of exemption (resident Chinese) to receive permits to visit China and return to the Cape Colony.[56] The Governor was to provide for such permits. However, the Governor also was granted the power to provide for 'the conditions as to identification.' The use of identification techniques was, however, limited to providing re-entry permits and strictly speaking did not relate to the certificates of exemption held by resident Chinese.[57] Some of these conditions of identification included fingerprinting, a physical examination for distinguishing marks, and a signature in

---

49 Section 5.
50 Section 6.
51 Section 17.
52 Section 11. The Act also empowered the Governor to appoint officials for its enforcement. Section 29.
53 Section 11.
54 Section 18 and 19. See also section 34 (deportation on second conviction).
55 Yap and Man, 1996: 64.
56 Section 1, Chinese Exclusion Amendment Act 15 of 1906 (Cape).
57 Section 2, Act 15 of 1906.

English and Chinese.[58] The Chinese Exclusion Act 37 of 1904 (Cape) was repealed only three decades later by the Immigration (Amendment) Act 19 of 1933 (Union).

EARLY MOBILITY REGIMES DIRECTED AT AFRICANS: PRE-UNION PASS LAWS

The term 'pass laws' refers to a variety of forms of regulation regarding the movement of Africans. Indeed, during the second half of the 20th century, 'pass laws' referred to a system of national laws and regulations controlling African movement. Pass laws were often understood to be one of the main features of apartheid. In 1986, the repeal of influx control was greeted with acclaim as the abolition of the hated pass laws. However, the continuous use of the term 'pass laws' obscures both the variety of regulations on movement and their changing styles and sources. The variation in pass laws as they existed around 1914 may be gleaned from an early parliamentary proceeding. In 1914, Parliament ordered its Select Committee on Native Affairs to consider the question of 'the consolidation of the pass laws' as well as a petition from seven African women of the Orange Free State.[59] A memorandum was presented to this Committee surveying what it termed 'the complex and diverse Pass Laws in force in different Provinces'. Entitled simply 'Pass Laws', Appendix A surveyed the pass laws on a province-by-province basis.

This official submission to Parliament identified many types of pass laws. For instance, pass laws in the Cape were described in four separate geographical areas of the province as well as recording a separate category of municipal passes and exemptions. For Natal, Appendix A 'roughly' identified four classes of passes: inward and outward passes, identification passes, reference passes and cattle removal passes. For the Transvaal, pass laws were grouped under three headings: general pass regulations, pass regulations for labour districts and pass regulations in municipal areas. In the Orange Free State, these laws were described in

---

[58] Yap and Man, 1996: 63–65.
[59] First-Second Reports of the Select Committee on Native Affairs (S.C. 8 of 1914); Third-Fourth Reports of the Select Committee on Native Affairs (S.C. 8A of 1914).

four classes: inward and outward passes, travelling passes, residential passes and cattle removal passes.

In 1920, another official analysis of the pass laws came in the Report of the Inter-Departmental Committee on the Native Pass Laws of 1920 (the Godley Report). Annexure B of the Godley Report revised and brought up to date Appendix A of the 1914 Select Committee adopting the same format as the earlier survey.

Even at this abstract level of classification, the constituent territories of the Union did not share a common understanding by which to describe their pass laws. Martin Chanock is thus correct in noting that 'considerable difference' existed between the African pass law regimes of the four soon-to-be-Union territories, with the Transvaal having the most detailed and comprehensive system of control.[60] Still, degree of control is not the only point of comparison.[61] The institutional form of implementing the migration regulation matters as well. Whereas official registration was fundamental to migration regulation for Asians, for Africans a system of private employer registration was used. As Douglas Hindson rightly notes with respect to urban areas: '[I]n all the areas which were to become provinces of the Union of South Africa after 1910, registration of service contracts was the basic mechanism by which the authorities attempted to exercise control over Africans.'[62]

At the risk of over-simplification, the pass laws at the time of Union can be divided into three types. The industrial pass system was characterised first by the enforcing of passes through large employers in the private sector (either exclusively or in addition to enforcement through the general police power), and second by using passes to reduce the bargaining power of labour by restricting its mobility. Then there was an urban pass system which was characterised first by the enforcing of passes through municipal police forces (even though these passes could be issued from the private sector), second, using these passes to promote urban policies which could include residential and labour policies. Third, there was a movement pass system characterised by enforcement

---

60   Chanock, 2001: 410.
61   Duncan, 1995; Wells, 1993.
62   Hindson, 1987: 31.

through registration processes that linked an individual to a particular area and by using these reference passes to serve as identification.

Laws affecting African mobility in the Cape

Although some claim otherwise, Africans were subject to a set of pass laws in the Cape. Pass laws controlling movement in the Cape at the time of Union were not a novel development. In one form or another, pass laws applying to Africans had existed in the Cape since 1760.[63] In 1809, Britain had introduced a pass law for native blacks wishing to enter 'white' areas. From the early 1800s, foreign Africans needed to carry passes while within the Cape Colony. From 1857, certificates of citizenship were issued to Africans who were British nationals. A foreign African 'who could prove he had lived for ten years in the Colony, constantly in service, and with a blameless record, was entitled to a certificate of citizenship'. The certificate stated that the bearer was not to be stopped on the supposition 'that he is a Kafir' (a foreigner) 'and thereby harassed or aggrieved'. The certificate of citizenship could thus be seen itself as a pass. According to Ellison Kahn, 'a registry of such certificates was to be kept, and production of the document could be demanded by an authorised police officer'. However, these legal provisions of the mid-1800s reportedly fell into disuse at least from 1867.[64] While no provincial law mandated a movement pass system, the Cape of the late 1800s had a piece of legislation 'the application of which could, and indeed in practice did, effectively take the place of movement passes in Natal and the Trekker States.'[65] Act 23 of 1879 (Cape) mandated strict rules concerning vagrancy.[66] According to this Act,[67]

> *the occupier of immovable property could summarily arrest anyone wandering about on his property without his permission. When brought before the nearest magistrate or special justice of the peace, the burden of proving his innocence rested on the accused ... It is not*

---

[63] Loveland, 1999: 9.
[64] Hindson, 1987: 19; Kahn, 1949: 275f.
[65] Kahn, 1949: 277.
[66] Act 23 of 1879 (Cape) (later amended by Act 27 of 1889 (Cape)).
[67] Kahn, 1949: 19.

surprising that many Natives, without being compelled to, carried passes — serving the purpose of passports — to show their bona fides. The operation of the vagrancy law thus constituted a de facto movement pass system that covered Africans travelling from one district to another.[68]

A second set of African pass laws dating from the 1870s in the Cape also bears mention. In the northern districts of the Cape Colony where the diamond mining industry operated, a fairly effective industrial pass system functioned from the 1870s.[69] Indeed, one can argue that the South African industrial pass system originated in Kimberley as the discovery of diamonds brought mine compounds and migrant labour to that town in the Northern Cape.[70] In Kimberley, these industrial passes were linked to the Masters and Servants legislation, an Act ostensibly geared to protect workers from arbitrary action by employers. As implemented, though, it operated more to keep workers within the grasp of the mines, even if a large proportion of their contracts were not registered. Within the proclaimed districts, a worker's copy of his service contract had to be produced on demand to an authorised official.[71]

The Cape enacted a law providing for urban passes (location passes) after the South African War. Act 40 of 1902 (Cape) established urban locations and provided for passes for Africans leaving and entering those locations.[72] The precise conditions of these urban passes (which were required for South African Africans as well as 'any other aboriginal native of South or Central Africa') were to be completed in accordance with regulation issued through the Governor-General's office. This law followed the earlier Act 30 of 1895 (Cape) that allowed local authorities to require 'night passes' for Africans to be in public spaces between 21.00 and 4.00.[73]

---

68 Hindson, 1987: 19.
69 Op cit: 21; Chanock, 2001: 410.
70 Hindson, 1987.
71 Op cit: 21.
72 Section 11(4), (12) and (13) of Act 40 of 1902 (Cape). Section 11(15) gave as a topic for regulation: 'Prescribing and regulating the issue of passes to Natives entering or leaving any Native Reserve Location and registering all such Natives.'
73 Act 30 of 1895 (Cape).

Laws on African mobility in Natal

At least from 1884 onwards, Africans residing in Natal were subject to movement pass requirements when entering or leaving the territory. These passes were obtained at a pass office, if temporary, and through the Secretary for Native Affairs, if permanent.[74] However, the administration of these provincial pass laws was reportedly lenient.[75] Control over movement became tighter in the late 1800s with the introduction of urban passes. In terms of a Natal provincial law, the municipalities of Durban and Pietermaritzburg had the power to frame by-laws for the registration of service contracts and their use as passes from 1888.[76] According to Chanock, from 1901, African employees were required to carry passes and their masters were required to keep registers of such passes. In 1904 this was extended to farm workers.[77] These passes would need to be produced upon demand. While Africans were thus subject to urban pass policing in pre-Union Natal, their passes did not derive from a central register, but rather from their employers.

African mobility regulation in the Transvaal and the Orange Free State

In the Transvaal, various pass laws applying to Africans had been in place from the mid-1800s under the government of the South African Republic. Some of these early movement pass laws aimed to retain labour. For instance, Law 3 of 1872 (Transvaal) required Africans resident in the Transvaal to pay the South African Republic if they wished to travel to the diamond fields in the Cape.[78] With the British annexation of the Transvaal in 1877, resident Africans could obtain a movement pass upon proof of payment of taxes, while foreign Africans were entitled to the travelling pass as a right.

However, the distinctive features of the industrial pass system that would come to dominate migration regulation in South Africa arose in the Transvaal only in the 1880s. At that time the developing gold

---

[74] Kahn, 1949: 277.
[75] Ibid.
[76] Ibid.
[77] Ibid; Chanock, 2001: 411. Kahn cites Act 49 of 1901 and Act 3 of 1904.
[78] Law 3 of 1872 (Transvaal).

mining industry in the Transvaal began to make increasing demands for pass laws to regulate the movement of the African population in order to secure adequate labour supplies. The Government of the Transvaal responded to a degree, by for instance, issuing a regulation in terms of the Gold Law 14 of 1894 (Transvaal) that required Africans on the diggings to have a monthly travel pass. However, the Chamber of Mines did not consider these measures adequate.[79]

Perhaps the most significant pre-Union state intervention in favour of the mining industry came in the form of an industrial pass system. This was implemented through two laws, both initially drafted by mining representatives.[80] The introduction of an industrial pass system was a critical moment in both the legal history of pass laws, as well as in the structuring of the migrant labour system upon which the low-wage cost structure of the mining industry was and would remain based.

The key territorial concept for the industrial pass law was that of a labour district. Law 22 of 1895 (Transvaal) required Africans to have a pass from their employer if they wished to move within the district, and a travel pass if they moved outside the district or across the border. Kahn also cites the Town Regulations (18 September 1899) that required coloured males above the age of 12 residing in any village or town to have a town pass. However, this may not have been put into place before the outbreak of the War.[81] Law 23 of 1895 (Transvaal) applied to the proclaimed gold areas and divided them into labour districts. Together, the two laws operated to facilitate the migration of African labour to the mines and to reduce the power of these migrant labourers. On travelling to and entering a labour district, an African was to exchange the state-provided travel pass for a three-day work-seekers' pass (a state-provided district pass). For a time,

---

79   According to the Chamber of Mines: 'Owing to the existing inadequate pass laws and regulations for the control of Native labour, it is impossible to secure such combination on the part of employers as would enable Native wages to be reduced to a reasonable level.' This lack of enforcement may even have been a benefit to the mining industry as it arguably allowed the labour monopsony of WNLA to be effective (Richardson, 1982: 10).
80   Kahn, 1949: 279. Kahn cites evidence given to the 1897 Mining Industry Commission and the Chamber of Mines by CS Goldmann, a member of the Executive Council of the Chamber of Mines. See 1895 Annual Report 106 (cited in Kahn).
81   Law 22 of 1895 (Transvaal); Kahn, 1949.

arm badges were mandated for work seekers.[82] Once African work seekers found employment, their employers retained their state-provided district passes and issued them with an employer's pass.[83]

The demarcation of a labour district dramatically lessened the bargaining power of migrant labourers, and in particular these pass laws lessened the power of those who had come from Mozambique using the 'tramping system', which was the majority of Africans working on the mines. According to Patrick Harries, the 'tramping system' refers to the practice established from the 1860s by groups of African migrants travelling overland to engage in wage employment. While their ultimate destination might have been employment on the mines, they would stop and work for short periods along the way to gather resources to continue the journey. The self-sufficiency these migrants generated through this system was important in forcing employers to pay at least a decent wage. By relying on their established tramping system, Mozambican migrants had, for instance, prevailed over the objectives of retaining labour of the assisted immigration to the Zululand sugar farms in the 1870s.[84] The alternative to tramping to the mines was to travel to the mines with the labour recruiters. Through the 1890s, the tramping system was strong enough for labourers to do battle with the employers.[85]

The creation of two organisational alliances signalled the advent of the industrial pass and the demise of tramping. First, the Transvaal Government, after hesitating in 1893, endorsed the mine owners' proposed industrial pass system in 1895. As Harries points out, 'Law No. 23 of October 1895 attacked the very basis of the tramping system by restricting the freedom with which black workers could withdraw their labour or move from mine to mine in search of better working conditions'. Its 'cardinal aim', according to the *Mining Journal*, was 'the reduction of the ridiculously high native wage'.[86] The second

---

[82] Ibid.
[83] One historian argues that the success of WNLA was based in part on the co-operation of the Mozambique officials (Katzenellenbogen, 1982: 111).
[84] Harries, 1994: 43–44. Harries discusses the failure of Immigration Law 1 of 1876 (Natal).
[85] Op cit: 127.
[86] Op cit: 128.

factor was just as significant and took place at the other end of the migrant labour nexus. From November 1895, the Portuguese colonial administration established effective control over the chiefdoms of southern Mozambique. The colonial authorities and the chiefs then in tandem used their control to regulate the flow of African labour to the mines. The Africans now faced migration regulation at both ends of their tramping journeys. The combination of a state-supported industrial pass system in the Transvaal and Mozambican state control over emigration reduced the Africans' mobility and broke the tramping system.

This three-way organisational alliance was demonstrated in the substance of what might otherwise be thought of as international or diplomatic negotiations. After direct negotiations between the Transvaal mining industry and the Mozambican government, officials of the Government of the Transvaal agreed with their Mozambican counterparts on a pact governing labour migration in 1897. A Portuguese official, the Curator, was allowed to operate on the Rand to suppress clandestine immigration to South Africa (especially permanent immigration), register Mozambican labour, and extract registration and endorsement fees from either the African mine workers or their employers on a per capita basis. The industrial pass system of the 1890s was thus established with the assistance of migration regulation enforced not at the borders of the Transvaal juridical territory, but rather by enforcement both in the labour districts of the Transvaal mines and in the colonial districts of Mozambique. One should note, however, that this does not mean the industrial pass system was totalistic. Charles van Onselen has argued that Africans remained able to exploit the pass law system of the pre-Union Rand even to the point of militarily challenging state authority.[87]

Nevertheless, once established, this industrial pass system was essentially ratified by the British Empire. The post-war British administration led by Lord Milner aimed to facilitate favourable conditions for the mining industry. To this end, Milner adopted the labour district system as well as the general pass regulations extant previously. Furthermore, he accepted the purposes of the Transvaal's pass laws in terms of providing labour control and also providing a

---

[87] Van Onselen, 2001: 368–397.

means of identification of Africans (a function which served the goal of labour control as well).[88] Although the harshest of the Transvaal's laws — considered inhumane — were repealed under pressure from London,[89] Milner found acceptable and left in place most of the pass laws, taking the stance that any evident evils were because the laws had not been well administered. He did, however, through a proclamation, abolish the administering of lashes as a penalty under the system.[90] The district pass was renamed a labour identification pass and the industrial pass system and other movement pass requirements for Africans were continued. Exemptions were made for non-Africans in terms of Proclamation 35 of 1901 (High Commissioner), Proclamation 37 of 1901 (High Commissioner) and Ordinance 28 of 1902 (High Commissioner).[91]

As one might expect, the complexity and variation of the laws regulating the movement of Africans was confusing to those subject to their provisions. Indeed, the articulated African demand was for clarity rather than repeal. In 1906, the Transvaal Native Congress had petitioned the British House of Commons for simplification of the pass laws. Its key demand was the free issue to every tax-paying native of a life-long identification certificate to replace the variously issued passes.[92] A multiplicity of legislation contributed to the confusion. For instance, by 1908, in addition to the industrial pass system, proof of payment of taxes had to be produced on demand in terms of Act 9 of 1908 (Transvaal).[93] Proclamation 18 of 1903, a municipal regulation, required that non-exempted persons have urban night passes, thus adding another source and layer of regulation.[94] In response to demands for clarity and effectiveness, Act 18 of 1909 (Transvaal) shifted control of the pass system from local authorities to the Transvaal central administration. This significant move bypassed the municipal layer of implementation and combined an industrial pass system with an urban

---

[88] Kahn, 1949: 280.
[89] Kahn, 1949.
[90] Chanock, 2001: 411–412. Proclamation 19 of 1901 (High Commissioner).
[91] Kahn, 1949: 280.
[92] Op cit: 281.
[93] Kahn, 1949.
[94] Ibid.

one. The 1909 Act replaced the labour identification pass with a system of registration of service contracts in the proclaimed urban areas.

The Orange Free State differed from the centralised administration of the Transvaal by continuing to give municipalities the authority to collect revenue through local pass laws. To a large extent, these urban passes remained separate from industrial ones. Further, the industrial pass system of labour districts established by proclamations extended to the mines of the Orange River Colony.[95] In the Free State, passes were a direct source of local government funding as well as facilitation of migration regulation by the mining industry. Indeed, the Parliament noted in 1914 that: 'it is to be regretted that the action of the municipalities has in some cases lent colour to the accusation that they regarded the natives under their control as a source of revenue.'[96]

THE CHINESE MINE-LABOUR SCHEME

Regulation pertaining to Chinese migrant labour in the Transvaal was population specific and dealt with both the mobility and the governance of that population. It was particularly important in the post-South African War and pre-Union period. It occupied a conceptual position somewhere between the African pass laws and Asian population registration, perhaps closer to the former. This migrant labour scheme had important effects upon the financial health of the mining industry as well as policing methods in the Transvaal. In response to a perceived need for labour on the mines, nearly 64 000 Chinese persons were brought to the Transvaal as indentured labourers between 1904 and 1907. Later, in response to changing labour supply conditions as well as political pressure from both South Africa and Britain, virtually all these Chinese labourers were repatriated and replaced, leaving only around 2 300 Chinese persons who were not mine workers and who had already been resident in South Africa when the indentured labourers arrived.[97]

---

95 Ibid. Kahn cites the Orange Free State Ordinance 28 of 1903 and then the Native Labour Regulation Act of 1911.
96 First-Second Reports of the Select Committee on Native Affairs (S.C. 8 of 1914), Appendix A: xiv.
97 Yap and Man, 1996: 134–135.

The mining industry joined forces in 1900 to form an industry labour recruitment agency, the Witwatersrand Native Labour Association (WNLA), in an attempt to control the costs associated with recruiting unskilled African labour. Once underway, WNLA supplied labour to the mining industry, which comprised 114 mines organised into nine groups for financial and administrative purposes. WNLA assured a regular supply of labour to all. '[U]nder WNLA, the allocation of African labour complements on the Group basis also allowed some of the poorer and less popular mines to secure adequate supplies of labour.'[98] In his book, *Work, culture and identity,* Harries is right to point out the gaps in WNLA's strength especially until 1920. However, its control over labour recruitment was extremely significant.[99]

As Peter Richardson notes, WNLA recruited two-thirds of its labour from the south of Portuguese East Africa (Mozambique). Labourers from this stream engaged in relatively long terms of service and had a history of working on the mines from the 1800s. Initially strong after the South African War (38 631 recruits in 1902 and 43 625 in 1903 when the Central South African Railways also applied to use Portuguese labour in the construction of new lines), the African labour supply to the mines weakened to only 27 633 recruits in 1904.[100] Furthermore, in the view of the industry, the existing African labour supply was costly. The need for cost-effective labour was particularly acute in view of the industry's policy of pursuing low-grade ore. Thus the mining industry explored several alternatives to its African labour supply: prison labour was tried but was not available in sufficient numbers; importing labour from India was considered but rejected.[101] As a perceived last resort, the mining industry adopted a pro-Chinese labour position, and in 1903 the industry began to campaign for such a Chinese labour scheme.

The campaign was successful. The resulting Labour Importation Ordinance 17 of 1904 (High Commissioner) passed by the Milner administration might be cited as a paradigmatic example of a public–

---

[98] Richardson, 1982: 11.
[99] Harries, 1994.
[100] Richardson, 1982: 21–22.
[101] Op cit: 24.

private partnership. A formal law governing the Transvaal from the date of assent on 11 February 1904 was initially drafted and subsequently revised by the Chamber of Mines itself. However, a Transvaal law did not by its terms make a scheme of indentured labour. International signatures were needed. With Milner's support, the mining industry was able to get the colonial office in London to negotiate with the Chinese government, which was initially hostile to the labour recruitment scheme. In negotiating, the Chinese government was clear that it would deal only with the British authorities in London, not the colonial authorities in Pretoria nor the mining industry itself.[102] As Richardson notes, this international context had a particular consequence:[103]

> *By virtue of Chinese insistence, the scope of government intervention in the Transvaal experiment was widely increased. Unlike the terms of the Ordinance which, although subject to Imperial consent and scrutiny, were essentially the result of factors operating in the Transvaal, the regulations for importation were largely the result of an international agreement to which the Transvaal authorities and the mining industry were to succumb if they were to be in a position to exploit the Chinese labour market at all.*

The regulations issued by the Minister under the Labour Importation Ordinance then were to be a mechanism by which Milner could satisfy Chinese as well as British demands. The Chinese labourers' regulations thus bear close resemblance to the scheme regulating the emigration of Indian indentured workers to the British colonies, including to Natal. The two principal legislative models were the Indian Immigration

---

102 The Chinese government stated: 'The Chinese Government wished it to be understood that any regulation to which they could give their assent as carrying out the provisions of the fifth article of the Anglo-Chinese Treaty of 1860, must be embodied in an Agreement to which His Majesty's Government themselves, and not merely a commercial agent from the Transvaal, nor even the Colonial Government, must be a party. The Chinese Government could not, for the purposes of an Agreement, take cognizance of any such person as the "importer" mentioned in the Ordinance.' Op cit: 33–34.
103 Op cit: 34.

Act of 1883 (Natal) and the Trinidad Immigration Ordinance of 1893. The regulations incorporated legislation from the Indian experience that established minimum conditions in respect of shipping and accommodation, food and water, and medical provision.[104]

The legal regime governing the labour scheme was complex. Its international legal basis was the Anglo-Chinese Labour Convention signed on 13 May 1904 in London.[105] But the 1904 Labour Importation Ordinance, concluded before that date in 1904, was to be used to implement the Convention. Under sections 2 and 3 of the 1904 Ordinance, a Superintendent of Foreign Labour was appointed and a Foreign Labour Department (FLD) created in 1904. The appointment of these public offices satisfied the terms of the Convention. They assumed an inspectorial role, combining the protection of Chinese labour and of the mining industry. The FLD was funded by passport fees, paid by the mining companies in respect of each Chinese labourer. The scheme itself was administered by the Chamber of Mines Labour Importation Agency, a sister corporation to WNLA and which was absorbed into WNLA at the end of the scheme.[106] The Chinese Consul established in Johannesburg was not permitted to monitor the scheme on site or to participate in its administration.

The legal complexity of the Chinese labour scheme extended across British South Africa. Natal enacted a specific statute as part of the scheme in anticipation of the Chinese migration scheme. The 1904 Natal Act allowed for labourers from overseas to pass through Natal as 'transit immigrants' on their way to a neighbouring colony or territory.[107] The details of this transit scheme were left to regulations. The border inspection system of the Immigration Restriction Act did not apply to these transit immigrants except as directed by a proclamation.[108] While the 1904 Act was facially neutral, within a month of its passage it was made applicable by executive proclamation to the Chinese migration

---

104 Op cit: 37.
105 Op cit: 37–38.
106 Op cit: 47–48.
107 Act 7 of 1904 (Natal).
108 Section 6 of Act 7 of 1904 (Natal). Apparently, no proclamation was issued and this power was never exercised.

scheme adopted by the Transvaal Colony.[109] The Act is also noteworthy for its demonstration of the particularly tight social control directed at the Chinese community. In the transit immigrants' legislation, Chinese persons who were not transit immigrants and were residents of Natal were authorised to obtain certificates to show that they were residents.[110] To obtain these proof of residence certificates, fingerprint identification was required (unlike the Cape provision relating to its re-entry permits). The Chinese community's objections to fingerprinting were to no avail.[111] This technically voluntary yet effectively mandatory document mirrored that discussed above, which provided for Indians not covered by the Indian immigrants' legislation.

White traders and merchants were nervous about economic competition from the Chinese. To satisfy these interests, the 1904 Ordinance provided for the Chinese to work exclusively on the mines and for compulsory repatriation after service.[112] From the point of view of the 64 000 Chinese indentured labourers, the scheme entailed two major restrictions on their freedom of movement. First, they could work only in the occupational area of 'exploitation of minerals'. Second, they could work only in the geographical area of the Witwatersrand. '[T]he labour power of the Chinese work force was exclusively at the disposal of the gold-mining industry.'[113] Kept in compounds, issued with occasional passes, subject to harsh treatment and stiff penalties for offences (criminal and civil) such as failure to work, the Chinese mine workers were clearly in a scheme of indentured labour. Indeed, this effectively indentured status was one shared with African mine labourers:[114]

---

[109] The Act was passed on 18 June 1904. The *Natal Government Gazette* published Proclamation 70 of 1904 on 12 July 1904.
[110] Section 8 of Act 7 of 1904 (Natal): 'Any Chinese or other person belonging to a race from which transit immigrants are at any time being brought to South Africa, but who is not himself a transit immigrant, may, on application to the Magistrate of his Division, and on satisfying the Magistrate that he is lawfully resident in Natal, obtain from him a certificate showing that such person is a resident of Natal.'
[111] Yap and Man, 1996: 45.
[112] Richardson, 1982: 30.
[113] Op cit: 24.
[114] Richardson, 1982: 187.

> *The system which has grown up, as far as unskilled labour is concerned is obviously a branch of the indentured labour system. The natives on the mines are, in all essential respects, indentured labourers. They are brought from long distances and mostly from other countries. They engage in the first place for fixed periods. They do not have their homes at or near their place of employment. .... They are even subject to a special code of law.*

The 1904 Labour Ordinance legalised an extensive racial definition of skilled trades and can be said to have marked the start of the class-colour bar that has ever since characterised the South African mining industry.

Within little more than a year, there was widespread desertion among the Chinese, in the order of 1 700 labourers a year. The Chinese deserters contributed to a perceived crime problem on the Witwatersrand,[115] but the industry saw the real problem to be a lack of production. A harsh new permit system under the Amendment Ordinance 27 of 1905 quelled the problem,[116] and increased many of the existing penalties. Flogging, fining and imprisonment were now contract enforcement options directly available to the mining companies. The superintendent was also given the powers of compulsory repatriation. Under the 1905 Amendment Ordinance, judicial independence was severely compromised as inspectors in the Foreign Labour Department assumed the powers of magistrates with respect to offences on mine property.[117] Although the Importation Amendment Ordinance of 1906 (High Commissioner) later limited some of these powers, it accepted the principle of non-judicial deportations.[118]

The end of the Chinese migrant labour scheme came about largely through British politics. The Liberal government in Britain elected into power in 1905 opposed the use of Chinese labour and attempted to end the importation scheme. By the end of 1906, the mining industry essentially acquiesced to this, perceiving a more favourable South

---

[115] Op cit: 174.
[116] Op cit: 175.
[117] Op cit: 31.
[118] Op cit: 174.

CHAPTER 2 Early practices of regulating mobility

African labour market.[119] The British government issued Letters Patent granting the Transvaal a Constitution for responsible government in 1906, and this withdrew the right to renew the contracts of service of the Chinese labourers and decreed that the 1904 Labour Importation Ordinance lapse one year after the first meeting of the Transvaal Government's legislature. The Transvaal government, in turn, enacted the Indentured Labour Laws (Temporary Continuance) Act of 1907 thus providing for a more gradual phasing out of the scheme over two and half years from June 1907 to February 1910. By 1910, almost all the 64 000 Chinese had come and gone.

The Chinese labour importation scheme had a significant and lasting effect on migration regulation in pre-Union South Africa by reinforcing the pattern for labour migration to the mines for the remainder of the century. Labour migration to the mines was to be an operation run nearly exclusively and in a turnkey fashion by the industry itself. Rather than the government, the mines themselves, through their corporate entity, provided the necessary civil services including law enforcement and repatriation. As an example of the apparently successful operation of importation, repatriation and, of course, control, the Chinese mine workers continued to make a lasting impression in the mining industry.

This legacy was particularly strong around identification practices. Having first tried a photographic system of identification and the complex Bertillon anthropometric descriptions, the FLD officials began in 1904 to use fingerprinting to identify the Chinese mine workers. The fingerprinting technique worked well for state control as the Foreign Labour Department (FLD) organised even financial payments from the mines to itself around fingerprints. After the last of the Chinese workers had been repatriated, the collection was destroyed. Significantly, the fingerprint officials of the FLD were transferred to the Asiatics division of the Department of the Interior. From 1907, this state department began the process of fingerprinting adult Asian males in the Transvaal. From 1909, the Native Affairs Department (NAD) supported decentralised fingerprinting and identification practices for Africans at the mines. In 1912, the police initially proposed amalgamating the

---

119 Op cit: 182–183.

NAD collection with their own, but balked at the link to the mines' own collections. While Breckenridge points out that there were many problems with the technique in practice, the Chinese episode underpinned the long-persistent idea that fingerprinting could solve the perceived failures of the pass laws.[120]

CONCLUSION

This chapter's survey of the various territorial laws on mobility existing prior to the formal unification of South Africa provides a baseline from which to assess the development of migration regulation and citizenship in the years after 1907. These laws regulating human mobility were a varied lot. The laws regulating the migrant labour of the Chinese to the Transvaal were the result of successful pressure applied by the mining industry to remedy a perceived lack of African mine labour. In contrast, the vagrancy laws of the Cape operated more as background regulation and appeared to have become embedded in social and political status. As I have suggested, these regimes spanned a spectrum between an emphasis on population registration and of control over individual mobility. This variety was about to be sharply reduced as the four constituent territories themselves surveyed these pre-existing laws and practices. However, each had also enacted comprehensive immigration laws during the period from 1897 to 1907, as discussed in the following chapter. .

---

120 Breckenridge, 2014.

CHAPTER 3

The rise of borders

This chapter traces the development and content of the pre-Union comprehensive territorial immigration statutes that were adopted between 1897 and 1907. It also traces the relationship on these immigration statutes to the pre-Union territorial laws of nationality. The migration regimes put into place by these laws purported to be comprehensive and based on territory — the territories of the political units that would join in the 1910 Union — and thus differ from the pre-existing population-based laws directed at Asians, Africans and Chinese. These laws — of the Transvaal, Natal, the Cape and Orange River Colony — look much more like the comprehensive territory-based regimes we today associate with nation states.

Although most studies of migration in South Africa that focus on law take the post-Union Immigrants Regulation Act 22 of 1913 as their guide, it is only from the perspective of national legislation that the year 1913 marks a beginning. Not surprisingly, given their histories, geographies and positions inside the British Empire, the four constituent territories that joined in the Union of South Africa in 1910 — the Cape, Natal, the Transvaal and Orange River Colony — had separate migration regimes. Each consisted of multiple layers of regulation. While they differed in significant respects of population coverage and method of enforcement, each of these laws nonetheless responded to a common South African phenomenon — a new wave of migration to British South Africa from India which began in the mid-1890s.

By 1907, each of the four candidate provinces would have facially neutral immigration laws based on similar concepts. Their laws put into place a system of colonial border inspection to which all persons, including Europeans, were formally subject. All responded to a concern about Asian immigration and this was reflected in the operation of the law and the exceptions allowed. Europeans were explicitly exempt from prohibited immigrant status in the Transvaal, Orange River Colony and the Cape. Indirectly, the same applied indirectly in Natal. A further significant aspect was that these immigration laws interacted with the nationality laws of the time in different ways. The Cape and Natal had laws that provided for a facially neutral citizenship. The Orange River Colony and Transvaal barred Asians from citizenship.

IMMIGRATION LAWS OF THE CAPE

After the South African War of 1899-1902, the Cape's migration regime was structured first by the Immigration Act of 1902[1] and then by the replacement Immigration Act of 1906.[2] These laws instituted the inspection of new arrivals at the borders by public officials and both applied to all immigrants entering the Cape territory. The Immigration Act of 1902 excluded migrants on several grounds: lack of literacy in a European language; lack of visible means of support/liability of becoming a public charge; information obtained from official channels; as well as three moral grounds (criminal conviction, lunacy and prostitution). In contrast to exclusionary provisions found elsewhere in the British Empire, infectious diseases was not listed among those at the Cape.[3] While the Immigration Act of 1902 itself applied to all nationalities and all races, the principal exemption was population-specific. The Act's border inspection regime did not apply to semi-skilled Europeans with a certificate of engaged employment. Section 3(g)[4] exempted

> European persons who are agricultural or domestic servants, skilled artisans, mechanics, workmen or miners, and are able to produce a certificate signed by the Agent-General of the Colony in England or others appointed by the Governor in England or elsewhere to grant certificates for the purposes of the Act, certifying that the person named therein has been engaged to serve, immediately on arrival in the Colony, an employer therein of repute at an adequate remuneration and for a reasonable period of time.

1　Immigration Act 47 of 1902 (Cape).
2　Immigration Act 30 of 1906 (Cape).
3　Section 2.
4　Section 3(g).

Another exemption was granted for all those domiciled in South Africa.[5] The exemption for Europeans who were semi-skilled was a migration policy peculiar to South Africa.

For the most part, the Immigration Act of 1906 continued the policies of the earlier Cape legislation. The 1906 Act largely re-enacted the six grounds for exclusion of the earlier Act, with section 3(a) including Yiddish as a European language.[6] Likewise, the 1906 Act again exempted from exclusion semi-skilled Europeans with a certificate of employment. This did not exempt these Europeans from the application of the Act but merely from the operation of the exclusion clauses. Hence European applicants with a certificate of engaged employment were required to present themselves for the procedures of inspection upon arrival, but there would be no substantive reason to object to their admission to the Cape Colony.[7] In a significant modification, the Immigration Act of 1906 recast the general domicile exemption. The 1902 Act had exempted from its application all persons domiciled in the High Commission territories in South Africa.[8] At this time, the Office of the High Commissioner for South Africa had jurisdiction over the four candidate provinces as well as Basutoland, Bechuanaland, Griqualand West, Rhodesia and Swaziland.[9] In other words, only new residents were subject to border inspection under the 1902 Act. In the 1906 legislation, this general exemption was replaced with two separate exemptions. The first was for all persons born in South Africa.[10] The second was for persons domiciled in South Africa as long they were persons of European birth.[11]

Asians domiciled but not born in the Cape received a lesser advantage than an exemption. Asiatic persons lawfully resident in the Cape were eligible to apply for permits authorising temporary absence from the territory. These permits for temporary absence were to be issued in terms

---

5 Section 3(f).
6 Section 3(a)-(f).
7 Section 4(h).
8 Section 3(f).
9 Kennedy and Schlosberg, 1935.
10 Section 4(f)(a).
11 Section 4(f)(b).

of the regulations.[12] This re-entry permit was thus a border inspection document (as opposed to the registration document for Asiatics in the Transvaal). While it was theoretically possible that a lawful Asiatic resident could leave the Cape without such a re-entry permit and return without falling within any of the exclusion grounds, the re-entry permit was a practical requirement for an Asian not born in South Africa to exercise the right to leave and return. Finally, the 1906 Act may also be regarded as the introduction into South Africa of a formalised practice of political asylum. It allowed immigrants fleeing religious or political persecution to be exempted from the exclusion ground of liability, that is of becoming a public charge or of having no visible means of support, but subject to receiving a licence from the Minister. This provision did not necessarily grant admission. For instance, an immigrant fleeing religious persecution could still be excluded on the basis of the other grounds of exclusion, such as a history of criminal conviction. Still, the 1906 asylum modification did remove the most significant obstacle to admission to the Cape: exclusion on economic grounds. Section 3 of Act 30 of 1906 (Cape) is thus the South African forerunner of its modern refugee protection legislation, the Refugees Act 130 of 1998 (South Africa). One should note that the term 'refugees' was also used in the Transvaal to refer to the Asian population. However, there it was used for persons returning to their places of prior residence after the War rather than for those fleeing persecution.

Both the 1902 and 1906 Acts of the Cape were implemented through deportation and inspection regimes. Immigrants found to have violated the provisions of the 1902 or 1906 Acts were liable to a sentence of hard labour or a fine as well as removal from the territory. This removal power did not specifically exclude persons born in South Africa but such persons were exempt from border inspection and thus unlikely to violate the Act.[13]

As with the earlier 1902 law, the enforcement provisions of the 1906

---

12 Section 4(g): 'Any Asiatic who having, when lawfully resident within the Colony, obtained from the Minister a permit issued under such Regulations as shall be proclaimed thereof by the Governor, authorising him to temporarily absent himself from the Colony, returns in accordance with the terms and conditions of such permit.'
13 Section 5. Compare with section 8 of the 1902 Act (Cape).

Act merely provided a framework for the appointment of officers. It mandated no particular structures for its administration, thus giving the Governor regulatory authority.[14]

LAWS PERTAINING TO NATIONALITY IN THE CAPE AND NATAL

The Cape immigration laws did not interact or overlap with any nationality regulation. In the Cape and other British colonies, the legal background of the Empire controlled nationality policy. As generally understood at the time, the English common law extended British nationality to all born within the territories.[15] Thus, Africans as well as Europeans born in the Cape were British subjects. Britain would deal with matters of nationality such as diplomatic protection. However, what was of direct relevance for the Cape Colony was the acquisition of nationality by non-British subjects. Here, as in other local jurisdictions, the Cape had explicit legislation. The Aliens Naturalisation Act 2 of 1883 (Cape) (originally and as amended by Act 35 of 1889 (Cape)) was not solely a naturalisation statute. It covered more broadly 'the Law relating to Aliens' and did so in a liberal manner. For instance, section 2 of the 1883 Act laid down the principle that persons of alien birth could 'purchase, acquire, own and dispose of immovable property in this colony in like manner as natural-born subjects of Her Majesty'. It had no minimum period of residence and was facially neutral, fitting within the generally liberal naturalisation policies of the Empire.[16] Nonetheless, from 1904 onwards, additional legislation disqualified Chinese persons from naturalisation. Section 33 of the Chinese Exclusion Act 37 of 1904 (Cape) precluded certificates of naturalisation being issued to Chinese persons.

In Natal, the Immigration Restriction Act 1 of 1897 also applied to all persons of any nationality and any race. Hitchins (Statutes of Natal (1900)) is careful to note that the Immigration Restriction Act refers

---

14 Section 7 of the 1902 Act (Cape). Section 8 of 1906 Act (Cape).
15 The common law rights of overseas subjects is a long-standing historical debate, Hulsebosch, 2003: 439–482.
16 Aliens Naturalisation Act 2 of 1883 (Cape).

to 'prohibited immigrants' irrespective of nationality. Nonetheless, the Act was intended at least in part to restrict passenger Indian immigration and came after a Natal commission of inquiry into Indian immigrants in 1887.[17] Unlike the earlier Natal laws specifically directed at Indian immigrants, the Immigration Restriction Act implemented a border inspection system. The Act prohibited immigration to Natal in six categories: persons unable to write a European language (the education/literacy test); paupers; insane persons; persons suffering from a loathsome or contagious disease; persons convicted of a two-year felony; and prostitutes.[18]

The use of an education/literacy test as a ground for exclusion was an imperial first, 'a device allowing for administrative exclusion of Indians rather than the statutory discrimination which the British Government was so anxious to avoid'.[19] The inclusion of this clause in this early Natal statute led to Empire-wide calls (some successful) for a 'Natal law' that would be effective in letting in the right people and keeping out others. As Adam McKeown has shown, colonies and officials across the Empire embraced this and a series of laws that were 'non-discriminatory on the surface yet allowed great leeway of interpretation by officials on the ground'.[20]

The Immigration Restriction Act of 1903[21] soon replaced the initial 1897 Act in Natal. By comparison with both its predecessor and the 1902 Immigration Act of the Cape, the 1903 Natal Act added an extra ground for prohibition, of persons deemed by the Minister to be undesirable immigrants.[22] However, persons domiciled in Natal were exempted from the application of the Act in 1903 as long as they were not prohibited immigrants.[23] This precondition differed significantly from the Cape Act, which had a different legal structure, in that exempting people from immigration legislation also effectively exempted them

---

17 Immigration Restriction Act 1 of 1897 (Natal); Peberdy, 2009.
18 Section 3 of Immigration Restriction Act 1 of 1897 (Natal).
19 Bradlow, 1978.
20 McKeown, 2008: 186.
21 Immigration Restriction Act 30 of 1903 (Natal).
22 Section 5(g) of Act 30 of 1903 (Natal).
23 Section 4(f). Section 6 of Act 1 of 1897 was to the same effect.

from prohibited immigrant status.[24] As discussed below, the Natal law was not comprehensive in this respect. Pre-dating the provisions of the 1904 Chinese Exclusion Act in the Cape, the 1903 Natal Act authorised the issue of domicile or residence certificates that were used by both Chinese and Asian persons to re-enter Natal, although an amendment in 1906, Act 3 of 1906 (Natal), tried to control the use of the concept of domicile.[25] Nevertheless, the 1903 Act set up a structure of specialised enforcement officers: the Principal Immigration Restriction Officer and Immigration Restriction Officers. In 1897, the law had enabled the Governor to appoint people to enforce the Act, but no specialised enforcement agency had been set up. Most contraventions of the Act were within the jurisdiction of magistrates. The 1897 Act prescribed a penalty of deportation and six months' hard labour for 'prohibited immigrants'. Despite the 1903 amendments to the administrative structure, the magistrates' courts retained jurisdiction over the enforcement of the Act.[26]

The population coverage of the Natal immigration laws also differed from the population coverage in the Cape in a significant way. Both the 1897 and 1903 Natal Acts did not apply to persons where another law or government scheme provided for their immigration.[27] It did not pre-empt or override other migration laws. Thus, the Natal Acts did not cover much of the indentured Indian population which remained under the 1891 Indian Immigrants Act (Natal). The 1903 Natal Act also innovated by creating a category of prohibited immigrants who had entered the territory but had not been admitted to immigrant status and might never be. It did this by extending the liability of immigrants to border inspection treatment after entry: for up to 12 months after entry, upon proof that a person was a member of any of the classes of prohibited immigrants, that person could be dealt with as a prohibited immigrant.[28]

The Cape laws, by contrast, provided an interlocking system

---

24 Supra notes 9–10.
25 Section 33. Bradlow, 1978; Yap and Man, 1996: 44–45.
26 Sections 35 and 41 of Act 30 of 1903 (Natal).
27 Section 2(b): 'This Act shall not apply to ... any person of a class for whose immigration into Natal provision is made by law or by a scheme approved by Government.'
28 Section 8 of Act 30 of 1903 (Natal).

of exclusion and exemptions within its immigration laws which substantively covered Asian as well as European migration. It should be noted that the 1904 Chinese Exclusion Act (Cape) was passed after the initial Immigration Act of 1902 (Cape) and subsequent to the Natal law of 1903.

The Natal comprehensive immigration laws were, however, similar to those of the Cape in not interacting or overlapping with any regulation of nationality. Natal followed the legal background of the Empire. So, for instance, Africans born in Natal were British subjects. Likewise, at least some Asians not covered by the Indian immigration laws were British subjects as well. Still, there was a major difference in local nationality policy in Natal compared with the Cape. From as early as 1874, naturalisation in Natal was limited to aliens of European birth or descent.[29] This restrictive naturalisation policy in Natal did not go uncontested. For instance, in 1886, 19 Chinese residents seeking naturalisation petitioned the Governor of Natal for a change in the law. This resulted in a drafted but never enacted amendment to this effect.[30] From 1905 onwards, however, aliens with five years of residence in Natal or one year of residence in Natal and four years elsewhere in the Empire could apply for a certificate of naturalisation. Naturalisation in the United Kingdom was recognised as naturalisation in Natal without application.[31] Within substantive areas, such as land policy, the principal aim of pre-Union migration regulation in Natal was to facilitate European immigration to Natal particularly from Britain.[32]

IMMIGRATION AND RELATED LEGISLATION IN THE TRANSVAAL

While the Cape and Natal territories operated directly against the background of the British Empire, the Transvaal was something of a different story. Situated inland and composed of a number of smaller

---

29 See Act 18 of 1905 (Natal) (repealing Law No. 23, 1874 (Natal) which repealed and re-enacted Law No. 8, 1874 'For further facilitating the Naturalisation of Persons of European Birth or Descent').
30 Yap and Man, 1996: 43–44.
31 Section 5 of Act 18 of 1905 (Natal).
32 Hattersley, 1950.

pre-existing Afrikaner republics, the Transvaal partook of the imperial legal regime only insofar as it bent to the influence of the British High Commission or was compelled by force of arms. However, the force of arms was exactly what defeated the Transvaal at the turn of the century. Under British control from 1877 to 1884, the Transvaal was again under British control from the end of the South African War in 1902. With his influence thereby dominant, Lord Milner and his military government had a relatively free hand in reconstructing the Transvaal as they saw fit. In so doing, Milner largely responded to the white population generally and to the mining industry in particular. As British High Commissioner, he established an Immigration Department in Johannesburg in 1902 to facilitate white migration. This administrative creation can be distinguished from the Immigration Department established by the Immigrants Restriction Act 15 of 1907.

Whether one counts from 1902 or 1907, the pre-Union Transvaal was the last of the constituent territories to adopt a general immigration law. From 1902, sections 19–24 of the Indemnity and Peace Preservation Ordinance 38 of 1902 enacted into law by the British High Commissioner regulated the return of 'refugees' into the Transvaal. In addition to new entrants being issued permits by the Governor, the military administration allowed previous residents or those who were actually resident at the end of the War to enter the territory. A year later, the 1902 Ordinance was updated with the similar Peace Preservation Ordinance 5 of 1903 (High Commissioner). The 1903 Ordinance left the details of the system to the wishes of the Governor, with the exception that permits could not be issued to burghers who refused to take the oath of allegiance.[33] Under the 1902 and 1903 Ordinances, returning residents could be white, Asian or coloured (which included African persons). Under the system as administered in this post-conflict situation, Asians required a registration certificate issued either by the pre-existing Transvaal government (in terms of Law 3 of 1885) or by the new military regime on the basis of former residence. A registration certificate allowed its holder to be considered a resident. In addition, a limited number of Letters of Authorisation were issued to Asiatics returning to

---

33   Peace Preservation Ordinance 5 of 1903 (High Commissioner), sections 3 and 4.

the Transvaal for the first time since the South African War. The Letters of Authorisation were halted from 30 November 1907.[34]

The Peace Preservation Ordinances put into place a strict enforcement and deportation regime, and, according to Shear,[35] linked control over mobility and political activity. Both the Transvaal and Orange River Colony ordinances provided for the offences of sedition and others. Shear argues that the repressive political culture of these little-analysed laws persisted through to the end of the 1920s.

People arrested in terms of the ordinances were to be brought before a magistrate who could order them to leave the Colony.[36] In addition, the Lieutenant-Governor could order a person to leave on reasonable grounds that the person was dangerous to the peace and good government of the country.[37] People ordered to leave but who failed to do so would be subject to a fine and imprisonment with hard labour.[38]

The enforcement of these ordinances with respect to Asians depended upon the bureaucratic registration system. Border inspection or direct policing of permits supplemented the scheme of Asian migration regulation accomplished through registration. Policing was not particularly extensive. For instance, although the power to do so was more broadly granted by the ordinances, only a small number of police officers and members of the South African Constabulary were actually authorised to order people to produce their permits, despite section 5 of the 1903 Ordinance providing that

> [a]ny person entering or residing in this Colony may be called upon by any member of any Constabulary or Police Force or other person authorised thereto by the Colonial Secretary to produce a permit issued under this Ordinance or to give satisfactory evidence that he

---

[34] Section 2. CIA 26, M2, vol 1: Registrar of Asiatics to Chief Staff Officer, SAC (1 June 1906). CIA 26, M2, vol 2: Chamney to Secretary, SAC Headquarters (27 November 1907).
[35] Shear, 1998.
[36] Section 6.
[37] Section 10.
[38] Sections 7 and 8.

belongs to one of the classes exempted from the necessity of having such a permit under the provisions of section two.

Resident magistrates also had the power to demand that a person produce a permit.[39]

The number of border inspection stations was likewise small and their capacity limited. Nonetheless, migration regulation through registration was fairly effective. The administering authorities claimed that their laws had nearly stopped new Asian immigration. The Registrar of Asiatics, Montfort Chamney, noted:[40]

> [T]he Government has at least done what very few Governments would attempt unless backed by special legislation, namely has stopped all Asiatic immigration. None but refugees are allowed to come in and as these formed a part of the domiciled population, their return cannot be called 'immigration'.

Up to 1907, these military ordinances and their administration (in civilian hands from 1905) took the place of immigration legislation in the Transvaal, with the 1903 Ordinance falling 'into desuetude against Europeans but [being] retained for use against Asiatics'.[41] In 1907, the legislature of the newly responsible Transvaal Colony enacted generally applicable immigration legislation, the Immigrants Restriction Act 15 of 1907 (Transvaal). This Act repealed the Peace Preservation Ordinance of 1903, except to the extent that the Ordinance was incorporated into the Asiatic Law Amendment Act 2 of 1907 (Transvaal), new legislation specific to the Asian population. The 1907 Immigrants Restriction Act innovated somewhat on the models of the pre-existing Cape and Natal legislation, combining features of both. The 1907 Act defined a category of prohibited immigrants using six standard grounds for prohibition: illiteracy in a European language; liability of becoming a public charge;

---

39   CIA 26, M2, vol 1: Secretary to the Law Department to Assistant Colonial Secretary (1 March 1906).
40   Yap and Man, 1996: 96.
41   Bradlow, 1978: 14.

danger to the public health (suffering from an infectious disease); and the three morality grounds — prostitution, criminal history and lunacy. There were also two grounds for executive discretion: official information, and reasonable grounds to believe a person was dangerous to peace and good government.[42] The Transvaal Act followed the practice of the Cape and of its own previous direct rule government (but not of Natal) in making its immigration regulation applicable to all people, even those subject to other migration regulation. In contrast with the Cape, however, but in company with Natal, there was no specific asylum provision. Also like Natal, the Transvaal Act was an immigration act that could be used for the removal of prohibited immigrants found within the territory.[43]

While the Immigrants Restriction Act of 1907 (Transvaal) applied generally to members of all population groups, exemptions to the grounds for exclusion contained within the Act did not. Europeans who had been at any time lawfully resident in the Colony were not prohibited immigrants. Moreover, semi-skilled Europeans were exempted from the exclusion of public charge.[44] There also was an exemption for any Asiatic who was eligible for or had received a certificate of registration in terms of the Asiatic Law Amendment Law 2 of 1907 (Transvaal) and who was not a prohibited person in terms of the morality, public health and executive opinion exclusion grounds.[45] Therefore it became necessary for Asiatics to register to escape the operation of the illiteracy and public charge exclusion grounds of the Immigrants Restriction Act. Under those grounds, Asiatics without a registration certificate could become prohibited immigrants and thus were not allowed to enter or re-enter the Transvaal. In addition, the Act linked some significant substantive rights to migration status: prohibited immigrants could not obtain a licence to carry on a trade nor could they acquire an interest in land.[46] Africans were exempted from the literacy and public charge exclusions without

---

42 Immigrants Restriction Act of 1907 (Transvaal), section 2(1)–(8).
43 Section 5.
44 Section 2(i).
45 Section 2(f) and (g).
46 Section 8 (using migration status as a bar to property ownership).

any certificate of registration.[47] Section 4 of the 1907 Act allowed the Governor to enter into an agreement with neighbouring colonies for the purposes of the Act.[48] The following year, section 1 of the Immigrants Restriction Amendment Act 38 of 1908 (Transvaal) narrowed the scope for Africans to avoid prohibited immigrant status. Africans — 'descendants of the Aboriginal races of Africa, South of the Equator' — would be exempt from most grounds for prohibited immigrant status only if they entered and remained as 'unskilled labourers'. Africans who entered illegally or overstayed in contravention of the laws (including the pass laws of the Transvaal) would be prohibited.[49] The exemptions of the Transvaal Act of 1907 thus provided a vision of the preferred and desired mix of populations in the Transvaal.

For its enforcement, the Immigrants Restriction Act of 1907 (Transvaal) authorised the establishment of an immigration department to prevent the entry of prohibited immigrants as well as to deal with those already present.[50] The Act provided for arrest on reasonable grounds of being a prohibited immigrant.[51]

> *Every person found in this Colony who is reasonably suspected of being a prohibited immigrant may be arrested without warrant by any magistrate, justice of the peace, police officer or officer of the department and shall as soon as possible be brought before a court of resident magistrate to be dealt with according to law.*

Removal was to be ordered by a magistrate and followed a process providing for fines, imprisonment and detention pending removal. People born in the Transvaal were not barred from removal.[52] The sole route out of such detention was by having two sureties pay £100 each and for the detainee to leave the Colony within a month. If a person was at liberty on surety and failed to leave, he or she was subject to removal

---

[47] Section 2(h) (later amended by section 1 of Act 38 of 1908 (Transvaal)).
[48] Section 4.
[49] Section 1 (amending section 2(h) of Act 15 of 1907 (Transvaal)).
[50] Section 3(1).
[51] Section 9.
[52] Section 5.

without the involvement of a magistrate in terms of section 6. This process also applied to those convicted under the Immorality Ordinance and with some safeguards to those deemed dangerous to the peace and good government.[53] In an adjustment a year later, which largely protected white people, judicial safeguards were made available to those persons deemed dangerous and liable to removal, while persons returning to the Transvaal after being subject to an order of removal were made subject to administrative detention and removal.[54]

Citizenship and nationality in the Transvaal

Citizenship in the Transvaal before the South African War was limited to burghers as a constitutional matter and thus to white male Dutch speakers. The issue of citizenship had been at the crux of the *uitlander* crisis and had formed part of the run-up to the conflict. In the pre-war Transvaal, the legal rights of citizenship included the right to vote but did not necessarily include the right to freedom of movement. After the war, this citizenship became explicitly entangled with the status of a subject of the Empire and with imperial nationality policy. From 1904, naturalisation within the Transvaal was facially neutral and available to persons upon five years residence in the Colony or one year in the Transvaal and four years elsewhere in the Empire.[55] As discussed below, Law 3 of 1885 (Transvaal) explicitly limited naturalisation by Asians in the Transvaal.

IMMIGRATION AND RELATED LEGISLATION IN THE ORANGE FREE STATE

The pre-Union Orange Free State adopted a general immigration law significantly earlier than the Transvaal. Chapter XXXIII of the Statutes of the Orange Free State, a 1891 codification of laws, had provided for the removal of white criminals from the state. In 1899, the Free State essentially adopted those provisions into its legislative scheme as well as mandating additional sections generally applicable to entry.[56]

---

53 Section 6(c); section 6(a) and (b).
54 Section 2 (amending section 6 of Act 15 of 1907 (Transvaal)).
55 Naturalisation of Aliens (Amendment) Ordinance 10 of 1904 (High Commissioner) (amending Naturalisation of Aliens Ordinance 1902).
56 Admission and Expulsion of Aliens To or From the Orange Free State Law 18 of 1899

Drawing most directly upon the Natal model, sections 2–6 of the 1899 law instituted a form of border inspection. Aliens were required to have passports showing satisfactory employment status. These passports had to be 'proper passports granted by or on behalf of the Government of the country to which [they belong], and vised by a Consul or Consular official of this State'. From their passports the authorities would determine whether such aliens could support themselves or obtain work. Letters of conduct could be used in default of passports. These aliens were to report to the appropriate officials who would issue travelling and residential passes as prescribed by the government.[57]

Substantively, the 1899 Act's formal presumption was that aliens 'shall be admitted into this State'. The six standard grounds of exclusion (literacy, public charge, lunacy, infectious disease, convicted felony and prostitution) would prohibit the entry of an alien.[58] An additional specific section targeted public agitators who were liable to an order of expulsion and a warrant of removal.[59] Only white persons were subject to a particular ground for expulsion: 'any white person' who had 'not yet acquired full burgher rights' found guilty of a grave crime committed elsewhere could be expelled from the state and would face harsh penalties of a fine and imprisonment with hard labour upon return.[60] The implication was that Free State citizens could not be deported, at least not on the ground of a grave crime committed elsewhere. In explicitly linking citizenship to protection against deportation, the Free State differed from its neighbouring territories.

While the 1899 Free State comprehensive law was generally applicable, there was one rather large exception: the entry provisions of the law did not apply 'to coloured people'.[61] For these people, pass laws would be operative. In addition, the 1899 law left in operation the portion of the Free State statutes providing 'against the influx of Asiatics'. The Free State thus followed the Natal model rather than that of the Cape

---

(Orange Free State).
57   Sections 2–6.
58   Section 9.
59   Section 10.
60   Sections 11 and 12.
61   Section 8.

or Transvaal in effectively limiting the application of its immigration legislation to those not covered by another law.

From the end of the South African War in 1902, migration regulation in the Orange Free State, now called the Orange River Colony, followed the pattern set by the Transvaal. Initially, the Orange River Colony was governed by the same sections 19–24 of the Indemnity and Peace Preservation Ordinance 25 of 1902 (High Commissioner).[62] Naturalisation was regulated by the Naturalisation of Aliens Ordinance 1 of 1903 (High Commissioner).[63] This ordinance granted eligibility to those with five years of residence in the Orange River Colony or one year of residence immediately preceding the application together with residence in the dominions of the Empire to make up five years.[64] A register of naturalised persons was to be kept and was to be open for inspection.[65] A 1905 amending ordinance added that persons with a certificate of naturalisation into British nationality were to be treated as having been naturalised in the Orange River Colony.[66]

CONCLUSION

Thus, six years before the passage of the Immigrants Regulation Act in 1913, each constituent territory of the Union had developed its own

---

[62] This law regulated sedition and other matters consequent on the lifting of martial law. The Ordinance allowed entry into the territory through a permit system (section 19). Persons who were already resident in the territory were allowed to enter as well as those mentioned in the Terms of Surrender and those in government service. The terms of the permit system were left nearly completely to the Governor, other than that any burgher of either the South African Republic or the Orange River Colony needed to take an oath of allegiance (section 20). Persons found in the Colony who entered it without permission could be called before a magistrate and ordered to leave, with harsh penalties for disobedience (sections 21 and 22). The substance of the public agitators clause persisted, the Lieutenant-Governor being granted the power to order a person to leave the territory upon 'being shewn to his satisfaction that there are reasonable grounds for believing that any person within this Colony is dangerous to the peace and good government of the country' (section 24).
[63] Naturalisation of Aliens Ordinance 1 of 1903 (High Commissioner).
[64] Section 1(1).
[65] Section 8.
[66] Section 2 of the Naturalisation of Aliens Amendment Ordinance 7 of 1905 (High Commissioner).

comprehensive immigration law. At the same time as the South African War, the development of these laws began in Natal, continued in the Cape and culminated in the Transvaal. Enacted from 1897 to 1907, these laws provided for classes of persons to be excluded or to be 'prohibited' as well as for certain classes of persons to be exempt from the operation of these laws. These legal prohibitions and exemptions established substantive criteria for immigration policy in racial, territorial and occupational terms but not in terms of nationality. Indeed, these laws largely operated separately from what little explicit regulation of nationality existed, the regulation of the acquisition of nationality (naturalisation). These laws also established formal deportation and enforcement structures that did not use nationality or citizenship as organising principles.

While in broad terms these laws were similar to each other (and to the 1913 Immigrants Regulation Act), they did contain significant differences with respect to population coverage as well as method of enforcement. To some extent, these laws built upon each other over the 10-year period of their adoption as they evolved towards population coverage rather than border control as a basis for enforcement.

The set of comprehensive immigration laws enacted from 1897 to 1907 was the result of political concerns held by established elites regarding a wave of migration by Indians to South Africa from the 1890s. Existing laws on mobility largely catered for the economic interests of the mining industry in the Transvaal and the large sugar plantations in Natal. European traders and shopkeepers, however, were threatened by Asian competition and found resonance with other Europeans through laws designed to limit the residence rights of their fellow British subjects. From the passage of the 'Natal clause' in 1897 through to the enactment of the Immigrants Restriction Act in the Transvaal in 1907, white political elites throughout British South Africa responded in increasingly collective ways to restrict Asian migration. In doing so, they set the stage for the elaboration of national laws regulating mobility before and after Union, the subject of the next three chapters.

CHAPTER 4

Union, the Act and the Registrar of Asiatics, 1907–1914

The unification of South Africa was a process driven by white South African political elites in response to economic issues. Four territories within the British Empire carefully and relatively smoothly negotiated with each other to form a Union. For the most part, processes and events within the territories that became South Africa propelled unification. Nonetheless, Britain and its Empire placed significant constraints on the structure of the chosen legal vehicle for unification, the Union. Formed out of four territories, the Union was an open legal form with carefully negotiated scope for other colonial territories in what was then understood as British South Africa to join and to be joined later.[1] Significantly, the new Union gave its central government constitutional competence over native and Asian affairs. Although the related issue of the franchise was much discussed, migration and citizenship matters were either given low priority or simply not treated at all. The governing assumption was that the nationality of Union subjects was and would continue to be determined by the law of the British Empire. In this law, the unifying legal structure is the crown: all individuals living under the crown are subject to its sovereignty, and thus are subjects rather than citizens.[2]

Two pieces of legislation followed hard on the heels of Union: the Naturalisation of Aliens Act 4 of 1910 (Union) and the Immigrants Regulation Act 22 of 1913 (Union). Both laws were demanded by the change in national form, a shift from four separate territories with various statuses to one unified self-governing territory. The Naturalisation of Aliens Act worked against the assumed background of imperial rules of nationality and concerned itself only with regulating how such a

---

1 Chanock, 1977.
2 Gorman, 2006: 9.

nationality could be acquired. It adopted the Cape model of the facially neutral acquisition of citizenship at the Union level.

The most significant law for the development of citizenship in the new Union of South Africa was undoubtedly the Immigrants Regulation Act. Like the laws it consolidated, the Immigrants Regulation Act 22 of 1913 was a comprehensive immigration law regulating the movements of all people. While it largely did not displace the existing provincial regulation of Asian affairs, the Immigrants Regulation Act established categories of prohibited and exempted persons, provided for deportation after procedural safeguards, and established administrative as well as judicial mechanisms for enforcing the rule of law. Drafted with Europeans and Asians in mind, one of its goals was to limit further Asian immigration. At its conception, the 1913 Act largely ignored African migration, both because it was consistent with the existing African pass laws and because African migration was then regulated by a different Union law, the Native Labour Regulation Act of 1911.[3] Partly owing to the structures set up by the pre-Union Transvaal legislation, the Transvaal migration practice and institutions had a determinative influence in shaping the Immigrants Regulation Act. In addition to having a role in shaping the law itself, the administrative practice of the Registrar's Office of the Transvaal was directly adopted as the governing instructions and interpretation of the Immigrants Regulation Act. This influence also resulted in the notorious deeming order directed against Asians.

ECONOMIC AND POLITICAL UNIFICATION[4]

The central economic conflict in pre-Union southern Africa concerned customs revenue and port competition. From 1903, a customs union attempted to enforce economic cooperation among the territories within British South Africa although without political cooperation.[5] However, conflict continued to brew between the inland territories (principally the Transvaal) and the coastal colonies (the Cape and

---

3 Native Labour Regulation Act 15 of 1911 (Union).
4 Thompson, 1960.
5 Op cit: 13.

Natal). In this conflict, the Mozambique Convention that Milner had negotiated with Mozambique on behalf of the Transvaal in 1901 was of particular importance.[6] This agreement facilitated labour migration to the Transvaal for employment on the mines and — even more importantly — the use of the Mozambican port of Delagoa Bay. As Leonard Thompson[7] noted: '[T]he Transvaal held the whip hand. Thanks to her possession of the one great industry in all South Africa, the coastal colonies had become dependent upon her, and thanks to the position of Delagoa Bay, she could afford to be independent of them.' With the mining industry and consequent international connections, the Transvaal thus held the dominant position in the economics of unification.

At this point, the constituting territories of British South Africa had varying statuses within the British Empire. In the aftermath of the second and final South African War, the Cape Colony and Natal were self-governing territories with responsible government. The Transvaal and the Orange River Colony were annexed by Britain and were no longer self-governing. Other territories were administered either by the High Commissioner (Basutoland, the Bechuanaland Protectorate and Swaziland) or even by a private corporation, the British South Africa Company (Southern Rhodesia, North-Western Rhodesia and North-Eastern Rhodesia). A Governor administered the Nyasaland Protectorate. The administration of some of these territories was vested in the same person wearing different hats. In particular, Lord Milner was not only the High Commissioner for Basutoland, the Bechuanaland Protectorate, and Swaziland (the High Commission Territories) to April 1905 but also served then as the Governor for the annexed territories of the Transvaal and the Orange River Colony.

There was elite support for unification from a variety of quarters in Britain and South Africa. From 1906, a loose collection of British officials in Milner's Pretoria-based administration (a group famously termed Milner's Kindergarten) pushed the idea of a South African union for various reasons. These officials particularly argued that making

---

6   The Mozambique Convention was also known as the modus vivendi.
7   Thompson, 1960: 55.

South Africa attractive to British immigration was their long-term hope and future.[8] General Jan Smuts of the Transvaal, and other local South African politicians, supported unification based on a different set of calculations. They felt that unification represented an opportunity for greater local autonomy (albeit within the British Empire). In their view, unification should come only after the assumption of governance by the annexed South African territories.[9] Once the Transvaal was granted responsible self-government in 1906 and soon thereafter also the Orange River Colony, the remaining issues among European politicians in the four most closely linked territories were how to effect unification and on what precise terms.

The practical route to unification lay through the already long-scheduled 1908 Intercolonial Conference. Its agenda was to revisit and revise the malfunctioning 1903 Customs Union arrangements. Politicians from the Cape Colony, Natal, the Transvaal and Orange River Colony attended the Conference in Pretoria. Representatives from Southern Rhodesia (a territory considered part of British South Africa) and Mozambique attended as well. Including these additional representatives made good sense to the conference delegates. Indeed, the representatives of the Transvaal hoped that Mozambique with its labour supply could be included in the South African federation.[10]

The delegates at the 1908 Intercolonial Conference decided quickly to pursue political unification as well as customs reform. A process of legal steps then unfolded rapidly over the next two years. The Conference first resolved to meet again in Natal as a national conference after having received specific mandates from their territorial legislatures to negotiate and draft an Act of unification. This National Convention then met in a Durban session in late 1908 and a Cape Town session in 1908–1909. The resulting draft South Africa Act was considered by the various South African legislatures and then again by the National Convention in its Bloemfontein session in May 1909. In June, the draft Act was approved by the parliaments of the Cape, Natal, Transvaal and Orange River

---

8   Op cit: 61–70.
9   Op cit: 70–82.
10 Op cit: 75–76.

colonies. In August, the Act was approved by the British Parliament and received royal assent on 20 September 1909. The Union of South Africa was inaugurated on 31 May 1910, a general election was held on 15 September 1910 and the Union Parliament opened on 31 October 1910.

One of the heavily debated issues from the time of the 1908 Intercolonial Conference was the franchise. In 1905 the South African Native Affairs Commission had been appointed to find a common native policy for British South Africa. It had recommended that natives not be placed on the common voters' roll, but rather be represented by a fixed number of representatives in each colonial parliament.

Disregarding this 1905 recommendation of the South African Native Affairs Commission, the South African politicians driving unification saw the way forward as a status quo compromise. The Transvaal and Orange River Colony barred coloureds, Asiatics and Africans from political rights. In the Cape Colony, the franchise was open to all men subject to simple educational and economic qualifications. Significant numbers of non-whites did, in fact, enjoy and exercise the franchise. In Natal, by contrast, where the principle of an open franchise applied, a series of laws and administrative practices effectively disqualified all but a handful of Indians and Africans. Realising that Union-wide adoption of the Cape franchise provisions was unlikely, the Cape's leading political figure, John Merriman, began to explore having the Union Constitution preserve the existing differences in the franchise laws, with an explicit and adequate security for the Cape franchise. The Durban session of the National Convention agreed to this. The Convention opted for a safeguard of a two-thirds supermajority in the Union Parliament to alter the Cape franchise. This status quo compromise left the precise laws governing qualifications for the franchise as well as the delimitation of constituencies to be regulated by the provinces. As it happened, however, the constitutional compromises decided upon with respect to qualifications and more importantly constituency demarcation were those that had been worked out in the Transvaal in the decade prior to Union.

CHAPTER 4 Union, the Act and the Registrar of Asiatics, 1907–1914

The contestation of franchise rights did not, of course, begin during the unification process.[11] For instance, in Thompson's view, the British missed an important opportunity for the provision of adequate franchise rights for native persons in 1902, in the Treaty of Vereeniging. In negotiating this peace treaty, which ended the South African War, Lord Milner took a more conciliatory position towards Boer demands to limit such franchise rights than did the British Colonial Secretary. Milner willingly gave up his relatively progressive initial positions on the franchise rights, in exchange receiving from the Boers better positions on language rights and constitutional development. As Thompson puts it: 'Britain thereby undertook not to admit any Africans to the franchise in the Transvaal or the Orange River Colony while she had the power to do so, and she ignored the Coloured inhabitants of those colonies.'[12] Maylam argues that Thompson does not take into account that the demand for exclusion of non-whites from the franchise came from English-speakers as well as the defeated Boers.[13] While these concessions made strategic sense from the point of view of encouraging European immigration, they left little scope for local non-European political citizenship. Milner is reported to have bitterly regretted this decision to yield to the Boers over the native franchise.[14]

The assumption by the Transvaal of self-government in December 1906 was perhaps another such missed opportunity. Despite Lord Milner's concessions, the Treaty of Vereeniging could be interpreted as at least not precluding a qualified non-racial franchise dispensation with educational and economic conditions such as existed in the Cape. Although they did not mandate it, the Treaty's terms arguably authorised a policy that at the outset admitted coloured and Asiatic men to such a qualified franchise for the future self-governing territories of the Transvaal and Orange River Colony. However, the Letters Patent issued by the British Government as the new Constitution for the responsible self-government of the Transvaal in 1906 did not attempt to

---

11 Loveland, 1999: 101–128; Thompson, 1960: 109–126, 212–226.
12 Thompson, 1960: 10–12.
13 Maylam, 2001: 147.
14 Op cit: 12–34.

take such a route. Instead, the vote was given to all white men over the age of 21, but not to non-Europeans, and not to women. The ideals of the devolution of responsibility to the colonies and of minimum standards for franchise rights were at odds here.[15] The Letters Patent did, however, contain a reservation clause under which the British Government could theoretically disallow discriminatory legislation. To be an effective substitute for franchise rights, this power would have had to be used more than it in fact was. In the next year, two pieces of Transvaal legislation, Acts 2 and 15 of 1907, which were explicitly discriminatory, were not disallowed.[16]

Some of these pre-unification debates over the wisdom of extending the franchise provided links between the issue of the franchise and the question of migration. In Natal, a 1862 legislative committee report opposing the extension of the franchise to Africans exercising individual land tenure simultaneously noted with alarm what the report termed 'a massive inflow' of African refugees over the previous two decades.[17] The link between franchise and migration was even clearer with respect to the action taken on Indian voting in Natal. In 1894, protests by local Indians and British imperial concerns over discrimination against British Indians delayed the passing of legislation that confirmed the disqualification of almost all Indians from the franchise.[18] In 1895, the Governor of Natal feared the power of Indians voting in the province and specifically predicated his fear on the prospect of 'fresh arrivals', while another speaker in the parliamentary debates felt that Africans would have more claim to the franchise than Indians, thus exemplifying the ambivalent position of the Indians.[19]

The significance of the franchise issue during unification has been appreciated — and perhaps over-appreciated — throughout South African historiography. However, the franchise issue was related in the debates to two other issues also on the table during the unification process: territoriality and nationality. One of these issues — the potential inclusion of the High

---

15   Op cit: 26–27.
16   Op cit: 27.
17   Evans and Philips, 2001: 96.
18   Op cit: 99–102.
19   Op cit: 99–100.

Commission Territories in the Union, that is territoriality — elicited significant debate during the unification process, while the other — the nationality regime of the newly unified country — attracted nearly none.

Among the delegates to these unification discussions the franchise issue did not stand alone. The question of franchise rights had a clearly perceived territorial aspect. As Thompson states: '[T]he question of the future of Basutoland, Bechuanaland Protectorate and Swaziland was linked to the franchise question.'[20] One link between the issue of territoriality and that of the franchise was political. After the 1908 Intercolonial Conference but before the National Convention, Smuts and other leading South African politicians became convinced that the Protectorates should be transferred to the Union immediately or at least soon after unification. The 1908 Conference had adopted the motion that Rhodesia could join the Union at a later stage. The three High Commission Territories were, however, not explicitly mentioned in the conference resolutions because it was 'advisable and discreet not to make any special mention of them for fear of raising a dangerous question, viz. — the treatment of Natives by independent African Administrations'.[21] Nonetheless, the commonly held expectation was that these territories would join the Union in due course.[22]

However, political opinion in London would not be so easily convinced. As Thompson notes, 'Britain recognised that she had special obligations to the Native inhabitants of those territories, and she was averse to allowing them to be included in the projected Union unless the Constitution provided some form of effective parliamentary representation for the non-Europeans throughout the country'.[23] South African expansionist aims were apparently thwarted by a genuine if paternalistic British concern.

Regardless of the actual motives, the discussion between the South Africans and the London Colonial Secretary on this point resulted in a schedule to the South Africa Act that would govern the future conditions

---

20 Thompson, 1960: 124, 375.
21 Chanock, 1977.
22 Op cit: 91.
23 Thompson, 1960: 124.

under which the British Government could agree to transfer the High Commission Territories to the Union's administration, although, according to Loveland, the most ever envisaged was the administration of these territories by the Union rather than their acquisition.[24] If this schedule were in the Union Constitution as agreed to by the Parliament, then any future transfer would not need to involve the Parliament but could be done directly by the British government. This schedule would form part of the Constitution of the Union of South Africa, but its provisions would lie dormant until the potential future inclusion of these territories.[25]

One of the envisioned conditions was a clause providing for relatively liberal free movement between the Protectorates and the Union. The South Africa Act, 1909, Item 18 stipulates: 'There shall be free intercourse for the inhabitants of the territories with the rest of South Africa subject to the laws, including the pass laws of the Union.'[26] Chanock argues that the schedule expresses a British native policy of protection of African land holding.[27] The schedule was never invoked and these conditions were never used for their carefully negotiated purpose. In fact, overtures by the Union for such transfer were rebuffed by Britain in the first two decades after Union, and when South Africa became a republic in 1961, the legal possibility of the conditions regulating the transfer of High Commission Territories to the Union fell away. Lesotho, Swaziland and Botswana themselves became independent of British rule in the 1960s.[28]

Towards the end of the unification process, the precise name of the unified territory came from a relatively late British amendment to the draft South Africa Act. The name 'the Union of South Africa' was given in distinction to the simpler 'South Africa' to avoid ambiguity, as the simpler term might also have been understood to mean British South Africa.[29] The South Africa Act itself, as passed by the British Parliament, thus embodied a distinction between 'South Africa' and

---

[24] Loveland, 1999: 120–121.
[25] Thompson, 1960: 271–279.
[26] The South Africa Act, 1909.
[27] Chanock, 1977: 29–31.
[28] Op cit: 80–81, 178–179.
[29] Thompson, 1960: 409.

the 'Union of South Africa'. The Union of South Africa consisted of the four British territories that had opted to join the Union. 'South Africa' or British South Africa consisted of the Union as well as the territories that continued to be administered by the High Commissioner for South Africa. The Union was a subset of 'South Africa', although the subset was not closed.

The second issue linked to the franchise question — nationality — was the topic of much less debate during the unification process, a reflection of the assumptions of the participants. Those involved with the new Union of South Africa understood the territory to be within the British Empire, and the uncontroversial assumption was that the legal position of British nationality would continue. This nationality would operate on the international plane and would coexist with the provincial regulation of other aspects of citizenship such as the franchise and land ownership. The assumption of British nationality fits with the political currents supporting unification. As Thompson points out, Milner had a vision of a South Africa stretching from the Cape to the Zambezi, which would be a federated South Africa within an imperial structure.[30] Smuts and other South African politicians also more pragmatically embraced the British Empire umbrella of the Union.

Within the conferences and committees there was thus little debate on the clauses that relate to nationality in the draft legislation of the South Africa Act. What debate there was concerned the acquisition of nationality. The naturalisation clause of the draft South Africa Act originated in a report of the franchise committee of the National Convention at its Durban session.[31] The initial proposal had a qualification that naturalising persons be 'of European descent'. This qualification was, however, dropped at the following Bloemfontein session. Furthermore, nationality of the Union would be Union-wide and would not be specific to any one province. As enacted, the South Africa Act

---

30   Op cit: 4.
31   Op cit: 225.

provided that the naturalisation of persons in any of the colonies should be valid throughout the Union.[32]

The unification of the four colonies and the structure of that union itself had considerable significance for citizenship. Reflecting the rather close economic ties among its European inhabitants, the Union was a unitary rather than a federated structure. In its formal political and legal composition, the Union was a single entity with a single executive and legislature rather than an entity comprising a collection of federal provinces. Unification thus implied that migration and nationality would be matters regulated at the national and not at the provincial level. Arguably, one of the most significant consequences of unification lay in the allocation of the legal competence over migration. This jurisdiction to regulate the movement of persons was legally built into the Union at the national rather than the provincial level (as was true for matters such as the franchise). The power to regulate migration was, for instance, linked to the potential accession to the Union of the High Commission Territories, therefore it was a national competence.

The legal structure of unification had population-specific consequences as well. The South Africa Act explicitly provided two population-specific bases for the distribution of legal competence within the new Union. In the terms of the Constitution, not only native affairs but also Asiatic affairs were matters that were vested separately in the Governor-General-in-Council.[33] The location of competence for native affairs in the Governor-General rather than in the provinces was the result of a South African drafting proposal. Competence over Asiatic affairs in the Union was also placed at national rather than provincial level. Indeed, the placement of this competence was a proposal that came from the Indian government via imperial structures, and was intended to protect Indian emigrants. The Colonial Secretary had requested this on behalf of the Secretary of State for India 'so that provincial governments would not be able to initiate discrimination against Asiatics'. The South African delegates readily agreed.[34] The administration of the affairs of these

---

[32] Section 138 of South Africa Act of 1909 (United Kingdom).
[33] Chanock, 2001: 257–261; Thompson, 1960: 201–202, 411.
[34] Op cit: 411.

two specific populations was thus assigned by the South Africa Act to a particular site within the Union: the Prime Minister acting together with the other ministers. The Union and not the provinces would have the constitutional authority and responsibility to regulate the movement and other affairs of Asians and Africans. This was a significant building block for the creation of South African citizenship.

UNION NATIONALITY AND IMMIGRATION LAWS

The first piece of Union legislation within the national competence of migration and nationality (and only the fourth statute to be passed by the Union Parliament) was the Naturalisation of Aliens Act 4 of 1910, under the charge of the Minister of the Interior.[35] Consistent with the last-minute amendment to the South Africa Act that dropped the 'European' qualification for eligibility to naturalise, the 1910 Act adopted as Union law the Cape facially neutral naturalisation model rather than the racially restrictive regimes of the other provinces. Repealing the naturalisation laws of the four component provinces, the Act replaced them with one uniform Union regime. Although dropping the European descent qualification had been considered a 'bone of contention', no opposition to its deletion and even some support was voiced in the parliamentary debate around the Bill.[36] In legal principle at least, the way to naturalisation for non-European aliens was thus open across the Union.

The 1910 Act understood nationality and citizenship against an imperial legal background. For instance, the Act defined 'alien' to mean a person who was not a British subject.[37] British subjects were thus not aliens, and even if they were not resident, domiciled or born in the Union, as British subjects they enjoyed rights as Union nationals. For those persons who were not British nationals, the 1910 Act allowed aliens over the age of 21 with two years' residence within the past five years to apply to the Minister of the Interior for naturalisation in South Africa as British nationals. Naturalisation would result in having the same rights

---

35   Section 2 of the Naturalisation of Aliens Act 4 of 1910 (Union).
36   *Debates of the House of Assembly (Hansard)* (14 November 1910) cols 72 and 74.
37   Section 2 of Act 4 of 1910 (Union).

as a natural-born British subject. In sum, the Act essentially put into a statute the background legal norm of nationality in the common law of the Empire with some specific South African procedures. At this time, the British Empire had relatively consistent legislative rules regarding naturalisation.

A parliamentary debate around a proposed amendment to the Bill revealed that the rights of British nationals in the Union, as opposed to rights granted at the provincial level, were understood in a purely formal sense. The proposal was to change the rights of a naturalised person to be the equivalent not of the rights of a British subject but rather the equivalent of the rights of a British subject born in the Union.[38] General Smuts, as the Minister of the Interior, rejected the proposed amendment primarily on the grounds that it would lead to the equality of rights among all British subjects born in the Union. He noted that the distinction between subjects born in the territory and those born outside was used only in several specific laws in the Cape. His objection thus was not to the proposed equality between naturalised and native-born national. Rather, Smuts was specifically defending the unequal state of political rights among all British nationals in the Union. The record of the parliamentary debate gives the following as his statement: '… natural born British subjects born in South Africa … did not have the same rights. [We have] a natural born coloured British subject, born in the Cape Province, who could get a vote in that Province, but not in other parts of the Union, so that even in South Africa [we do] not have natural born British subjects all having the same rights. It was impossible to go into all these inequalities. [We know] that there [are] these distinctions, and there were special laws for each case; and these laws would apply.'[39] General Smuts's remarks used the example of franchise but also indicated a South African (and colonial) understanding of the status of British nationality (whether of British subjects or of British subjects born in the Union) whereby the rights associated with that status could be unequal and contested.

38　*Debates of the House of Assembly (Hansard)* (10 November 1910) col 180.
39　Ibid.

The second piece of Union legislation within the national competence of migration and nationality was the Immigrants Regulation Act 22 of 1913. As detailed in Chapter 3, each of the four constituent provinces had facially neutral and comprehensive immigration laws by 1907, with varying implementing bureaucracies. Nonetheless, in contrast to the quick passage of the naturalisation statute, it took the Union Parliament nearly three years to consolidate these provincial laws into the Union-wide Immigrants Regulation Act 22 of 1913.[40]

Before examining the Act itself, it is necessary to understand what the Act did and did not do. The 1913 Act did replace most of the facially neutral provincial statutes that regulated migration across provincial borders, both with other provinces and with other states.[41] It thus consolidated the provincial facially neutral migration laws at a national level. However, the Act did not replace the population-specific migration statutes, including the African pass laws. Furthermore, in at least one aspect relating to economic citizenship, the Immigrants Regulation Act supplemented the provincial migration regime in all provinces. Section 8 forbade prohibited immigrants without lawful residence from conducting a business or trade through a licence as well as from holding immovable property. In 1962, the Froneman Commission termed this the 'greatest disqualification to which foreign Bantu are subject'.[42] Nor did the 1913 Act consolidate or repeal most of the provincial laws that regulated Asian affairs. The Natal laws relating to Indian immigrants were not repealed, nor was the Chinese Exclusion Act in the Cape. With respect to the Free State, the 1913 Act had a specific savings provision for Chapter XXXIII of the Orange Free State Statutes.[43]

The 1913 Act accomplished three tasks. First, it established substantive criteria for making some persons prohibited immigrants and exempting others, while at the same time it authorised the Department

---

40 Bradlow, 1978; Peberdy, 2009.
41 The Immigration Act 30 of 1906 (Cape), the Immigration Restriction Act 30 of 1903 (Natal), the Immigrants Restriction Act 15 of 1907 (Transvaal) and the Admission and Expulsion of Aliens To and From the Orange Free State Law 18 of 1899 (Orange Free State).
42 Froneman Commission Report, 1962: para 75.
43 Section 7 of Act 22 of 1913 (Union).

of the Interior to issue migration documentation in the form of temporary permits and re-entry certificates to some prohibited persons. Second, it authorised the deportation of persons from the Union mostly after formal procedures. And third, it established a national framework for its administration and implementation that allowed for limited judicial oversight over migration yet provided for some internal organs of administrative justice.

As its first function, the Immigrants Regulation Act established substantive criteria for classifying immigrants. These criteria were laid out in two separate sections, one listing grounds for prohibition and the other the grounds for exemption. Persons could be declared prohibited immigrants either in respect of the Union or of a particular province. The Act included as grounds for declaring a person a prohibited immigrant the seven grounds given in the Natal 1903 statute. Using the 'Natal clause', the 1913 Act, in relevant sections, declared as prohibited those persons unable to read and write any European language; those likely to become a public charge; persons deemed undesirable from information received from the government; any prostitute or person living on earnings of prostitutes; persons convicted of certain offences; idiots and the insane, and persons with certain diseases.[44]

In enacting these grounds of exclusion, the Immigrants Regulation Act of 1913 section 4(1)(a) was phrased in facially neutral terms. In this it mirrored the 1903 Act of Natal from which it had borrowed some elements. The 1913 Act gave the Minister broad powers to deem a class of persons to be prohibited immigrants. This deeming power effectively meant the Minister, at his discretion, could declare a group of persons to be prohibited immigrants. This deeming power effectively constituted a discretionary substantive criterion for prohibited immigrant status.

In a separate section from its listing of grounds for prohibited immigrant status, the Act established grounds for exemption from this status. In terms of substantive policy, the positively stated grounds for exemption must be understood together with the grounds for prohibited immigrant status. It is in these grounds for positive exemption that the Immigrants Regulation Act directly employed population-specific

---

[44] Section 4(1)(b)–(h).

terms. Section 5(h) exempted 'persons of European descent who are agricultural or domestic servants, skilled artisans, mechanics, workmen, or miners and who have entered the Union under conditions which the Governor-General has approved ...'[45] Other exemptions were non-discriminatory at face value. Section 5(f) exempted persons domiciled in any province. Applicable generally to wives and children of people domiciled in the Union, the exemption in section 5(g) was later slightly broadened in response to resistance from the Asian population.[46] Section 5(e) exempted from the Act people born of parents domiciled 'in any part of South Africa included in the Union'.[47]

In a significant indication of the influence of the mining industry, section 5(d) of the Act exempted from prohibited immigrant status 'any person who entered the Union under conditions as may be prescribed from time to time in accordance with any law or under any convention with the Government of a territory or state adjacent to the Union' with certain provisos.[48] This statutory provision essentially incorporated the Mozambique Convention whereby workers came to the mines of the Transvaal from Mozambique in terms of an agreement originally negotiated by the mines with the Transvaal and

---

45   This exemption draws on section 4(h) of the 1906 Cape Act and section 2(i) of the 1907 Transvaal Act. The Natal Act did not have a skilled European labour exemption.
46   Section 3 of the Indian Relief Act 22 of 1914 (Union) granted exemption to the second wives of exempted men and to the children of these second wives, at least under certain conditions. One of the spurs to the resistance leading to the Indian Relief Act 22 of 1914 was the Cape decision of *Esop v Union Government* which decided (contrary to the position in the Transvaal) that potentially polygamous marriages were not marriages for purposes of immigration of the spouses. Loveland, 1994: 139–40.
47   This phrasing demonstrates the use of the term 'South Africa' to refer to territory beyond the Union. Section 5(e) exempted 'any person born before the commencement of this Act in any part of South Africa included in the Union whose parents were lawfully resident therein and were not at that time restricted to temporary or conditional residence by any law then in force, and any person born in any place after the commencement of this Act whose parents were at the time of his birth domiciled in any part of South Africa included in the Union'.
48   Immigrants Regulation Act of 1913, section 5(d) includes the following provisos: ... 'provided he is not such a person as is described in sub-section (1)(c), (d), (e), (f), (g) or (h) of the last preceding section; and, provided further he is not a person domiciled north of twenty-two degrees south of the equator in such a territory or state.'

Portuguese governments.[49] Section 5(d) was of great significance for Africans: persons covered by this section were exempted from the ministerial declaration of section 4(1)(a) as well as the European literacy requirement of section 4(1)(b). Thus mineworkers entering in terms of the Mozambique Convention were exempt from the 'Natal clause'.

Another exemption of the 1913 Act of benefit to Africans was the exemption granted to persons born in the Union before 1913 if their parents were lawful residents and were not restricted to temporary or conditional residence. Exemption also applied to those born after 1913 if their parents were domiciled in the Union.[50] Because Africans were not as a class declared prohibited immigrants (unlike Asians), they could take advantage of this exemption.

The effect of all these exemptions was limited to the national sphere. They did not trump the operation of other provincial statutes that regulated movement, nor did they exempt people from the operation of the pass laws. Moreover, these exemptions had an ambiguous relationship to the deeming order under section 4(1)(a). The exemptions would take precedence over the effect of a ministerial deeming order under section 4(1)(a) only in respect of entry to the Union. With respect to inter-provincial movement and a section 4(1)(a) deeming order, the exemptions did not operate.[51] In the conception of the 1913 Act, the Union was a collection of provincial borders.

In fulfilling its second function, the Immigrants Regulation Act provided for the deportation of people from the Union. The removal power could be exercised in terms of any of four specific provisions. The first two provisions were subject to quite strict safeguards. The most general removal section, section 4(1), directed the immigration officers to remove prohibited immigrants whose entry or presence was unlawful. In terms of this section, all persons to whom the Act applied were thus under threat of removal if they were prohibited immigrants. This meant that people subject to the section 4(1)(a) order deeming them to be prohibited immigrants were liable to removal should their legal status

---

49   This convention was also known as the Portuguese East Africa Agreement.
50   Section 5(e).
51   Section 5 of Act 22 of 1913.

lapse. There was, however, a significant safeguard which demonstrated that deportation in terms of this section was a fairly formal procedure. Section 4(3) stated that a list of all persons who had been declared prohibited and been removed had to be tabled in Parliament for each of its sessions. The second removal provision, section 6(1)(b), authorised the deportation of any person previously dealt with in terms of the Act. Such a person could be convicted of an offence and removed under a warrant of removal. This section thus focused on what could be termed 'habitual' migration law violators. Although it would trigger the safeguards of the criminal process, the section 6 removal provision was generally applicable and not limited to people born outside the Union.

The other two removal powers contained in the Immigrants Regulation Act could be exercised after either an administrative or a judicial process. Applicable to those who had previously been removed or who had failed to comply with an order to leave the Union, section 21 allowed for arrest without a warrant and summary removal. Section 22 provided for removal upon expiration of sentence.[52] These last two provisions could not be used against people born in the Union.

As its third function, the Act established a framework for its implementation that allowed for limited judicial oversight over migration. In its first section, the Act established an immigration department under the control of the Minister of Interior.[53] The functions of the department were very broad: 'the performance of all work, whether within or outside the Union, necessary for or incidental to the prevention of the entrance of prohibited immigrants into the Union or into any Province where their residence is, under this Act or any other law, unlawful, or necessary for or incidental to their removal from the Union or any such Province.'[54] In addition to its broad delegation of power to this department, the 1913 Act limited the jurisdiction of the general courts of law over migration. Magistrates' courts and the High Court no longer had jurisdiction with

---

52 The Froneman Commission Report refers only to the first of these removal power sections. Froneman Commission Report, 1962: para 76.
53 Section 1(1) of Act 22 of 1913 (Union).
54 Section 1(2) of Act 22 of 1913 (Union).

respect to activities undertaken in terms of the Act.[55] However, the courts still had power over naturalisation activities.

In place of the jurisdiction of the ordinary courts, the Act set up a system of immigration boards appointed by the Governor-General.[56] These boards were intended to be chaired by magistrates.[57] Aliens as well as British subjects could appeal to the boards against actions taken against them in terms of the Act. As discussed further in Chapter 5, these boards granted certain procedural protections, and there was a strong duty to provide reasons in writing to the persons detained, restricted or arrested.[58] However, questions of law could be reserved for the courts of law only by motion of the board, an immigration officer or a British subject appellant.[59] Essentially, this meant that access beyond these boards to the courts of law was guaranteed only to British subjects declared prohibited immigrants.

In accomplishing each of these three tasks (prohibiting immigrants, deporting persons and adjudicating migration status), the Immigrants Regulation Act was neither substantively based on nationality nor organised administratively around that concept. Nationality is mentioned only once in the Act and then in a peripheral context in section 4(3). Nor did the Act distinguish between nationals and non-nationals. Instead, the Immigrants Regulation Act was based on the

---

[55] Section 3(1) of Act 22 of 1913 (Union).
[56] Section 2(1) of Act 22 of 1913: 'The Governor-General shall appoint so many boards as he may deem desirable for the summary determination of appeals by persons who, seeking to enter or being found within the Union or any Province, have been detained, restricted, or arrested as prohibited immigrants. Each such board shall have jurisdiction in respect of such port or ports of entry and such areas in the Union as the Governor-General may determine.' See further Government Notice 1185 of 1913 (*Gazette* No. 399 of 1 August 1913) 734.
[57] Section 2(3) of Act 22 of 1913 (Union).
[58] Section 2(5) of Act 22 of 1913 (Union): 'Whenever leave to enter the Union or any particular Province is withheld by any immigration officer or police officer, or when any person is detained, restricted or arrested as a prohibited immigrant, notice of that fact and the grounds of refusal, detention, restriction or arrest shall be given by such officer in writing to the said person and, if such persons has been restricted on arrival by sea, also to the master of the ship on which he has arrived.' It is not clear if 'person' includes a non-British subject here.
[59] Section 3(2) read with section 3(3) of Act 22 of 1913 (Union).

concept and status of a prohibited immigrant. It is migration regulation without citizenship, based on a contemporary understanding of immigration. Its deportation provisions and their overall omission of birth or citizenship bars to deportation underline the Act's relative blindness to nationality. Conceptually and practically, British subjects and white South African residents were as susceptible to deportation as any others. Their vulnerability was demonstrated in a dramatic fashion in the 1914 general strikes. The nine labour leaders deported after the strike were British nationals, all born outside South Africa. Nonetheless, the deportation could have been applied to them regardless of their place of birth.[60] Their deportations led to a lively and extended debate in the House of Assembly, which focused more on the processes of law not being followed than on their deportations despite British nationality.

Instead, the Immigrants Regulation Act 22 of 1913 was organised around the mobility of the different population groups: European, Asian and African. It was drafted with Europeans and Asians clearly in mind. By its terms, European as well as Asian arrivals were subject to national not provincial migration regulation. Still, the effect of the Act on those two groups differed greatly. For Europeans, the new Act effectively limited the potential scope of the registration provisions of Act 36 of 1908 (Transvaal). Persons exempted from being declared prohibited immigrants on the grounds of habits of life, literacy, public charge and undesirability or those granted a temporary section 25(1) permit under the new Act did not have to comply with the Transvaal provincial registration.[61]

Although clearly within the parameters of the Act, Asians did not enjoy the exemptions granted to Europeans and thus remained subject to the pre-existing Transvaal registration provisions. Furthermore, section 25(2) allowed for the issuing of certificates to any person 'apprehensive that he will be unable to prove on his return that he is not a prohibited immigrant'. These permits were thus re-entry certificates and appear in practice to been used mostly by the Asian community.

---

60   Trew, 1938: 251–69.
61   Section 28 of Act 22 of 1913 (Union).

Reflecting the Act's link to the administration of Asian affairs in practice, the Immigrants Regulation Act 22 of 1913 was modified immediately after its passage in response to resistance from the Indian community. The Indian Relief Act 22 of 1914 made some significant adjustments to the population-specific provincial migration regime in Natal. For example, it provided for the appointment of marriage officers to solemnise Indian marriages and that the procedures of such marriages remained regulated by provincial laws.[62] It also stated that an Indian wishing to take advantage of the free passage back to India had to apply within 12 months of the expiry of his or her indenture.[63] Furthermore, it authorised the Minister to offer other Indians a free passage to India on condition that they relinquished their rights of residency and domicile in the Union.

Most importantly, after the 1914 Act was passed, the Asian community succeeded in obtaining the repeal of a number of onerous Natal statutory provisions: Indian immigrants at the end of their indenture were no longer required to take out a pass to remain in the Colony,[64] and neither were their children.[65] The employer sanctions for employing persons without such passes were also repealed.[66] Apart from these changes, the 1914 Act was careful to note that the marriage sections of the Indian Immigration Law of 1891 (Natal) were not changed.[67]

By contrast with the European and Asian populations, the Immigrants Regulation Act did not explicitly deal with African migration. In some respects this left Africans in a better position than Asians. There was no direct bar to the movement or residence of Africans in the Act, making them eligible to be granted rights and privileges in terms of the legislation. Unlike the Asian population, Africans were never officially deemed prohibited immigrants in terms of section 4(1)(a). However, even as individuals Africans could not lay claim to the skilled

---

62 Section 1 of Act 22 of 1914 (Union).
63 Section 5 of Act 22 of 1914 (Union) (amending section 3 of Act 17 of 1895 (Natal)).
64 Section 8 of Act 22 of 1914 (Union) (repealing section 6 of Act 17 of 1895 (Natal)).
65 Section 8 of Act 22 of 1914 (Union) (repealing sections 2, 3, 5 and 6 of Act 2 of 1903 (Natal)).
66 Section 8 of Act 22 of 1914 (Union) (repealing Act 39 of 1905 (Natal)).
67 Section 4 of Act 22 of 1914 (Union).

Europeans exemption to prohibited immigrant status.[68] This was true even though the occasional educated or wealthy foreign African could (and occasionally did) satisfy the Act's entrance provisions in the same way as a European or Indian. To illustrate this point, the *1921 Year Book* reports arrivals in the category of 'Mixed Race and Other' for 1915 as 39, for 1916 as 34 and for 1917 as 20. This category was differentiated from 'European' and 'Asiatic'. Likewise, nine 'Central African Natives' were recorded as prohibited immigrants for 1918.[69]

It may be most accurate to say that the 1913 Act simply did not consider Africans at all — it turned a blind eye to African mobility. The exemption granted to Africans effectively incorporated the pre-existing Mozambique Agreement as well as the pre-existing set of pass laws without attempting to revise or change either. Section 5(d) of the Act granted an exemption to persons (in practice nearly uniformly African) entering in terms of a law or an agreement with adjacent territories or states. This exemption allowed the mining industry to continue with the status quo and also effectively determined that the Act was supplemental to and did not replace existing local and provincial pass laws.

As we have seen, local authorities regulated the movement of Africans through the pass laws. These completed the more social regulation undertaken by private employers of African labour, such as the mines through their systems of urban compounds. While these laws were indeed varied and complex, there was some uniformity of method, at least with respect to the legal control of movement of African men into urban areas.[70] The pass laws were a form of migration regulation that depended on identification issued by private employers.[71] Interestingly, in practical terms in the Orange Free State and legally in the Transvaal, the pass laws were not applied to African women.[72]

The 1913 Act did not disturb this pattern of control over the movement of Africans. For instance, there was little doubt that municipalities, through the provinces, had the competence to enact pass laws. Since

---

68   Section 5(h).
69   *1921 Year Book*, 1921: 163, 167.
70   Corder, 1984: 141–143; Loveland, 1999: 150. See also *R v Detody* 1926 AD 198.
71   Hindson, 1987: 31.
72   Wells, 1993.

there were no conflicting substantive rules regarding control over movement (except in the case of the Chinese population), pre-emption and conflicting policies between national and provincial laws presented few problems. If nothing else, the proviso placed into the incorporation conditions of the High Commission Territories in the schedule to the Act of Union made it clear that the pass laws were understood to be complementary to the regulation of the Immigration Act.[73] After the Act was passed, the Union Parliament specifically chose not to change the inherited hodgepodge of pass laws. In 1914, a parliamentary select committee convened to examine the issue reported that it was inadvisable to consolidate 'the complex and diverse pass laws in force in different provinces'.[74] These laws were nonetheless the subject of popular protest, with one articulated demand being a call for their rationalisation.[75] Thus, after Union, Africans (whether foreign or not) continued to experience migration regulation more ordinarily and directly at a local rather than a national level.[76]

In one important respect, the Union Parliament did make a significant policy choice regarding African regulation through the Immigrants Regulation Act. The proviso to section 5(d) in the 1913 Act meant that 'person[s] domiciled north of twenty-two degrees south of the equator' — Africans often known as 'tropical natives' — could not be brought into the Union through the mines' or any other recruitment scheme. The primary concern behind the ban on the recruitment of these Africans was one of public health. Africans from north of that line died in mine employment in truly alarming numbers.[77] Jeeves argues that cost-cutting group administration prevented individual

---

73 Interdepartmental Committee on the Native Pass Laws Report, 1922: 2.
74 First–Second Reports of the Select Committee on Native Affairs (S.C. 8 of 1914) and Third–Fourth Reports of the Select Committee on Native Affairs (S.C. 8A of 1914).
75 Hindson, 1987: 34–35; Wells, 1993.
76 Maylam, 2001: 158–162. Maylam divides urban segregation and apartheid in 20th century South Africa into three main forms and provides a historiography of them: 'the segregation of space — residential, commercial, and recreational — along racial lines; the restriction of access to urban areas according to racial (and other) criteria; and the racial differentiation of local government'. Although these three forms are clearly interrelated, this study covers only the second form, the control over movement.
77 Jeeves, 1985: 73–92.

mine administrators from appreciating the need to address the mortality rate.[78] However, public health was not the only reason for the ban. Restrictions on the entry of Africans from the tropics in the decade around Union were also justified as a measure to combat illicit recruiting. By allowing the government to cancel the contract of a native from north of that line, the original intention of these restrictions was understood 'to eliminate the factor of the Labour Agent's profit in connection with the recruitment of tropical labourers, and thus to secure the cessation of illicit recruiting'.[79] When the decision was announced by the Minister of Native Affairs, the Witwatersrand Native Labour Association (WNLA) considered a legal challenge. However, the passing into law of section 5(d) put the matter to rest.[80] Thus, this provision of the Immigrants Regulation Act should be understood alongside the passage of the Native Labour Regulation Act 15 of 1911.

THE REGISTRAR OF ASIATICS AND THE ACT

It is a notorious and infamous South African fact that, as soon as the Immigrants Regulation Act was passed in 1913, the Minister of the Interior exercised his deeming power in terms of the Act to declare Asians as a class of prohibited persons, an action that became publicly known only several days later through the operation of the Immigrants Appeal Board in Natal. Indeed, many have interpreted the order made in terms of the Act as evidence that British paternalistic non-racialism was subverted by South African racist intent.

The generally accepted history of this event proceeds more or less along the following lines. Under pressure from Britain that the Immigrants Regulation Act 22 of 1913 (Union) should not contain explicit racial legislation, the Act was passed with a Canadian clause for deeming a class of persons unsuitable to the requirements of the Union or any of its provinces. The relevant section, section 4(1)(a), was the product of a three-year legislative process and was modelled on a

---

78   Jeeves, 1985.
79   CIA 36, M130, vol 2: Secretary for Native Affairs to the Imperial Secretary (24 June 1914).
80   Jeeves, 1985: 235 (citing *Hansard* 8 May 1913).

similar Canadian provision. It was assumed during the negotiations that this provision would be immediately exercised, and indeed, the administration of the 1913 Act by the newly created Department of the Interior immediately demonstrated the link between immigration and racism. In a portent of later South African bureaucratic despotism, this racial policy was carried out at the level of ministerial directive.[81]

Indeed, the terms of section 4(1)(a) of the Immigrants Regulation Act were nearly as broad as possible. This section of the 1913 Act authorised the Minister to declare as a prohibited immigrant 'any person or class of persons deemed by the Minister on economic grounds or an account of standard or habits of life to be unsuited to the requirements of the Union or any particular Province thereof'. Further, section 4(1)(a) seems to have been legislatively designed to be used as there were no procedural safeguards on the exercise of the deeming power, such as requiring the Minister to table in Parliament notice of his intended use of this power. To a small extent, this power was limited in section 4(2) by the pre-existing status in three provinces. For instance, in the Transvaal, lawfully registered Asiatics could not be deemed prohibited persons. Instead of any procedural restrictions, the Minister was directed to give written notice of his intention to use the power granted to him by section 4(1) to the immigration officer concerned and to every board. In addition, section 4(4), which authorised the Minister to limit the ports of entry of persons declared prohibited in terms of section 4(1)(a), also required that this action be published in the *Gazette*.[82] Both the wide ministerial discretion and the lack of parliamentary safeguards for section 4(1)(a) fit with the racist intent subtext of the standard legal history.

The standard account is accurate as far as it goes. However, such an account does not take our understanding very far.[83] The standard history of the deeming order has at least one important gap: an account of the

---

[81] Bradlow, 1978; Peberdy, 2009.
[82] Section 4 of Act 22 of 1913. (Note there may be a typographical error in section 4(2)(a) of the 1913 Act: it refers to section 5(a) of the 1903 Natal Act, but that section provides the prohibited immigrant declaration ground, not the ground for exemption which is in section 4.)
[83] Chanock, 1977: 2. Chanock argues that 'studies of imperial history in south and central Africa should be liberated from the form of argument which claims benevolence for

interpretation, application and implementation of the Act. The interplay between sections 4 and 5 of Act 22 of 1913 is also often left out of this story. The Minister's deeming order meant that the people affected were not exempted from the Act entirely (as some others were under section 5), but instead were deemed prohibited immigrants and thus left within the structure of the Act.

When we investigate and fill the gap referred to above, we can see the Act as less of a pure expression of nefarious racism and more as the legalised expression of a set of bureaucratic practices developed over the preceding several years. In other words, we can view the Immigrants Regulation Act as the parliamentary adoption of the Registrar of Asiatic's administrative practices developed before and during unification. Developed in the Transvaal and consistent with the law of the British Empire, these bureaucratic practices led directly first to the Act and then to the deeming order.

The bureaucratic origins of the deeming order began before unification with a series of instructions given out in the Transvaal. The first of these were the 4 February 1909 instructions issued by the Registrar of Asiatics and Transvaal Chief Immigration Officer, Montfort Chamney, to his immigration officers, which codified Transvaal migration regulation practice with respect to Asians. However, this codification process would not be strictly limited to the Transvaal. On 13 December 1909, Chamney wrote the immigration officers a confidential minute cancelling his previous instructions and 'describing the procedure to be adopted in respect of the ingress of Asiatics to the Transvaal'.[84] Significantly, although it covered immigration to the Transvaal, Chamney sent copies of his December 1909 minute beyond the Transvaal to Cape Town and Lourenço Marques in Mozambique, as well as to the four frontier posts, the Commissioner of Police in Pretoria and the Principal Immigration Restriction Officer in Natal. There were two office copies.[85] In substance, Chamney's instructions of 13 December

---

Britain on the one hand and is answered by the indignant *exposé* on the other'.

84   CIA 26, M2, vol 3: Chief Immigration Officer and Registrar of Asiatics to Immigration Officer Komati Poort (13 December 1909).
85   CIA 26, M2, vol 3: Chief Immigration Officer and Registrar of Asiatics (4 February 1909). The confidential minutes accompanying the instructions requested

1909 merely updated his 4 February 1909 instructions. The 11 points were reduced to 10 with some alterations and amendments. However, the instructions issued in December 1909 also were intended to consolidate his authority. He added a preamble — written first by hand on a copy of the 4 February 1909 instructions[86] — that made his vision of centralised administration clear. In this preamble, Chamney was particularly concerned to assert his own authority:[87]

> *In rare occasions special authority authorising Asiatic immigration may be found necessary or expedient on urgent or political grounds, but I shall be obliged if you will take particular note that such special authority must be issued by the Registrar of Asiatics or the Chief Immigration Officer alone. Irregular passes or authority of any kind issued by any other officer must be disregarded and the documents collected and forwarded to my office.*

His assertion of authority came against a background of confused and overlapping mandates with respect to provincial border control. After the formal date of Union, one of the pressing bureaucratic issues for the police and the immigration authorities became how to coordinate their functions pending the passing of national immigration legislation.

---

confirmation of receipt and the Registrar's files contain confirmation of receipts from Transvaal Customs, Lourenço Marques; the Immigration Restriction Department, Natal; and the Chief Immigration Officer, Colonial Secretary's Office, Cape Town. CIA 26, M2, vol 3: Immigration Officer George Marshall to Registrar of Asiatics (15 December 1909); G Dick, Principal Immigration Restriction Officer to Registrar of Asiatics (17 December 1909); C Cousins, Chief Immigration Officer to Registrar of Asiatics (20 December 1909).

86 CIA 26, M2, vol 3: Chamney to The Immigration Officer (4 February 1909). Chamney's handwritten notation on these instructions of 4 February 1909 took the following form: 'Letters to frontiers asking them to communicate at once if the instructions are not sufficiently clear. Point out that any special authority to immigrate not named in the instructions but which may be found necessary or expedient on ... or political grounds must be issued by R of A or CIO alone. Irregular passes or authority of any kind issued by any other officer must be disregarded and the document forwarded to my office.'

87 CIA 26, M2, vol 3: Chief Immigration Officer and Registrar of Asiatics to The Immigration Officer Komati Poort (13 December 1909).

Both the police and the immigration authorities had been involved in the enforcement of the immigration laws in each of the provinces. The immediate consequence of Union was that inter-provincial border control was dropped for whites, yet maintained with respect to Asians. Chamney summarised the instructions he circulated on behalf of the Department of the Interior as follows:[88]

> *You will observe that white persons entering the Transvaal no longer require written authority and I have instructed the Immigration Officers at Volksrust, Vereeniging and Christiana to discontinue interrogating white persons or calling for their passports. As, however, the laws and regulations relating to the movements of Asiatics continue in full force it will be necessary to retain the permit examiners at the frontier stations as previously.*

Soon thereafter, on 9 September 1910, Chamney issued further slightly amended instructions on the ingress of Asiatics. These instructions were nearly the same as those of 13 December 1909, though some of the points were amended and their number reduced to nine.[89]

Unification thus presented a new opportunity for negotiating the relative mandates of the police and the immigration bureaucracy. From the point of view of the police, unification among the provinces presented an opportunity to shed some onerous tasks of border control and reduce the personnel complement at posts at the provincial borders.[90] Chamney, however, resisted this attempted reduction of

---

88 CIA 26, M2, vol 3: Chief Immigration Officer to Commissioner of Police (16 June 1910). Apparently, the archives contain no copy of the enclosed instructions themselves. See also Chief Immigration Officer to Commissioner of Police (29 June 1910) ('It has been decided that as few arrests as possible should be made at present in respect to persons who have been registered but who have destroyed their certificates. Asiatics who have not been registered and whose presence in the Transvaal is in consequence illegal should still be taken before a Magistrate under Section 7 of Act 36/08. I am aware that the Police experience considerable difficulty in distinguishing one class from the other.').
89 CIA 26, M2, vol 3: Registrar of Asiatics and Chief Immigration Officer (Transvaal) to The Immigration Officer (10 September 1910).
90 As the Acting Secretary of the Transvaal Police asked: 'I am directed by the

resources on the part of the police, asserting his jurisdiction and drawing on the force of the circulated instructions and the authority of the Department of the Interior.[91]

For the next three years, migration administration pretty much rested there in terms of official policy. The next documentary form of migration administration was in July 1913. On the eve of the commencement of the Immigrants Regulation Act, the Secretary for the Interior wrote to his principal immigration officers regarding, most significantly, the Minister's deeming order. As the Secretary put it, he was to inform them that[92]

> *the Minister has formally deemed, under the powers conferred on him by paragraph (a) of sub-section (1), Section four of the Act, every person of Asiatic Race (except such in respect of whom the Act provides an exemption, and such as may be in lawful possession of certificates or permits entitling them to enter the Union or a particular Province) to be unsuited on economic grounds to the requirements of the Union, and to the requirements of every Province of the Union:— (a) in which such person is not domiciled, or (b) in which such person is not, under the terms of any statute of such Province, entitled to reside. Following this act of the Minister every such person becomes a prohibited immigrant.*

The actual content of this deeming order was nothing other than the Transvaal administrative practice dating back to 1909. Indeed, the actual Transvaal documents were used and extended nationally. The Immigrants Regulation Act came into effect on 1 August 1913. On 3

Commissioner to ask you to be good enough to inform me, seeing that the Union of the Colonies has now been accomplished, how long the arrangement of Examining Permits at the Border is likely to continue.' CIA 26, M2, vol 3: Acting Secretary, Transvaal Police to Registrar of Asiatics (10 June 1910).

91 Writing as the Chief Immigration Officer of the Transvaal, Chamney replied enclosing 'instructions issued by the Acting Secretary for the Interior to the Under-Secretaries for the Interior at Cape Town, Pietermaritzburg and Bloemfontein on the subject of immigration'.

92 CIA 35, M126, vol 1. Secretary of the Interior to Principal Immigration Officers (30 July 1913).

August 1913, Chamney noted on his pre-Union 13 December 1909 file copy of instructions: 'Strictly Confidential. Instructions not to be shown to any person other than an Immigration Officer. Minister's Instructions re deeming Asiatics undesirable. MC 3.8.13.' At the bottom of the document, Chamney wrote, 're further elucidation. MC 5.8.13'. Moreover, immigration officials interpreted the Secretary's circular — the governing instructions for the Immigrants Regulation Act — directly through the sets of earlier circulars. This meant that the 1913 circular was taken to refer to the earlier circulars of 1909 and 1910.

In terms of ministerial policy as well as of practical application, the effective content of the ministerial deeming order was the Asiatic policy from the Transvaal. The instructions of the Registrar of Asiatics developed over the five years before the passage of the Immigrants Regulation Act had become the explicit and precise policy of the Union Minister of the Interior in implementing that Act. The practice of the Transvaal became the law of the Union.

CONCLUSION

In the process of Union, the political elites in four of the constituent territories in British South Africa jointly negotiated their unification first with themselves and then with Britain. British officials hoped unification would lead to greater immigration from Britain while local elites desired greater autonomy from the Empire. In any case, the Union was less of a political statement than it was a vehicle for the management of problems already perceived as common and thus national, such as relations with the African population and, because of the intervention of the Indian Government, the Asian population as well. While Mozambique did not formally join the Union, the terms of unification and the subsequent Immigrants Regulation Act provided for continued labour migration from that territory to the newly minted Union territory, including the mining industry in the Transvaal.

While the Union was primarily a status quo development, a pouring of old wine into new bottles, the new legal entity nonetheless provided new opportunities for bureaucratic expansion and political and economic advance to its officials and inhabitants. From 1907 to 1914, building on the similarities that already existed among the comprehensive immigration laws adopted in the constituent territories from 1897 to 1907, the Transvaal immigration bureaucracy (the office of the Chief Immigration Officer and the Registrar of Asiatics) exploited the unification process. Its officials did so to ensure that the content of the Immigrants Regulation Act would be in line with the bureaucracy's own policies as well as to maintain or expand the influence and jurisdiction of these agencies. At the same time, elites within the Indian community (increasingly coordinating their action between locations in the Transvaal and Natal) managed to repeal a number of onerous Asian affairs provisions in the Natal laws that had restricted the freedom of descendants of indentured Indians. By 1914, the result was dominant Transvaal influence over the new national powers of immigration and of Asian affairs. The dynamics of the spread of that Transvaal model into the other provinces of the Union from 1914 to 1927 followed from this dominance. As the next chapter indicates, the model itself changed as a result of the diffusion process as well as imperial pressures, so that by 1927 a new national structure for jointly regulating the mobility of the European and Asian populations had to be established.

CHAPTER 5

Nationalisation of the immigration bureaucracy, 1914–1927

This chapter sketches largely bureaucratic developments at the national level from Union till 1927. The focus is on the Asian population and the institutions mandated to register and regulate its members. Regulation of the mobility of the Asian population propelled the nationalisation of migration regulation over this 20-year period. This nationalising process culminated in the formal establishment of the Commissioner for Immigration and Asiatic Affairs (CIAA) within the Department of the Interior in 1927.

Three developments drove this process. One was the increasing influence of the immigration officer based in Pretoria over the entire national immigration bureaucracy. Not only the formal laws, but the bureaucratic practice of migration regulation also became increasingly uniform across the Union from 1908 to 1927. In part, this was because the administration of migration regulation became more and more institutionally linked with the national administration of the resident Asian population. The immigration and Asiatic bureaucracy in Pretoria occupied an increasingly dominant position and assumed growing nationwide responsibilities.

A second development was the entrenchment of a particular understanding of the rule of law within this nationalising bureaucracy. The immigration bureaucracy operating in terms of the Immigrants Regulation Act did develop and exercise a practice of the rule of law in an administrative style from 1913 to 1927. As shown by the interactions between the bureaucracy and the courts as well as by the operation of institutions such as the Immigrants' Appeal Boards, the immigration laws during this period were administered in a manner that was bureaucratic in style yet also arguably adhered to the substance of the rule of law.

The third development — establishing the office of the Commissioner for Immigration and Asiatic Affairs — resulted from the nationalising of the migration bureaucracy and from negotiations between South African, Indian and imperial political elites that accepted the permanence of the Indian community within the Union. Establishing the office of the Commissioner for Immigration and Asiatic Affairs in 1927 may be seen as the culmination of the development of the national immigration bureaucracy. It was a change in South Africa's political culture that contributed to establishing this post: the Indian community had won an important battle in its struggle for the right to residence within the Union as evidenced most clearly by the Cape Town Agreement, which illustrated that by 1927 South African elites publicly and durably accepted that the Indian population was in the country to stay. This outcome was further influenced by negotiations within the British Empire and in particular between the dominions of South Africa and India. Establishing the Commissioner's office yielded a powerful bureaucratic force: a single national official charged with the two functions of providing for the Asian population and regulating immigration into the Union.

THE NATIONALISATION OF MIGRATION ADMINISTRATION

From 1908 to 1927, the organisations and structures regulating mobility became national in scope. As seen in Chapter 4, in the five-year process of considering and adopting the Immigrants Regulation Act 22 of 1913, the Transvaal-based Registrar of Asiatics successfully pushed to extend his office's jurisdiction over other state elements regulating movement and to ensure that the legislation would operate in line with the model of the Transvaal provincial legislation. This dual trend of nationalisation and increasing dominance of the Pretoria-based immigration office persisted after 1913 and continued with similar dynamics through to 1927. Undoubtedly, the reason for centralisation in the Transvaal was its geographical position inland of the two coastal colonies combined with the heavy volume of traffic in that province. Much of the immigration work at the coast was associated with residents of the Transvaal.[1]

---

[1] This volume of work was remarked upon in the 1911 Natal Annual Report: 'Practically the whole of the Embarkation Passes and the about three-fourths of the Visiting Passes issued may be associated with the movement of Indians having a claim to reside in the

This trend was driven at the bureaucratic rather than the legislative level. As we have seen, the Immigrants Regulation Act 22 of 1913 did not explicitly set up a coordinated bureaucratic structure. Furthermore, from 1914 (with the passage of the Indian Relief Act adjusting the Immigrants Regulation Act) to 1927, although several pieces of immigration legislation were proposed, little national immigration legislation was passed.[2] Instead, under the influence of the Registrar of Asiatics and Principal Immigration Officer in the Transvaal, the migration bureaucracies of the various provinces increasingly co-ordinated their work and began to undertake joint activities. The administration of migration became less provincial and significantly nationwide in scope. Procedures and institutions also became increasingly formal and centralised, such as the operation of the Immigrants' Appeal Boards from 1913.

From Union onwards, the practical administration of migration regulation became more (but not entirely) national in range. In the immediate aftermath of Union, the pre-existing border posts of the pre-Union provinces were rationalised and reduced 'in the interests of economy and efficiency'. For instance, in 1911, the work of the Inland Station of the Immigration Restriction Department (Natal) at Charlestown was shifted to the police in Volksrust. In these reduction processes, the authority of the Principal Immigration Officer (Pretoria) at times expanded. Another example was in 1913 when the Komatipoort border post (on the Transvaal–Mozambique border) came under the jurisdiction of the immigration office in Mozambique, but that office could liaise with the Principal Immigration Officer (Pretoria) as desired.[3]

In 1917, border inspection was described as operative at the ports but not at the land borders. While dwindling in number, the provincial border offices were not eliminated entirely and increasingly appeared to

---

Transvaal. This movement is continuous and involves heavy and exacting work in the way of scrutiny and finance and the preparation of credential documents.' BNS 684, 2/129, vol 1; 1911 Natal Annual Report.

2   The sole statute enacted was the Naturalization of Aliens South West Africa Act 30 of 1924 (Union).
3   CIA 35, M126, vol 1. Secretary for the Interior to Principal Immigration Officers (30 July 1913).

function as checkpoints for the Asian rather than the white population.[4] Whites appeared to be exempted in practice if not in law. From 1913, the Immigrants Regulation Act regulated entry of white people into the Union under a system of border inspection. All provincial legislation regulating the provincial entry of white persons was repealed with the enactment of the Immigrants Regulation Act 22 of 1913. Thus the only law substantively governing provincial entry of Europeans was the Immigrants Regulation Act itself. Section 4(1) made its border inspection regime applicable to entry to a province as well as to the Union. Technically, the same seven prohibited immigrant grounds applied to provincial entry as to Union entry. A white person not lawfully resident in a province could thus legally be refused provincial entry on the basis of the Immigrants Regulation Act.

As a result the following was reported by border officials. In 1926, the Natal Border Office at Volksrust on the provincial border with Transvaal (whose officers' request in 1916 to be placed under the direction of the Principal Immigration Officer, Natal and not the Transvaal had gone unheeded) reported examining and permitting entry to 1 533 Indian, 48 Chinese and two Japanese persons.[5] 'Asiatics' would be allowed entry upon proof of lawful domicile, although the 1913 Act also imposed further restrictions on this population.

Even those Asians allowed Union entry could be restricted by the Immigrants Regulation Act of 1913 in terms of inter-provincial travel. The section 4(1)(a) deeming order meant that the movement of even free Indians was presumptively restricted. However, there was a further provision in section 4(1) that turned the presumption into an absolute bar, with the sole exception of lawful residents of that province (section 4(2)). With regards to provincial entry, none of the exemption grounds were allowed to trump the deeming order (proviso to section 5). Asiatic entrance to a province was thus completely blocked, except to previously lawful residents of that province.

Indentured Indians were in a different situation from free Indians, closer to the situation of Africans. The 1913 Act set a framework for

---

4 *1917 Year Book*: 185.
5 BNS 684, 2/129 (1916 Natal Annual Report).

rather than directly governed their Union entry. The exemption of section 5(d) of the Immigrants Regulation Act exempted indentured Indians in Natal from the national 1913 Act by placing them under the labour migration provisions of the provincial law, the Indian Immigration Law 25 of 1891 (Natal). However, the deeming order continued to have force with respect to provincial entry in terms of the proviso to section 5. Further, since indentured Indians were lawfully resident only in Natal, they were unable to take advantage of the lawful residence exception of section 4(2). Somewhat superfluously, the Indian Immigration Act itself limited travel outside the province.[6]

Soon after unification, the reporting practices of the three principal immigration officers were standardised. On 8 March 1913, the Secretary for the Interior requested such a common format for the statistical reporting of admissions, deportations, issuance of permits and Immigrants Appeal Board activities based on the returns submitted by the Cape. The Natal office was specifically requested to reduce the amount of information submitted.[7] Each of the three principal immigration officers continued to prepare standard although separate annual reports through to 1926. In a step beyond common reporting at principal immigration officer level, the Director of Census and Statistics began to collate and prepare the statistics for passengers arriving at ports, giving, for instance, their reason for entry as well as their race and nationality. This centralisation resulted in delays, to the annoyance especially of the Natal office.[8] In another sign of nationalisation, the *1924 Year Book* was the first of these official national statistical publications to report on Asians in the Union rather than in each of the provinces.[9]

---

[6] Section 90, Law 25 of 1891 (Natal).
[7] BNS 864, 2/129, vol 1.
[8] 1919 and 1925 Annual Report. BNS 864, 2/129, vol 3. An author of the 1919 Annual Report stated: 'I have found it quite impossible to use for purposes of comparison the figures supplied by the Census and Statistics Department and consequently found it necessary to require members of the staff to work on several evenings in order to work up the information required to enable the returns to be of any use and intelligible.'
[9] *1924 Year Book*: 134 (noting also that the matter is covered in the Report on the Census of 1921).

Official policy towards the Asian population — rather than European immigration or African mobility — encouraged the move towards a national immigration bureaucracy. The 1920 Lange Commission (also termed the Asiatic Inquiry Commission) was charged with surveying the administration of Asian affairs in the Union. Its interim report (later confirmed by its final report of 3 March 1921) recommended that a single official be charged with the administration of the government's Asian policy.[10] In terms of policy, the Commission rejected compulsory repatriation on practical grounds and recommended a voluntary repatriation scheme.[11] Although it called for no relaxation in the enforcement of the immigration laws, the Commission noted that the majority of the Indian indentured community in Natal were born and educated in South Africa. In 1921, the response of the government to the Lange Commission recommendation was to appoint an Indian Repatriation Commissioner and to take over the functions of the employer-oriented Indian Immigrants' Trust Board.[12] The Commission and the response to it were important moves towards the public assumption of Asian welfare and repatriation as government and public responsibilities. Nonetheless, the government response remained within the policy framework of repatriation as the primary and preferred national solution to the Asian question and, despite the call for a single official, did not formally take on the administration of Asian affairs as a significant national responsibility.

To a great extent, the Immigrants Regulation Act also facilitated this centralisation of migration administration. The Act provided at the least a common language among the provincial bureaucracies. For instance, the chief of each organisation was the principal immigration officer. Yet the Act itself was hardly an unambiguous centralising instrument. As already seen, the Act regulated inter-provincial migration as well as migration into the Union. Indeed, albeit without a full-scale border

---

10   Bradlow, 1978: 118.
11   U.G. 37-20, Interim Report of the Asiatic Inquiry Commission; U.G. 4-21, Report of the Lange Commission.
12   The decision of *Govindsamy v Indian Immigration Trust Board, Natal* 1918 AD 633 (subsequent decision in Privy Council) provides some foreshadowing of the takeover of the Trust Board in 1921. Corder, 1984: 176.

inspection regime at the provincial borders, the business of the principal immigration officers retained a large provincial component for at least 15 years after Union. For instance, in 1926, of the 1 407 persons who had arrived at the port during the year and whom Natal deported, 1 277 were sent to either the Cape or the Transvaal. The vast majority of prohibited persons in terms of the Immigration Act were thus 'deported' within the national boundaries of the Union, rather than being transported outside the Union and to their country of origin. For example, Natal's 1926 Annual Report states that all 89 Chinese declared prohibited were passed on to the Transvaal or the Cape; of the 1 231 Indian nationals deported, 548 were sent to the Cape and 637 to the Transvaal. Not included here are a lesser number of people arrested in Natal and deported mainly outside the Union. Only two of 31 persons deported after arrest in Natal were sent to the Transvaal, while the rest were deported to India, China, the United Kingdom and Italy.[13]

THE IMMIGRATION BUREAUCRACY AND THE DEVELOPMENT OF THE RULE OF LAW

The operation of the increasingly nationalised immigration bureaucracy from 1908 through to 1927 developed and demonstrated adherence to a concept of the rule of law. The rule of law has, of course, a number of different definitions and meanings, many that focus heavily on judicial institutions. By contrast, an administratively focused understanding places emphasis on the rational and reasonable exercise of discretion within formal bureaucratic limits.[14] The understanding developed within the immigration bureaucracy was of adherence to the rule of law with a bureaucratic style.[15] Using this administratively focused definition, the

---

13   Immigration Statistical Summary, 1926 Natal Annual Report, BNS 684, 2/129, vol 4.
14   Salyer, 1995: xviii. This minimalist concept of the rule of law became dominant in the US during the Progressive era (1890s–1920s) as part of a historic shift towards efficient and expert administrative agencies. Lucy Salyer has used this concept in examining the development of the American immigration bureaucracy. While government bureaucracies in South Africa differed significantly — not having the capacity (and in particular the legal specialists) of their American counterparts — this conception of the rule of law can still be useful in examining the operation of the immigration bureaucracy in South Africa at this time.
15   Shear, 1998: 40. This argument, in theory and application, is consistent with Shear's

orientation to the rule of law in the immigration bureaucracy in this period was developed and can be seen in three specific registers.

One register for the rule of law is the institutional relationship between the bureaucracy and the courts. In general, the immigration bureaucrats were respectful and heedful of the courts, both the magistrates' and the Supreme Courts. Even where the Principal Immigration Officer (Natal) expressed irritation with excessive numbers of court interdicts, the tone of the objections in his annual reports is not dismissive nor questioning of the courts' authority.[16] Those annual reports also carefully note the number and the results of the appeals taken against the Department of the Interior, as well as sometimes noting the outstanding issues for decision between 1911 and 1915.[17] The Principal Immigration Officer (Natal) was involved in a number of early

---

view that a rule of law orientation linked to the 1902 Ordinance persisted for three decades but then faded in the 1930s. In particular, Shear has argued that Smuts's 1908 amendment was 'a telling instance of South African rulers' responsiveness to local and British public and Colonial Office opinion in developing repressive powers within a "constitutional" framework'.

16 BNS 684, 2/129, vol 1. 1911 Natal Annual Report: 'The readiness of the Courts to grant Interdicts (which have in every case but one been issued on ex parte statement, notwithstanding that my presence at the hearing of applications could have been secured in fifteen minutes) constitutes an interference with me in the performance [sic] of my duties, which operates against a prompt and effective administration of the Act, and I repeat the advice already tendered that the position is one which requires serious consideration.'

17 The Principal Immigration Officer of Natal understandably welcomed the initial decision upholding his decision to exclude MM Nathalia. 1911 Natal Annual Report: 'A very valuable judgment was delivered [by] the Supreme Court on the 18th December in the matter of an application of one M.M.Nathalia to bring in as his son a youth named Essop, whose alleged relationship to Nathalia I had reason to doubt. Shortly stated, the Court held that, the matter having been shewn to have received proper consideration, it could not, in view of the wording of Section 3 of Act 5, 1906, interfere with my decision. It is noteworthy, however, that the Court regretted that it should have had to record such a decision. The applicant, possibly encouraged by this expression of sympathy, has taken his case on appeal to the High Court.' In 1912, the eventual success of Nathalia (after losing the appeal (*Nathalia v Principal Immigration Restriction Officer* 1912 AD 23) ('In other words, the matter is left to the absolute discretion of the Immigration Restriction Officer.') but re-entering Natal after leaving to be again excluded and to again appeal) was noted without comment. Nathalia appears to have made two trips to India in the course of his effort to immigrate.

CHAPTER 5 Nationalisation of the immigration bureaucracy, 1914–1927

cases that set the parameters of the Immigrants Appeal Board.[18] The solution to interfering courts was not to ignore their orders but rather to change the system so that the Minister would be 'the sole judge of all cases in which the Immigration Officers' decisions might be excepted to'.[19]

The immigration bureaucracy often discussed issues relating to the relationship with the courts within a legal framework of providing fairness, albeit from a point of view favouring bureaucratic considerations. For instance, when, in 1916, the Natal Principal Immigraton Officer proposed that a £5 deposit be required for each special case sent from the Immigrants Appeal Boards to the courts, the suggestion was referred to the 'Law Advisers'. It seems the Department did not have its own lawyers at this time. Instead, it depended on the Law Advisers, that is, government lawyers, for legal advice, as had been the practice in the pre-Union Transvaal. The drive towards internal rationalisation thus had a more bureaucratic than a legal style. This approach was the prevailing South African norm at that time. These government lawyers rejected the suggestion as being 'in effect a restriction upon the administration of justice and ... ultra vires [the Act]'.[20] The only comment that the Principal Immigration Officer of Cape Town had on the suggestion and its rejection was 'I quite agree'.

Another register for the rule of law can be found in the degree of consistency between judicial and bureaucratic interpretations of administrative discretion. There was a significant interrelationship between the regulation of Asian communities and the development of administrative law in South Africa.[21] Among various cases of significance and interest, take, for example, the doctrine formulated in the immigration context in the 1912 case of *Shidiack v Minister of*

---

18 *Bibi v Immigration Officer for Natal* 1913 AD 495 (no appeal from an answer given by a provincial division to a question reserved in terms of section 3 of Act 22 of 1913); *Immigration Officer for Natal v Ratanjee* 1913 AD 498 (same even where provincial division has purported to grant an order).
19 BNS 684, 2/129, vol 1. 1912 Natal Annual Report.
20 CIA 34, M91. Acting Under Secretary to Principal Immigration Officer (Natal) (8 July 1916).
21 Chin, 2002: 1; Corder, 1984; Lourie, 1927: 10–23; Salyer, 1995.

the Interior.[22] Arising in the immigration context, *Shidiack* is a case still taught in classes of general South African administrative law for the principle that 'the court would not interfere with the bona fide exercise of discretion by a public officer'. One apparent consequence of this case was that the statutory wording of section 4(1)(b) of the Immigrants Regulation Act — finally drafted in 1913 — specifically authorised immigration officers to evaluate the educational test of intending immigrants.[23] At the final judicial stage of this matter, the judges of the Appellate Division decided that where the statute provided that an educational test be completed to the 'Minister's satisfaction' it was inadequate for an immigration officer and not the Minister to evaluate a test taken by potential immigrants. The court thus ordered the educational test to be administered again to two sons of the Syrian appellant. After the administration of this second educational test, the Minister himself evaluated the results and was not satisfied; thus the sons were excluded. The Minister and the bureaucracy demonstrated compliance with the judicial legal interpretation, but the judiciary also abided by the Minister's opinion.

Still, the practice of educational tests as administered by officials of the Department of the Interior in this period was hardly a series of good

---

[22] 1912 AD 642. Another significant development was the series of events leading up to *R v Padsha* 1923 AD 281. This ruling of the Appellate Division validated the Minister's deeming order with respect to Asiatics in terms of section 4(1)(a) of the Immigrants Regulation Act. The Cape Provincial Division had held this order ultra vires in *Mahomed v Immigrants Appeal Board* 1917 CPD 171. The Natal Provincial Division had continued its support for administrative interpretations of the Act and upheld the order in *In re Seedat* 1914 NPD 198. *R v Padsha* was the Transvaal case that made it as far as the Transvaal Provincial Division and thence to the Appellate Division. Some earlier Transvaal Immigrants Appeal Board matters had stated the validity of section 4(1)(a) as a case for Supreme Court decision but those cases had not progressed further up the judicial hierarchy, despite intense interest in the matter among the various principal immigration officers. CIA 35, M126, vol 2. Principal Immigration Officer (Cape Town) to Principal Immigration Officer (Pretoria) (13 November 1917) (asking for copy of Supreme Court ruling on section 4(1)(a) validity once decided); in the matter between Abdul Latief Jamaludin and Sheik Ally Jamaludin and Principal Immigration Officer (Transvaal) (reservation on question of law regarding validity of section 4(1)(a) deeming). Corder, 1984: 177–181.

[23] Op cit: 175.

faith evaluation exercises by immigration officers respectfully monitored by the courts. Instead, it was a series of internal policies specifically directed and channelled within the organisation, as was even the initial decision to administer an educational test as well as the later decisions made in evaluating their results. The principal set of instructions implementing the Immigrants Regulation Act communicated to immigration officials a set of rules for the differential application of the education test. Directly after relaying the substance of the section 4(1)(a) deeming order, the Secretary of the Interior stated that[24]

> *it is not the policy of the Government to apply the Education Test (paragraph (b) of sub-section 1, Section four) rigorously in the case of Europeans. Europeans who appear to be desirable persons, notwithstanding the fact that they may be unable to read or write, or that they are not possessed of means, should not be restricted unless it appears practically certain that by allowing them to enter they would become a public charge. The Education Test should be brought into operation only in the case of Europeans who are obviously undesirable. It is the wish of the Government that the Act should be so administered as to encourage as much as possible the entry of all desirable Europeans, and to prevent the entry of Asiatics who are not already entitled to reside in one or other Province of the Union.*

---

[24] CIA 33, M64, Secretary of the Interior to the Principal Immigration Officers (30 July 1913). This instruction also ratified earlier practice. See HN Venn to Principal Immigration Officer (Pretoria) (19 July 1913) ('I have to inform you that in administering the Education Test as provided in paragraph (b) of Section 4(1) of the above Act, it is the wish of the Minister that the test should not be applied to Europeans who in their appearance are desirable persons and against whom nothing is known, notwithstanding that they cannot read or write or are not possessed of means, unless it appears practically certain that by allowing them into the Union they would become a public charge.'); see also Under Secretary of the Interior to Principal Immigration Officer (Pretoria) (19 March 1914) (noting possible voyages to South Africa of 'a number of people of the Hebrew persuasion', yet reminding the officer of the general policy not to administer the educational test to Europeans desirable in appearance). As discussed in the following chapter, the Secretary of the Interior also instructed that the Education Test was in general not to be administered to Asiatics.

In 1922, the Minister announced a further policy of allowing female relatives of persons domiciled in the Union to enter without passing the Education Test.[25] The effective limitations on the discretion of the immigration officers during this period were thus not those provided by judicial monitoring, but rather instructions from above in the managerial hierarchy.

The compliance of the immigration bureaucracy with the *Shidiack* decision itself put into operation an understanding of administrative discretion more slanted towards bureaucratic authority than the understanding expressed in the court judgments of the matter. The copy of the *Shidiack* decision kept by the Department and circulated among immigration officers as the relevant decision in this matter was not the 30 September 1912 judgment of the Appellate Division on the principal issue (the judgment analysed and taught in the law schools), but rather the judgment of a later stage of proceedings held on 2 November 1912 where the panel of judges evaluated the compliance by the immigration officer and the two intending immigrants with the order by the court.[26] In the brief latter stage, the court stated that the particulars of the test demanded by the Principal Immigration Officer (Cape Town) were reasonable and that it was not improper for the immigration officer to have dictated the particulars of the test to the intending immigrants even though this was not provided for in the interim order of the court. This one-page portion of the case expansively supports the discretion of immigration officers as to both the substance and the procedures of educational tests. While both stages of the proceedings are included in the law reports, immigration bureaucrats were apparently primarily if not exclusively aware of and working with the more bureaucratic friendly decision of the final stage rather than the 11 pages of the principal hearing.

A third register of the rule of law can be found in the adoption and use of internal institutions and procedures intended to provide

---

25 CIA 33, M64, Secretary of the Interior to the Under Secretary of the Interior (21 June 1922), Secretary for the Interior to Secretary, Office of the High Commissioner, London (12 July 1922).
26 CIA 33, M64, *Shedieck (sic) v Minister of the Interior* (2 November 1912).

some measure of administrative justice. During this period, the principal immigration officers set up and operated a national system of immigrants appeal boards in order to make available to intending immigrants a measure of administrative justice. In doing so, the officers were complying with their empowering statute. This institution had statutory grounding. Section 2(1) of the Immigrants Regulation Act provided for boards 'for the summary determination of appeals by persons who, seeking to enter or being found within the Union or any Province, have been detained, restricted, or arrested as prohibited immigrants'. The institution of the appeal boards emanated from the earlier 1911 and 1912 proposed Bills. The 1911 Bill had been opposed in part on the rationale that the Minister had surrendered too much control to an immigration department. The 1912 Bill thus included advisory boards at ports of entry. These boards were still regarded as useless, in particular in the face of white fears that the Department would exclude Jews. The 1913 Bill (to become law) contained full-blown appeals boards, drawing on the Canadian model. The appeal boards were perceived in this debate to be as much as the recipients as immigration officers of instructions from the Minister in terms of his discretion.[27] Three Immigrants Appeal Boards were constituted in Cape Town, Durban and Pretoria respectively to cover each of those provinces. Initially, the Orange Free State together with Kimberley and the northern territory of the Cape Province as well as some districts of the Transkei were consolidated with Pretoria. In 1917, consequent to a reshuffling of the jurisdiction of the principal immigration officers, the Orange Free State was shifted to the Natal Board and the Cape Board's remit extended over its entire province.[28] The majority of the cases before the Appeal Boards apparently concerned Indians. For instance, in each year for which the nationality of appellants was recorded in Natal between 1914 and 1926, Indian nationals constituted the majority of appellants and often constituted nearly the full number of appellants.

The Boards were careful to ground their policies in defensible interpretations of judicial decisions. For instance, in 1915, the chairman

---

[27] Bradlow, 1978: 45, 48, 59, 65, 68.
[28] GN 1185 (*GG* 399 (1 August 1913)). *1917 Year Book*: 184; Op cit: 80.

of the Natal Immigrants Appeal Board found a 20 July 1914 House of Lords decision to be 'most valuable ... in overruling Counsel when bei[n]g pressed for the procedure before the Board to be strictly in accordance with Law Court practice and the law of evidence'. The British case, *Local Government Board v Ablidge* (House of Lords, 20 July, 1914), held that a statutory appellate body could decide its own procedure. Under that case, the statutory body did not need to disclose which officer had taken the decision, nor orally to hear the applicant, nor allow the applicant to see materials adverse to his case. While the specific content of the case would not conform to modern notions of administrative justice, the practice of basing the appellate procedure in a judicial decision was an example of this register of the rule of law.[29] Even in deciding own procedures, the principal immigration officers deferred to the opinion of the magistrates.[30] Additionally, by means of the office of the Under Secretary of the Interior, copies of judicial decisions and supporting materials were at times circulated to the other principal immigration officers. However, these materials were often used to support legal interpretations of bureaucratic procedures that would fall short of a judicial understanding of the rule of law in the operation of the courts. For instance, the same 1914 House of Lords case was retrospectively used as the basis for the Acting Under Secretary to justify making an order that the Board could 'take cognisance of any fact within its knowledge no matter how it is placed before them'.[31]

The Appeal Boards also demonstrated a concern for legality through their exercise of the statutory authority to reserve and state cases to the courts for decision on questions of law. As the 1916 Natal Annual Report claimed: 'Great care is exercised by the Immigrants Appeal Board in

---

[29] CIA 34, M93. Acting Secretary for the Interior to Chairman Immigrants Appeal Board, Cape Town, Durban and Pretoria (Minute 1/A/149 of 3 May 1915); Acting Secretary for the Interior to Chairman, Immigrants Appeal Board, Pretoria (Minute 4/A/149 of 28 May 1915).

[30] CIA 34, M95. Principal Immigration Officer (Transvaal) to Resident Magistrate (6 January 1915) (asking 'whether you have any objections to the procedure laid down'); Memorandum: Immigrants Appeal Board (30 May 1927) (setting Board procedures).

[31] CIA 34, M93. Acting Secretary for the Interior to Chairman, Immigrants Appeal Board, Pretoria (Minute 4/A/149 of 28 May 1915).

CHAPTER 5 Nationalisation of the immigration bureaucracy, 1914–1927

stating these cases and the results of those dealt with during the year have been fraught with important issues in the administration of the Immigrants Regulation Act of the Union.'[32] Additionally, legal issues were frequently referred to the Law Advisers (government lawyers) for decision.[33]

Although the Department of the Interior adopted the position that the Boards were in principle administrative and not judicial bodies, the Boards nonetheless adopted procedures that in many respects mirrored existing court practice. As a rule, attorneys and advocates were allowed to be present and to present both legal argument and evidence. At least the Cape Town Immigrants Appeal Board made transcripts of its proceedings. Other Boards carefully considered the degree of minute- and note-taking that should be provided for. The Natal Board provided an interpreter for Indian applicants. In some instances, it was the Department rather than the applicant's legal representative that proposed greater procedural formalities for the Boards.[34]

A controversial issue concerning the independence of the three-member Boards — one of the points of parliamentary debate raised by Morris Alexander in his effective opposition to the 1912 Bill — was disputed within the framework of the rule of law. Despite the matter having been raised in legislative debates, the Immigrants Regulation Act had not resolved this issue, noting only that the chairman 'shall whenever possible be a magistrate'.[35] In 1913, each of the principal immigration officers was initially appointed as a member of the relevant Board on a six-month trial basis. Soon the Natal Board was sitting in the Principal Immigration Officer's office, an arrangement which the officer noted was to the convenience of attending attorneys and advocates.

---

32   BNS 686, 4/129C. 1916 Natal Annual Report.
33   CIA 34, M102. Under Secretary for the Interior to Principal Immigration Officer (Pretoria) (1 December 1913) (relaying opinion as requested by Law Advisers to the effect that all three members of the Board had to be present to achieve a quorum).
34   CIA 35, M126 vol 2. Immigrants' Appeal Board (Transvaal) Report No. 96 (14 November 1917) (statement of question of law by Department). Principal Immigration Officer (Transvaal) to Principal Immigration Officer (Natal) and Principal Immigration Officer (Cape Town) (23 September 1930) (suggesting written argument by counsel and written responses by Department).
35   Section 2(3); Bradlow, 1978: 48.

Smuts, as Acting Minister of the Interior, saw no 'difficulties' with these arrangements.[36] However, opinion in the Indian community was to the contrary as an article entitled 'Prosecutors sit as judges' indicates.[37]

The Boards operated with some degree of autonomy with respect to the principal immigration officers. For instance, embarrassing publicity through an Appeal Board hearing in Durban on 11 August 1913 became an immediate source of controversy.[38] The internal instruction containing the Minister's deeming order with respect to Asiatics was publicly revealed by the magistrate who was the Board chairman. Both the Minister's order and the objection raised to it (as ultra vires) were reported in the media. The disclosure of internal instructions was more of an issue than the attendance by members of the public at the hearings, which was apparently permitted.

Still, the autonomy of the Boards was limited by the policies of the Immigrants Regulation Act. In 1925, after 10 years of operation, the Boards developed a practice of forwarding to the Department appeals for exemption by Indians that had good grounds for success, an approach the Department had encouraged from the inception of the Boards. Records of immigration appeal statistics suggests that this practice was formalised around 1925.[39] Most significantly, the policy and practice of the Boards was to discourage the admission of Asiatics and to prohibit such persons from even attempting the Education Test (which was reserved for Europeans of undesirable appearance). Bradlow, however, contends that in the Boards' first term of office the Act was strictly applied against Asiatics.[40]

---

36 Op cit: 81.
37 CIA 35, M126, vol 1. *Indian Opinion* (16 August 1913).
38 Bradlow, 1978: 76, 77. CIA 35 M126 vol 1. *Indian Opinion* (16 August 1913); *Indian Opinion* (23 August 1913) (referring also to a report in the *Natal Mercury*).
39 CIA 35, M126, vol 1. Under Secretary for the Interior to Principal Immigration Officer (Pretoria) (20 July 1914) (noting also that the PIO should keep a separate register for such cases additional to the register kept in terms of the 1908 Transvaal Act).
40 Bradlow, 1978: 80–82.

THE ESTABLISHMENT OF THE COMMISSIONER FOR IMMIGRATION AND ASIATIC AFFAIRS

The establishment of the office of the Commissioner for Immigration and Asiatic Affairs within the Department of the Interior in 1927 followed the signing of the Cape Town Agreement.[41] This agreement was the conclusion of a conference between the governments of South Africa and India in January 1927. The conference and the agreement capped and linked two significant developments within South Africa's political elite, one internal in character, the other external.

By the 1920s, a significant demographic trend with respect to the Indian population had become accepted among white political elites in South Africa. The 1911 and 1921 censuses, which made a specific return in respect of the Indian population in the Union at the request of the Indian government, had revealed powerful figures.[42] The 1921 count showed that nearly two-thirds (65 per cent) of the Indian population in the Union was South African-born. That status put the vast majority of Asians in the Union in a strong legal position. As people born in the Union, they could not be deported without a change to the Immigrants Regulation Act. Indeed, for some time the official repatriation policy of the South African government had been little more than the provision of inducements for assisted repatriation.

Despite this acceptance, both before and after a change in the South African government in June 1924, legislative proposals were introduced to effect a degree of resident and trading separation between Asians and Europeans. These proposals from both sides of the governments of the time responded to calls from across the white electorate to deal with the Asian population through some effective means, with widespread calls for segregation and persistent but lessened calls for repatriation.[43] Although they did not provide for compulsory repatriation, these proposals were far-reaching. For instance, the 1925 Areas Reservation and Immigration and Registration (Further Provisions) Bill contained a clause that would have empowered the Minister to withdraw domiciliary

---

41   Pachai, 1971.
42   *1917 Year Book*: 186; *1923 Year Book*: 162.
43   Bradlow, 1978: 124–137.

rights already acquired or might be acquired in another province from Asians born of parents legally resident in the Union, as well as restrict the entry of wives or children of domiciled Indians. Indians born in the Cape Colony objected to this limitation of inter-provincial movement and wanted the same privileges as Cape Malays. A new version of this Bill was introduced in 1926.[44]

These 1924–1925 legislative proposals were technically consistent with the governmental interpretation of the Smuts–Gandhi agreement of 1913 not to discriminate against Indians in South Africa, but only on the narrowest of interpretations. In this view, Smuts had promised Gandhi only that the specific vested rights of traders under provincial laws such as the Transvaal gold laws would not be altered by subsequent legislation.[45] Such a promise was not applicable to Union legislation. Not surprisingly, the 1924 proposals were condemned by the Indian community for their substance and as a violation of Smuts's undertaking to prohibit discriminatory legislation. As part of their campaign, the Indian community resident in the Union called for an inter-governmental conference between the Union and the Dominion of India.

The specific idea of an inter-governmental South Africa–India conference had its proximate origins in discussions South Africa was conducting with India. Despite South Africa's proclaimed definitive position that political rights would not be extended to the Indian population, the Indian and South African governments had long been involved in significant negotiations concerning the legal protection of Indians in the Union.[46] Much of this negotiation and positioning

---

44 Op cit: 136, 138, 142.
45 Op cit: 129.
46 Account in *1924 Year Book*: 134: 'The Asiatic question in the Union has an Imperial context to which brief reference may here be made. The Imperial Conference of 1917 accepted the principle of reciprocity of treatment between Indian and the British Dominions in the matter of immigration. The Conference of 1918 elaborated the principle, and laid down that Indians already permanently domiciled in the other British countries should be allowed on certain conditions to bring in their wives and minor children. At the Imperial Conference held in 1921 the position of Indians in the British Empire was further discussed, and a Resolution was passed which, while approving the Resolution of the 1918 Conference on the subject, expressed the opinion that in the interests of solidarity of the Empire it was desirable that the rights of British

took place within formalised imperial forums and channels. Smuts proposed an imperial resolution at the 1923 Conference affirming the right of each dominion to 'regulate citizenship as well as immigration as domestic questions for its own handling'. Bradlow points out that '[t]he Indian government was prepared to waive its request that Indians be given the right of free movement within the Empire, and concentrate on the issues which ... were regarded as first priority; the promise of just treatment for Indians domiciled within the Empire (including the right to bring in wives and minor children) and a grant to educated persons of the freedom to travel, visit and study in the Dominions'.[47] In 1924–1925, these discussions threatened to deepen into a disruptive dispute, with India, in February 1924, passing its own legislation to allow its government to retaliate against persons coming from a dominion that discriminated against Indians (eg South Africa).[48] Attempting to retain some form of consensus in the Empire, the Imperial Secretary of State for the Colonies visited South Africa in September 1924 and promoted the idea of an inter-governmental conference to address, among other issues, the citizenship of Indians born in South Africa. In the ensuing exchange of fact-finding deputations, the Indian deputation gave evidence before a select committee of the House of Assembly on the proposed legislation, while negotiations continued at a governmental level on the groundwork for a conference. With respect to the proposed

---

Indians to citizenship should be recognised. This Resolution was not accepted by the South African representatives, and the Indian delegates expressed the hope that by negotiation between the Governments of India and the Union the objections of the latter could be overcome. The question was again raised at the Conference of 1923, when the Indian representatives made certain proposals with a view to giving effect to the policy laid down in 1921. In the case of the Union, the suggestion was that the Union Government should agree to the Government of India sending an agent to South Africa who would protect Indian nationals there and act as an intermediary between them and the Union authorities. In rejecting the proposal, General Smuts on behalf of the Union stated that he could hold out no hope of any further extension of the political rights of Indians in South Africa. He defined the issue in the Union to be the question of economic competition, and not of race or colour, and declared that the white community in South Africa felt that the whole question of the continuance of western civilisation in that country was involved in this issue.'

47 Bradlow, 1978: 111, 128.
48 Bradlow, 1978: 138–140; Pachai, 1971: 108–120.

conference, the negotiations between India and South Africa posed the question whether the conference should 'be held with the idea of considering the best method of repatriating the Indians here or is it to be held with the idea of improving conditions of the Indians as permanent residents in South Africa?'[49]

By 1926, an important political understanding had been developed — internally and externally — regarding the place of Indians in South Africa. This understanding was on display at the Indian–South African Conference of 1926–1927. The Conference itself took about three weeks, sitting from 17 December 1926 to 11 January 1927. The resulting Cape Town Agreement of 1927 constituted a significant watershed in South African political culture. However, despite the country-to-country aspect of its preceding negotiations, the agreement did not constitute a formal treaty, but was instead an honourable understanding, consistent with the dominion context.[50] Article 2 of the agreement provided: 'The Union Government recognise that Indians domiciled in the Union, who are prepared to conform to western standards of life, should be enabled to do so.' The proposed Areas Reservation and Immigration and Registration (Further Provision) Bill was dropped. Additionally, the Indian government agreed to assist in the operation of the voluntary repatriation scheme and an Agent-General for the Government of India in the Union was appointed.[51] Although representatives of the South African government continued to state that the agreement was merely a way to enlist Indian aid in the voluntary repatriation scheme, the agreement, in fact, is best interpreted as indicating a formal acceptance of the permanent presence of Indians in South Africa.

As the most significant practical result of the Cape Town Agreement, the Union Government finally appointed a single national official to deal with Asiatic affairs, a markedly different response from its earlier response to the Lange Commission. Thus in May 1927, HN Venn was initially appointed to an office as the Commissioner for Asiatic

---

49 Bradlow, 1978: 143.
50 Op cit: 145.
51 *1926 Year Book*: 890.

Affairs.[52] Only six months later, the title and terms of his appointment were changed to that of the Commissioner for Immigration and Asiatic Affairs.[53] It is indicative of the frame through which the government viewed immigration that the post was originally conceived of related to Asiatic affairs. Nonetheless, the second title reflected the reality of government practice (which combined migration and Asiatic affairs administration) better since the provincial immigration bureaucracies, having inherited a pre-Union situation, had till now been charged with administration of Asiatic affairs. The Protector of Indian Immigrants remained an office separate from the Principal Immigration Officer (Natal) at least through 1916, although the Protector closely cooperated with the Immigration Officer, for instance in issuing permits for Indian immigrants to visit India.[54] However, the changed title also indicated that immigration matters preceded Asiatic administration in perceived significance.

At its debut, the Commissioner of Immigration and Asiatic Affairs was a powerful bureaucratic post within the Department of the Interior. The first Commissioner, HN Venn, had been the Under Secretary for the Department for seven years prior to this appointment on 27 May 1927.[55] After the Secretary, the Under Secretary was the most powerful civil servant post in the Department. As a former Under Secretary, Venn was familiar with and skilled in operating the procedures of the Department of the Interior.

---

52 *Government Gazette* 1634, 3 June 1927, GN 904. *Debates of the House of Assembly (Hansard)* (1927), vol 9 (24 June 1927).
53 *Government Gazette* 1658, 11 November 1927, GN 1964.
54 1917–1921 *Year Books* states: '[A]part from the Transvaal, and the indentured Indians of Natal whose interests are watched by the Protector of Indian Immigrants, the administration of Asiatic affairs is centred under the various Principal Immigration Officers as a normal part of their duties, and under a system of Boards provided by law for the revision of restrictive decisions appealed against by any person whose freedom of entry or of movement has been challenged.'
55 Venn had been Acting Under Secretary in 1919 and Under Secretary from 1920 to 1925.

Still, the Commissioner's power was not plenary. The terms of his appointment gave Venn power to deal with 'all Asiatic matters including immigration and give decisions, provided there was no departure from fixed policy and when a policy had not been definitively adopted, no new policy was involved'.[56] In terms of his original appointment, the CIAA was competent to keep the register of Asiatics in the Transvaal and of Chinese in the Cape. Within six months, the office picked up the competence to administer the immigration laws of the Union. The CIAA's competence did not include administration of the Indian immigrants in Natal. These remained under the Protector of Indian Immigrants (until 1942) and the Indian Immigration Bureau (until 1948).[57]

CONCLUSION

Within the migration policy negotiated and set by economic and political elites at the time of Union, bureaucratic consolidation proceeded relatively unhindered for the following 15 years. The immigration bureaucracy based in the Transvaal succeeded at steadily expanding its power and influence, absorbing some pre-existing inter-provincial offices and even some officials in Natal. It also adopted some functions previously performed by other officials with respect to the Asian population there. In this period, the bureaucracy developed rule-based internal procedures to make migration decisions with respect to European and Asian immigrants. The expanding power of the Transvaal office, as well as its twin sources of power in immigration and Asian affairs, was a contributing factor in the government's creation of a new office, the Commissioner for Immigration and Asiatic Affairs in 1927. Establishing this office was further influenced by domestic and external pressure applied by the Indian community in favour of such a move. White South African political elites gave in to this demand (without granting the Asian population political rights), because of the demonstrated demographic position of the Indian generations born in South Africa and because of a desire to maintain imperial

---

56 Bradlow, 1978: 166.
57 Ibid.

relations, particularly with India. While effectively concerned only with European and Asian migration at the establishment of this office, the new Commissioner would soon coordinate with the Department of Native Affairs, the national entity engaged in regulating the mobility of Africans during this period.

CHAPTER 6

African mobility and bureaucracy, 1911–1927

The Native Affairs Department (NAD) was the central bureaucracy charged with exercising some degree of control over the mobility of Africans from 1911 to 1927. As is well known, it did so in an ambiguous position with local governments and the Department of Justice[1] but also to some degree with immigration officers. The treatment of Africans and especially foreign Africans in the Union during this period cannot be completely separated from the operation of the immigration bureaucracy. As demonstrated below, the Native Affairs Department and the increasingly nationalised immigration bureaucracy did have contact and overlapping mandates even before 1927, particularly with respect to foreign Africans.

Migration regulation of foreign Africans occurred along two tracks or approaches during this period. One saw the regulation of large-scale legal recruitment of foreign Africans, which was mediated largely by the employer's relationship with the migrant and was supplemental to the local operation of the Union-era pass laws. In the 1920s, the Department experimented unsuccessfully with the operation of a labour depot in line with this approach. A second approach saw the largely unregulated migration of foreign Africans clandestinely and individually. In some areas, such migration gave rise to brutal recruiting practices. From 1921, official policy continued to tolerate the entry of protectorate and Mozambican Africans, but began to place barriers (with varying degrees of effectiveness) in the way of immigration by Africans resident in places further north. The capacity and effectiveness of law enforcement for both approaches was minimal. For instance, the practice of border deportations was acknowledged as ineffective and alternative deportations procedures were too costly.

---

1   Dubow, 1989; Evans, 1997.

In an attempt to deal with this situation as well as that of Union natives, the 1920s witnessed the rise of internal boundaries at the city limits. White elites came to agree that greater control could and should be exercised over African migration to urban areas. After considering different strategies, Parliament chose to put into place a system that depended upon labour contract registration, comprehensive policing and the internal removal of non-compliant offenders. While simultaneously opening new frontiers for migration regulation as well as the restructuring and empowerment of the Department, this strategy continued to rely heavily on private firms and the cooperation of local governments for its success.

TWO APPROACHES FOR REGULATING EXTRA-UNION AFRICANS

With respect to regulating the recruitment and mobility of extra-Union Africans, the Native Affairs Department as well as the immigration bureaucracy followed two separate approaches between 1911 and 1927. For both the regulation of movement was liberal. The differences between the two approaches were those of legality and scale of recruitment. The first approach was a legalised one of overseeing and monitoring foreign labour recruitment. Along with the Native Labour Regulation Act 15 of 1911, the Immigrants Regulation Act 22 of 1913 was used to enforce the prohibition of large-scale labour recruitment. The second approach was at times barely legal but more often a clandestine one that tolerated and exploited the individual entry of Africans into the Union. Here the policy was as much a social fact as it was a mandated policy. In terms of the enforcement of this second approach, foreign Africans were essentially treated the same as Africans from within the territory.

Prior to 1911, labour recruiting for the most prominent of the large recruiters — the mines of the Witwatersrand — had been minimally legalised although hardly closely regulated through an international agreement. As discussed in Chapter 3, the Portuguese East Africa Agreement (originally and in its subsequent form as the Mozambique Convention) governed labour migration from Mozambique to South Africa (although primarily the Transvaal) from 1897. Broadly, this Agreement exchanged the right to recruit mine workers for railway traffic and customs privileges.² At the time of Union, this Agreement allowed for the recruitment of labour in Mozambique on condition that a fee was payable to the Government of Mozambique for a passport for each labourer.

The passage of the Native Labour Regulation Act 15 of 1911 (NLRA) did bring some regulation of these operations. This Act was a response to calls for regulation of the worst practices of recruiting Africans from inside and outside the national borders, as well as the worst excesses of the African workplace.³ In terms of the Act, recruiters of foreign labour needed to be licensed and were required to conclude written contracts with their recruits.⁴ Neither the NLRA nor the Immigrants Regulation Act contained any policy to block entry by individual Africans. Along with the Mozambique Convention (which was essentially incorporated and ratified in terms of section 5(d) of the Immigrants Regulation Act), the 1911 Act was recognised as embodying the migration policy for Africans.⁵ Thus, the NLRA was a broad filter set up to monitor the larger recruitment agencies. Indeed, it is arguable that the law's effect was to ratify the operation and dominance of the two largest recruitment arms of the mining industry and to force a number of smaller recruitment agencies out of the field.

Beyond directly regulating recruitment, the NLRA also put into place a labour district system that began legally to consolidate the then-existing set of pass laws.⁶ Furthermore, it strengthened the system of identification used in some of these laws by requiring workers to have their fingerprints taken as well as to register their service contracts in the pass office of their district of employment. A duplicate of the registration certificate would be an effective pass since it would need to be produced upon demand.⁷

Although the NLRA strengthened the system of identification used in the pass laws, the regulation of African mobility remained dependent

---

2   Katzenellenbogen, 1982.
3   Native Labour Regulation Act 15 of 1911; Duncan, 1995: 109–110.
4   Froneman Commission Report, 1962: para 19.
5   Op cit: paras 18–19.
6   Kahn, 1949: 281.
7   Hindson, 1987: 24.

on private institutions, such as the mining houses themselves. This arrangement became an issue when a proposal to merge the fingerprint collection of the police and those of the Native Affairs Department in 1912 was being considered. While initially receptive to the idea, the police became disenchanted upon realising that the Native Affairs' collection was loosely linked to a much larger and less well-organised set of private collections, administered by each separate mining house. So, instead, the police chose to continue to expand their own collection largely from prison records.[8]

Thus, despite some attempts at the regulation of recruitment, the pre-existing state of affairs with respect to African mobility largely continued after Union notwithstanding the passage of the Native Labour Regulation Act of 1911 and the Immigrants Regulation Act of 1913. At the time of Union, it would have been overstated to hold that any element of the national bureaucracy took cognisance of or catered for individual Africans in the Union. Instead, the relationship of individual Africans to the national bureaucracy was usually a mediated one, most often through the employer, bolstered with the various pass laws then in force.

The clandestine approach of labour migration was perhaps as significant as the legalised one. From around 1910, the acknowledged policy of the Native Affairs Department was to prohibit any large-scale recruiting (apart from the legalised recruiting of the mines) or immigration of Africans but to tolerate and not penalise individual entrants. For instance, as the Principal Immigration Officer (Pretoria) informed his superiors in December 1921: 'If Natives are recruited and brought in in large numbers they will be detected. The few who filter in on foot are generally engaged by farmers before they get far south of the Union border and the Native Affairs Department are of the opinion that such Natives should not be interfered with.'[9]

In terms of this de facto policy, substantial numbers of foreign Africans entered the Union clandestinely after 1910. This migration was demonstrated in part in the mining industry, where many did eventually

---

8   Breckenridge, 1998.
9   CIA 36, M130, vol 2: Acting Principal Immigration Officer (Pretoria) to Secretary for Interior (29 December 1921).

find work. The numbers of 'non-recruited' Mozambicans on the mines rose slowly but steadily from 1910, peaking in 1925.[10] The officials of the Witwatersrand Native Labour Association (WNLA) complained that Mozambicans entering clandestinely could readily obtain passes and jobs in the Transvaal.[11] To crack down on this migration, WNLA agents were given powers as enforcement officers for Mozambique's emigration laws in order to arrest any unlicensed recruiters. Furthermore, channelling all migration through WNLA would give the Mozambicans the passport fee for the emigrating worker.[12]

However, some of this 'clandestine' migration was encouraged by the mines' recruitment agencies. For instance, after 1912, the Native Recruiting Corporation (NRC) (often using the personnel from independent recruiters who had been put out of business) would entice recruits over the border, offering 'meat feasts' as well as their choice of a specific mine on which to work.[13] In addition, some of this clandestine migration was welcomed by the Union Government.

Despite the ban on recruitment and employment of Africans from the tropics, the flow of clandestine entrants continued.[14] In official policies from 1914, Africans from the tropics who did enter the Union were often allowed to enter into employment providing their health was not at risk.[15]

Since the 1890s, extremely competitive and brutal recruiting practices had been occurring related to the clandestine approach, particularly at the intersection of Rhodesian, Mozambican and South African territory, the major route followed by this undercover labour migrating to South Africa from Rhodesia and Nyasaland. These labourers avoided the high costs of more formal transport and circumvented the WNLA recruiting

---

10 Katzenellenbogen, 1982: 160.
11 Op cit: 110–111.
12 Op cit: 108.
13 Op cit: 109–110.
14 Jeeves, 1985: 235.
15 CIA 36, M130, vol 2: Secretary for Native Affairs to the Imperial Secretary (24 June 1914). 'Indeed, should the voluntary labourer from North of Latitude 22 degrees be assisted by Government agency to proceed to the Labour Bureau Compound, the Administration will accept the charges for his fare and rations and find employment for him in a suitable environment.'

routes which had been forced to close (see Chapter 4). Together with the high mortality rate of Africans from the tropics on the mines, regulation of these slave-like practices had motivated a ban on recruitment and employment of 'tropical labour' — labourers residing north of 22° S latitude — in the Immigrants Regulation Act 22 of 1913.

The lawless character of recruitment practices in this area continued after 1911. This intersectional border area had only scattered settlements, few resident whites and no police posts. Recruiting foreign Africans here depended on unlicensed touts and their black runners, often in networks based near a trading store at Makulekas. These men used guns and ambushes as well as fraud and food to obtain their recruits. Only at places further in the interior, such as Sibasa and Pietersburg, did state officials maintain a presence. The establishment of the NRC in 1912 led to a short-lived alliance between it and one of the main labour recruiters — Mr H Seelig at Makulekas — in 1913. Thereafter, the NRC dealt directly and illegally with the touts, the 1913 ban on employment perhaps worsening the situation.[16] Officially banned from employment, migrants arriving in South Africa were not only without legal rights to sell their labour, but were officially ignored with even their mortality rates on the mines no longer monitored. The illegal touting for labour in this region diminished only gradually during the 1920s once state authorities began to extend relatively effective supervision over the far north-eastern Transvaal and adjacent Rhodesian and Mozambican areas.[17]

Some small but significant changes were made with respect to official policies along both these approaches of regulation from about 1921. Regarding large-scale legalised recruitment, the Department of Native Affairs, building on its limited efforts to regulate recruitment in the decade after Union, began to make some institutional attempts to do so now again within the Union. However, even in the 1920s, the Department was largely unable to regulate effectively the private labour recruiting networks operating inside the Union's demarcated space, including the border area around Makulekas.

---

16 Jeeves, 1985: 241.
17 Op cit: 235–252.

One part of the recruitment regulation policy of the Native Affairs Department entailed establishing a labour bureau. As Helen Bradford has shown, from 1921 onwards, foreign Africans clandestinely entering the northern Transvaal seeking work were technically to report to a monopoly labour bureau (or labour depot) run by Native Affairs at Louis Trichardt.[18] This bureau did not seek to deport extra-Union Africans but instead to allocate them to places of employment.[19] In practice, it had little opportunity to influence recruitment practices, as it provided an insufficient counterweight to the existing networks and was only able to monitor the labour market and to parcel out some groups of Rhodesians.[20] As Bradford argues, a 'labour bureau with monopoly rights, was ... no match for merchants of men'.[21] Labour touts exploited an alternative market to the mining industry: they 'sold' black immigrant labourers to large potato and maize farmers in the Transvaal.

In 1924, the National and Labour Parties representing the Afrikaners and white English-speaking workers came into power as the Pact Government. It attempted with brief success to bolster the operation of the depot at Louis Trichardt, a move whose legality Bradford questions.[22] Foreign Africans brought to the depot — often as pass-law offenders — had a choice of repatriation or a 12-month farm contract at lower wages and for longer hours than the agriculture industry standard. This arrangement was justified as an alternative to the costs of deporting Rhodesian Africans. The depot charged the farmers less per head for these labourers than did the private recruiters and a lottery

---

18 Bradford, 1993: 96–125.
19 CIA 36, M130, vol 2: Sub-Native Commissioner (Louis Trichardt) to Principal Immigration Officer (Pretoria) (18 September 1923) ('Provided the natives do not come through in large numbers, I consider it would not be desirable to turn them back if they get as far as Louis Trichardt.')
20 CIA 36, M130, vol 2: Sub-Native Commissioner (Louis Trichardt) to Secretary for Native Affairs (Pretoria) (20 August 1923) ('The position to day is that Rhodesian labour is still coming into the Union, not in such large numbers as hitherto, but in fair quantities and approximating to 200 weekly. No difficulty is now being found in placing these Natives in various parts of the Union with approved employers, authorised to employ this class of labour.').
21 Bradford, 1993: 100–103.
22 Beinart, 2001: 82; Bradford, 1993: 103.

allocated the recruited labourers to various farms.[23] However, despite such government support, this system collapsed within a year, with the bureau eventually closing in 1933 during the Great Depression.[24] In the meantime, large numbers of black immigrants deserted en masse from the farms once they were sent there. Furthermore, African migrants simply altered their travel routes to avoid the depot.[25]

With regard to clandestine individual entry, some significant changes in official policy also became apparent from about 1921. From this time regulation in this sphere pertains to three principal groups of Africans, the Principal Immigration Officer (Pretoria) having formalised policies with respect to each of these groups.

The entry of Africans from the protectorates continued to be determined by a relatively liberal policy from 1921. Indeed, it was more liberal than an earlier set of instructions that had at times been interpreted by immigration officials restrictively.[26] The 1921 instructions allowed 'non-tropical Natives', including those from Bechuanaland, to enter South African territory.[27] According to the instructions issued: 'Aboriginal Natives entering the Union from Bechuanaland on foot are

---

23 CIA 36, M130, vol 6: Sub-Native Commissioner to District Commandant, South African Police (Pietersburg) (18 March 1927) ('The fact that they are given no option in the selection of employers would act as a deterrent to these transborder natives entering the Union of South Africa in search of employment. There is no doubt that being sent to work on farms at a low rate of wage is not altogether to their liking.').
24 Upon its closure, the Additional Native Commissioner Louis Trichardt queried what should be done with prohibited immigrants who reported there: 'Are they to be handed over to the Immigration Officer for deportation at Government expense? As regards Nyasaland Natives in particular, ... [can these] be put over the Rhodesian border in view of the fact that they are not domiciled in that Territory?' CIA 38, M130, vol 11. Secretary for Native Affairs to Secretary for the Interior, 1 Feb 1933: Additional Native Commissioner Louis Trichardt (1933/1934).
25 CIA 36, M130, vol 6: Secretary for Native Affairs to Secretary for the Interior (3 November 1926).
26 CIA 36, M130, vol 1: Under Secretary for Interior to Principal Immigration Officer (Pretoria) (14 November 1921); see also CIA 36, M130, vol 2: Acting Principal Immigration (Pretoria) and Registrar of Asiatics to Secretary for Interior (3 January 1922) (responding to request for history of circumstances of revised instructions).
27 CIA 36, M130, vol 1: Acting Principal Immigration Officer and Registrar of Asiatics to Principal Immigration Officer (Cape Town) (29 November 1921).

not to be interfered with.' This policy was adopted partly because of a lack of enforcement capacity.[28]

Africans who entered clandestinely from Mozambique were structurally treated more liberally. These Africans were allowed to enter the Union and seek work on an individual basis, a practice formalised from at least 1913.[29]

With respect to 'tropical Natives', Africans from north of latitude 22°S, the policy embarked upon in 1921 was initially more restrictive than for protectorate or Mozambican Africans.[30] The provisions of the Immigrants Regulation Act were nominally enforced with respect to these Africans,[31] and was in line with the ban on the recruitment and employment of Africans from the tropics.[32] Nonetheless, in practice, immigration officials were quite tolerant of immigration by natives from the tropics. In 1921, Rhodesians (classified as residing north of latitude 22°S) working on farms in the area were not to be disturbed.[33] In 1922, the formal policy was further changed in a liberal direction.

---

[28] CIA 36, M130, vol 1: Acting Principal Immigration Officer and Registrar of Asiatics to Secretary of Interior (7 November 1921) (quoting District Commander of Marico District: 'Natives from the Bechuanaland Protectorate are constantly coming into the Transvaal, they usually come on foot, and if all who come over without written offers of employment, are to be returned by the Police, my men will be able to do very little else except take prisoners back across the border'.) Directions from Interior stressed the need to 'work in close co-operation with and be advised by the Native Affairs officials'. CIA 36, M130, vol 1: Under Secretary for Interior to Principal Immigration Officer (Pretoria) (14 November 1921).

[29] CIA 36, M130, vol 1: Agent of the Union of South Africa (Lourenco Marques) to Principal Immigration Officer (Pretoria) (20 November 1913).

[30] CIA 36, M130, vol 1: Acting Principal Immigration Officer and Registrar of Asiatics to District Commandant, South African Police, Rustenburg (12 December 1921).

[31] Jeeves, 1985: 250.

[32] CIA 36, M130, vol 2: Secretary for Native Affairs to Resident Commissioner, Bechuanaland Protectorate (13 December 1921). See eg CIA, M130, vol 2: Principal Immigration Officer (Pretoria) to Immigration Officer (Mafeking, Messina) (25 October 1922) ('The main object aimed for at the moment is to return to their country of origin workless natives who are entering the Union to seek employment and to see that other unattached natives leave the Union when the object of their Temporary visit has been attained.')

[33] CIA 36, M130, vol 1: Acting Principal Immigration Officer and Registrar of Asiatics to Principal Immigration Officer (Cape Town) (29 November 1921).

Africans from north of the designated line were allowed to enter the Union, provided such a person had a 'travelling pass' from the Rhodesian or Bechuanaland authorities to seek work or was proceeding to definite employment or was visiting.[34] However, within six months, under pressure from the Secretary for Native Affairs, this additional dispensation with regards to work-seeking Africans was limited.[35]

The national bureaucracies during this period had only minimal capacity to enforce the laws governing the recruitment and mobility of foreign Africans.[36] This lack of capacity was demonstrated in particular by practice with respect to deportations. Whether foreign Africans were deported by immigration officers or the South African Police, the results were not encouraging.[37] Officials during this period understood the deportation duty with respect to Africans to be fulfilled by simply placing the persons on the other side of the physical border and warning them that re-entry could subject them to three months' imprisonment.[38] Neighbouring governments as well as immigration officers of

---

[34] CIA 36, M130, vol 2: Secretary for Interior to Principal Immigration Officer (3 March 1922); Principal Immigration Officer and Registrar of Asiatics to Immigration Officer (Messina) (18 October 1922).

[35] CIA 36, M130, vol 2: Under Secretary for the Interior to Principal Immigration Officer (Pretoria) (23 October 1922); Acting Secretary for the Interior to Principal Immigration Officer (Pretoria) (21 August 1923) (reflecting pressure from the Native Affairs Department and suggesting that the better course would be to limit the passes issued by the Rhodesian authorities).

[36] In this period, African migration regulation can be understood as moving from a state of retreatism towards one of unauthorised discretion. Consistent with both these bureaucratic styles, Keith Breckenridge has argued that the written relations between Africans and their employers as well as state bureaucrats during this time had an essential 'archival' quality to them. These written archival relationships allowed individual Africans to exercise a certain degree of autonomy within their relationships with large organisations such as municipal pass offices, central state departments and their employers. (Breckenridge, 1998).

[37] CIA 36, M130, vol 2: Principal Immigration Officer (Pretoria) to Secretary for the Interior (22 August 1923) ('Machinery exists for the removal of natives from Rhodesia who have entered the Transvaal without authority and if the Native Affairs Department will bring such cases to my notice I will see that the natives in question are removed.').

[38] CIA 36, M130, vol 2: Principal Immigration Officer (Pretoria) to District Commandant, South African Police (Pietersburg) (3 August 1923); Principal Immigration Officer (Pretoria) to Immigration Officers (22 August 1923) (referring to section 6 of Act 22 of 1913).

neighbouring provinces complained of persons being dumped across the borders of the Transvaal.[39] Others complained of problems during the return trip of their migrants, leading to these migrants losing their wages.[40]

In any case, most if not all officials agreed that this practice of border deportations was not particularly effective. One immigration officer, after receiving a set of October 1922 instructions regarding deportation stated: 'Mafeking town is already swarmed with this class of native and speaking from previous experience it is almost fruitless placing them over the Union border which is only a matter of 18 miles from Mafeking. They are no sooner put across the border by the escort when they take either an Easterly or a Westerly direction and re-cross at some other point.'[41]

Moreover, as the officials recognised, deportations, if conducted further than across the border, would be very costly. For instance, the Principal Immigration Officer (Pretoria) suggested that deported Africans be put on a train to Francistown in the north of the Bechuanaland Protectorate. This suggestion was rejected on the grounds of cost

---

39   CIA 37, M130, vol 8: Secretary for the Interior to Secretary for External Affairs (27 February 1928) (deportations at Komatipoort on border with Portuguese East Africa); Principal Immigration Officer (Cape) to Secretary for the Interior (28 June 1927) ('In fact, to put it briefly, no one seems to care what happens to them in the Transvaal if they obtain work. If they don't, they are sent over the Border and it is left to another officer in a different Province to take the required action.').

40   CIA 37, M130, vol 8: Secretary for South West Africa to Secretary for the Interior (4 January 1928) (complaining of lack of rations and native purchase touts [labour brokers]).

41   CIA 36, M130, vol 2: Immigration Officer (Mafeking) to Principal Immigration Officer (Pretoria) (3 November 1922); Immigration Officer (Mafeking) to Principal Immigration (Pretoria) (29 August 1923) ('Since the first of January last about 120 natives from Rhodesia have been deported from Mafeking and placed over the Union border by police at Ramathlabama. I am inclined to think that a good few of these went into the Transvaal by way of "Groot Marico". Only a few days ago Two were taken in to custody at that place by the police who on searching them discovered by the endorsement on their passes that they had been deported by me. I would also bring to your notice one native who was deported by me and reached Johannesburg. I may add that deported natives usually destroy the prohibition notices served upon them.'); Immigration Officer, South African Police (Zeerust) to Principal Immigration Officer (Pretoria) (18 September 1923).

by the Secretary of the Interior who instead suggested continuing to work with the authorities in Rhodesia to discourage labourers from moving to the Transvaal.[42] Many officials saw the fundamental problem of deportations to be one of cost. In November 1928, a magistrate in Bloemhof initially wanted to deport four East Africans, but was told by the immigration authority to charge the four rather than deport them because the police did not want to bear the expense of escorting them to the exit point.[43] For apparently similar cost reasons, the policy of the Commissioner for Immigration and Asiatic Affairs (CIAA) was to deport only those whose birthplace was known.[44] Faced with difficulties of deportation, the Department of the Interior did not persist. Its policy went so far as to accommodate even those Africans refused permission to re-enter their countries of origin.[45]

THE RISE OF AN INTERNAL BOUNDARY

The development of urban influx control in the 1920s significantly modified the regulation of African migration in the Union. As seen in Chapter 4, the initial choice of the Union Parliament had been to leave the complex and varied system of inherited pass laws in place. However, this national sense had changed by the end of World War I and the beginning of the 1920s. A political consensus had emerged that

---

42 CIA 36, M130, vol 2: Principal Immigration Officer (Pretoria) to Secretary for Interior (3 January 1924); Under Secretary for the Interior to Principal Immigration Officer (Pretoria) (24 January 1924).

43 CIA 37, M130, vol 8: Immigration Officer (Bloemhof) to Chief Immigration Officer (Pretoria) (4 November 1927); Immigration Officer (Bloemhof) to Chief Immigration Officer (Pretoria) (10 November 1927).

44 CIA 38, M130, vol 9: CIAA to Principal Immigration Officer (Durban) (5 June 1928).

45 CIA 36, M130, vol 2: Under Secretary for the Interior to Principal Immigration Officer (Pretoria) (18 October 1922) ('As you are aware, cases have recently occurred in which natives from Madagascar, East Africa and similar places have been declared to be prohibited immigrants in the Union but whose admission to their supposed countries of origin has been refused and they have been compelled to return to the Union. In ordinary circumstances such natives are not prohibited from free inter-Provincial movement, and once they have been refused admission to overseas countries and are returned to the Union there is no option but to accept them as part of the native population, in which circumstances they cannot be regarded as prohibited immigrants.').

a need existed for some uniform state controls over the movement of all Africans into urban areas. Despite this consensus on greater regulation of African movement into the city, differing strategies were advanced.

Two stark alternatives were presented to Parliament in 1923: the Native Registration and Protection Bill and the Native (Urban Areas) Bill. The former proposed abolishing pass laws and replacing them with a national identification system including registration in urban areas.[46] This Bill distinguished between those Africans with permanent status and residence in urban areas and those Africans without such status. Its rationale was that co-opting the permanent African population would lead to effective urban control and stability. The national identification system with a fixed system of racial classification was supported by Patrick Duncan, the Minister of Mines (previously Minister of the Interior).

This Bill of 1923 originated with the Godley Commission (also known as the Interdepartmental Committee on Native Pass Laws).[47] Although the Godley Commission did not have the Native Labour Regulation Act within its mandate,[48] nevertheless its report recommended the repeal of existing pass laws and the provision of a lifelong registration certificate to each male African. As Douglas Hindson notes:[49]

> [T]wo forms of documentation and registration were envisaged. Population registration and the issuing of identity documents throughout South Africa would make it possible to monitor movement from rural to urban areas. Registration of contracts of service was designed to enable control over employment and unemployment within urban areas, through maintaining records of all Africans' employment histories.

---

46 Hindson, 1987: 39; Posel, 2001: 87–114.
47 U.G. 41 of 1922. The report is that of the Interdepartmental Committee on the Native Pass Laws (The Godley Report).
48 Duncan, 1995: 96–97.
49 Hindson, 1987: 35–36.

The Godley Report thus proposed using the urban boundary as a means to control the movement of Africans, while also proposing to recognise substantial rights for those permanently resident in urban areas.[50]

The Godley Report touched only briefly upon the question of 'alien natives'. However, it did not call for greater control over the entry of Africans into the national territory, nor for the expulsion of extra-Union Africans from the cities. It noted that its earlier recommendations assumed that Africans were domiciled in the Union and recommended 'that all alien natives, excluding indentured labourers for employment within proclaimed industrial and urban areas, shall be registered under prescribed regulations on entry into the Union'.[51] Thus the Godley Report advocated a 'regularise[d] and legalise[d]' strategy with respect to extra-Union Africans.

In contrast to the Native Registration and Protection Bill, the Native (Urban Areas) Bill of 1923 took a clearly restrictionist approach. This Bill's approach is often identified with the earlier Stallard Commission, which investigated and reported on the situation in the Transvaal. According to the Stallard Commission, 'the Native should only be allowed to enter urban areas, which are essentially the white man's creation, when he is willing to enter and to minister to the needs of the white man, and should depart [therefrom] when he ceases so to minister'.[52] Africans in urban areas were to be temporary sojourners only.

Both of these proposed pieces of legislation could fit within the framework of the Immigrants Regulation Act 22 of 1913. Both adopted strategies of migration regulation that did not depend upon the nationality or citizenship status of Africans nor upon their territorial

---

50 As Hindson, 1987: 37 states: 'No legal obligation should be placed on a person to carry a pass within their registered place of domicile ... but anyone who left their home area had to produce his identification certificate on demand. So Africans who resided permanently in urban areas would not be required to carry passes, while newcomers to town would.'
51 Report of the Interdepartmental Committee on the Native Pass Laws (The Godley Report) 1922: para 78.
52 Posel, 1991: 40.

birth status.[53] Likewise, both Bills provided for Africans to be removed from urban to rural areas and did not cross national boundaries, although they differed significantly in procedure. 'To deal with the "idle, dissolute, or vicious", [the Godley Report] advocated setting up a special court, with powers to order an African out of the urban area, send him to a labour colony, indenture him to a farmer or place him under the control of his chief.' Here, the difference with the Stallard Report is clear. That Report envisioned summary administrative removals, although undertaken by municipal native affairs departments.[54]

Both proposals shared the aim of creating a new internal boundary around urban areas in order to regulate the movement of Africans. Given the origins of the conceptual structure of the Act in the control of the inter-provincial movement of Asians, this common aim did not violate the regulatory scheme of the Immigrants Regulation Act of 1913.

Although it had more in common with the restrictionist approach of the Stallard Commission, the Natives (Urban Areas) Act of 1923 adopted by Parliament opted for neither the reformist nor the hard line, the two approaches to the problem of influx control identified by Posel, and the contest between which she argues 'continued within the state throughout the next three decades'.[55] Instead, the 1923 Act adopted the principle that Africans would be liable for expulsion from urban areas if they were unemployed. There were some exemptions including parliamentary voters and property owners in urban areas. Work seekers' permits and visitors' permits were also provided for. As a consequence of this Act the Transvaal model of fused industrial and urban pass laws was potentially extended to the Cape Province, if taken up by municipalities there.[56] Conceptually, the law was a regulation of African mobility.

The Act provided for enforcement through the practices of registration, policing and removal. All African males needed to register their contracts of service with the Native Affairs Department (NAD) for approval. Based on the NAD register of these contracts, the Department

---

53 Baldoz, 2011.
54 Hindson, 1987: 36–39.
55 Posel, 1991: 40.
56 Duncan, 1995: 105; Hindson, 1987: 40–41.

would issue the African with a single registration document.[57] Registration was carried out through local but centrally supervised Native Affairs Department offices. (This decentralised and partially privatised system of registration thus rejected the draft Native Registration and Protection Bill's comprehensive national identification system.) However, as Hindson notes,[58] 'in the smaller towns, mainly in the rural districts, Africans continued to carry a plethora of passes: tax certificates, registration certificates, service contracts, and inward and outward passes specific to different districts and provinces'.

The registration document 'had to be produced on demand to police or state officials checking the men's right to be in urban areas'.[59] If an African could not demonstrate a right to remain, he would be liable to be removed as well as to be charged with a criminal offence. In practice, the removal provisions of the 1923 Act were implemented through the practice of 'endorsing out', which meant that the holder of a registration document was given a period of time to depart voluntarily.[60] People permanently unemployed or convicted of criminal offences could also be charged with criminal offences, as well as being removed to labour colonies or back to rural areas in terms of section 17. These offences included return by those who had been 'endorsed out'.[61] As Posel has noted, the implementation of this Act through these practices would depend on 'ubiquitous policing'. In some locales and situations, policing was effective.[62]

---

57 Hindson, 1987: 41.
58 Op cit.
59 Posel, 1991: 41.
60 Section 12.
61 Hindson, 1987: 41.
62 Hellmann, 1948: 17–18. Ellen Hellmann wrote a classic ethnographic survey of a yard housing Africans close to the centre of Johannesburg in 1933. In discussing the sale of beer in these yards, she notes: 'The Native who slips out with a "special" or the Native who has to return home in an inebriated condition after a convivial beer drink is well aware that the shorter the distance he has to travel the more he minimises the danger of meeting a policeman on his beat. Further, as one informant pointed out to me, "If he has to walk far, he will fall down in the road and be found there".' Posel, 1991.

Even though it opened up a new frontier of regulation and provided greater resources and authority to the Native Affairs Department, the 1923 Natives (Urban Areas) Act as implemented continued to reflect substantial private sector involvement in the regulation of African mobility. According to Hindson:[63]

> *Registration of service contracts came into effect immediately in thirty-one areas of the Transvaal. Almost all already had pass offices, run by the Native Affairs Department since the time of the Transvaal Republic. Under the new legislation these remained under central government control. Cape Town, Kimberley, Bloemfontein and three smaller Free State towns were also proclaimed. In Natal the pass offices already in operation in Durban and Pietermaritzburg continued to be run by local authorities under the Natal Act of 1888.*

CONCLUSION

Pass laws would remain a reality until the Urban Areas Act was applied.[64] The employer remained central to the scheme of regulation. It was the employer who issued the contract, the decentralised offices of the national government or the municipalities themselves who registered that contract, and police officers who monitored compliance based on the contract. The enforcement scheme of the Act also afforded plenty of opportunities for evasion by Africans and their employers, as well as by local municipalities. From the standpoint of control over African movement, the Natives (Urban Areas) Act of 1923 did little more than set up a loosely demarcated set of city states. It is interesting to note that the Natives (Urban Areas) Amendment Act 25 of 1930, essentially a continuation of the 1923 model, provided increased powers to remove surplus Africans. It gave greater powers to the local authorities, making their permission (and not solely a contract of service) necessary for an African to enter and reside in proclaimed urban areas. Still, only

---

63 Hindson, 1987: 42.
64 Op cit: 40.

11 municipalities implemented these powers and their most strict application was limited to the Transvaal. [65]

The opinion of the Principal Immigration Officer (Pretoria) in 1926 was that Africans were 'freely entering from British Bechuanaland, Rhodesia, Swaziland and Portuguese East Africa'.[66] Far from ignoring this African movement, in his view it substantiated the view that 'the provisions of the Immigrants Regulation Act No. 22 of 1913 are practically a dead letter'. It might have been more accurate to have said that enforcement of the immigration laws over African mobility from beyond the borders of the Union had hardly been seen or conceptualised as a live option, either by immigration officials or those from the Native Affairs Department, except with respect to large-scale labour recruitment of Africans from outside of South Africa. Nonetheless, just at this time, reflecting a significant new political understanding among the white population, an internal boundary at South Africa's cities was formed. Political pressure demanded that the presence of all Africans in the urban areas be limited. The operation of this internal boundary would soon give greater capacity to the Native Affairs Department and deepen its co-ordination with the soon-to-be-established national bureaucracy regulating population mobility.

---

[65] Op cit: 44–45; Posel, 1991: 42.
[66] CIA 36, M130, vol 6: Principal Immigration Officer (Pretoria) to Secretary for the Interior (23 November 1926). Dutifully, this letter goes on to state the then-existing policies on entrance for Africans from British Bechuanaland, Rhodesia and Swaziland.

CHAPTER 7

The Commissioner's population, 1927–1937

The establishment of the Commissioner for Immigration and Asiatic Affairs (CIAA) in 1927 and his implementation of existing laws catalysed several important movements which added complexity to the meaning of South African citizenship in the following 10 years. In the first place, and as the focus of this chapter, the Commissioner oversaw the paradoxical development of migration regulation over Asians. On the one hand, movement between provinces for people termed 'Asiatics' became significantly restricted through administrative and legislative developments. On the other, Asians were increasingly treated as South African nationals. National registration effectively replaced provincial registration. The Commissioner's handling of the repeal of the Cape Exclusion Act in 1933 demonstrates a similar paradoxical development.

THE RESTRICTION OF MOBILITY AND A NATIONALISED POPULATION

As already noted, the movement of Indians between provinces was relatively unrestricted after the passage of the Immigrants Regulation Act 22 of 1913 and its amendment in 1914.[1] Indians living in South Africa and passing an education test could enter and reside permanently in all provinces except the Orange Free State on the same terms as they could enter the Union. The education test was required by the 1913 Act and the Union Government accepted the recommendations of the Solomon Commission[2] regarding inter-provincial movement, although this mobility remained subject to official discretion. In the Cape, the

---

1 Immigrants Regulation Act 22 of 1913 (Union); Indian Relief Act 22 of 1914 (Union).
2 The Solomon Commission (1913–1914) comprised a South African and an Indian representative and investigated some of the grievances of Indians in South Africa. Its recommendations led to the Indian Relief Act of 1914 as well as a number of administrative instructions. Bradlow, 1978: 91–95.

education test was administered restrictively by the Principal Immigration Officer. Passing the test was a 'passport' to mobility.[3]

Under concerted pressure from the Asian community, even greater freedom of movement was granted to Indians in the decade after Union. For instance, a 1921 meeting between the Minister of the Interior and a deputation of Indians from the Transvaal resulted in two 'very important departures from the established practice'. Indians living in two provinces were allowed free movement between those provinces (ie Transvaal and Natal). Those holding special letters of exemption for religious or teaching purposes and admitted for permanent residence were allowed free movement within the Union (except in the Orange Free State).[4] These practices favoured the movement of dual (provincial) citizens and of elite professionals.[5]

Chinese people did not enjoy the same degree of freedom to visit the Cape Province. Nonetheless, until reversed on the advice of the Law Advisers, Pretoria interpreted the effect of section 25(1) of the Immigrants Regulation Act as the Minister being able to issue visiting permits to allow the Chinese to visit the Cape Province despite the Exclusion Act.

However, from 1927, this relative degree of freedom to move between provinces began to decline, and Asians became increasingly restricted in their movements by the newly established national bureaucracy of the CIAA. The restrictions on the movement of Asians between provinces was effected through both criminalisation and administrative means.

The Immigration and Indian Relief (Further Provision) Act 37 of 1927 had one criminalising section with a clearly restrictive effect.[6] From 1927 onwards, illegal entrants into a province committed a criminal offence if they did not notify an immigration officer within eight days

---

3   Bradlow, 1978: 78, 92–94, 102–104.
4   CIA 34, M74, vol 1: Secretary of the Interior (signed HN Venn) to Principal Immigration Officer (Pretoria) (3 December 1921) (also noting 'The publicity of these decisions may very well be left to the Indian community itself and I do not wish you to take any action in this regard.').
5   CIA 34, M86: Acting Principal Immigration Officer and Registrar of Asiatics to Deputy Commissioner, C.I.D., Johannesburg (8 January 1920); Acting Under Secretary for the Interior (Venn) to Principal Immigration Officer (Pretoria) (19 September 1919).
6   Immigration and Indian Relief (Further Provision) Act 37 of 1927 (Union).

of entry.[7] Significantly, the Act criminalised this illegal entry only for persons deemed prohibited. The criminalisation of illegal movement across a provincial border in terms of the Immigrants Regulation Act was thus primarily limited to the Asian population.

This criminalisation of entry in the 1927 Act also provided opportunities for later administrative restrictions on movement between provinces. In response to a number of Natal-born Indians travelling to Cape Town to work there, the Minister of the Interior ruled that those taking up residence in the Cape after the passage of the 1927 Act should return to Natal, while those resident in the Cape prior to the Act were not so restricted.[8] This restriction on the inter-provincial movement of Asians meant that non-domiciled Indians would need section 25(1) visiting permits to travel to other provinces, and by 1934, the restricted issuing of inter-provincial visiting permits was a significant complaint of the South African Indian Congress.[9]

Much of the erosion of the freedom of Asians to move between provinces took place through increased national registration. From 1920, the Union Government, through the Indian Immigration Bureau, had taken over the functions of the Indian Immigration Trust Board in Natal. With respect to Indian immigrants and their descendants, the Bureau carried out functions in relation to births, deaths and marriages as well as the collection of revenue and administration of the assisted repatriation scheme.[10] The 1927 Act completed and formalised an ongoing process of nationalising registration and controlling the movement of Asians. This legislation nearly completely removed the registration responsibility from the Registrar of Asiatics (a Transvaal provincial official) and made it the charge of the Commissioner (an official of the Union Government).

Although Act 37 of 1927 deleted certain sections of Act 36 of 1908 (Transvaal) (ss 3, 4, 5(1), 6, 8, 16 and 17(6)) relating to registration requirements and procedures for issuing Transvaal Asiatic Registration

---

7   Section 8 of Act 37 of 1927 (amending section 19 of Act 22 of 1913); *Debates of House of Assembly (Hansard)*, (9 May 1927) col 3371.
8   Bradlow, 1978: 104–105.
9   CIA 60, M574: CIAA to Secretary for the Interior (17 May 1934).
10   See *Debates of House of Assembly (Hansard)* (10 March 1949) col 1948.

Certificate (TARC) documents and exceptional permits, vested rights were maintained and minor children of these certificate holders could accede to certified status at the age of 16. Thus section 5(2) of Act 36 of 1908 (Transvaal) was not deleted and, moreover, vested rights of trading status and the like were also maintained. By repealing Act 28 of 1897 (Natal), the 1927 Act also removed the mandate of the Protector of Indian Immigrants in Natal to issue passes to uncovenanted Indians in Natal. In future, such persons would be able to register nationally only in terms of the Immigrants Regulation Act 22 of 1913 (Union). In Parliament, the Minister explained that the 'dead branches' were merely being taken out of the provincial law and that such provisions were 'really re-enacted in our existing immigration law'.[11] Provincial certificates issued earlier would remain valid for migration purposes, alongside national documentation such as the certificate of identity issued in terms of section 25(2) of the Immigrants Regulation Act.

A clear step forward in the nationalisation of migration regulation concerns the position of Asians in the northern districts of Natal, magisterial districts adjacent to those of the Transvaal. The Asiatics in the Northern Districts of Natal Act 33 of 1927 applied the same registration provisions to Asiatics as then applied in the Transvaal.[12] At this point, four years before the 1931 Act, a provincially issued registration certificate affected people's mobility. A Transvaal provincial certificate allowed an Asiatic to enter and reside in the Transvaal for as long as that person remained domiciled there. However, this regulation would not be available to Asiatics introduced into the northern districts on labour employment or domestic service contracts.

The effect of the Asiatics in the Northern Districts of Natal Act was to extend the registration and policing regime of the Transvaal to these districts of Natal. Registration depended on the 'registrar' who was defined as 'the officer appointed by the Minister [of Interior] to keep the register of Asiatics and any person lawfully acting in such capacity'.[13] The policing of movement was set out in section 7(1) of Act

---

11 *Debates of House of Assembly (Hansard)* (23 June 1927) col 5662.
12 Asiatics in the Northern Districts of Natal Act 33 of 1927 (Union).
13 Section 17 of Act 33 of 1927 (Union).

33 of 1927 (Union).[14] As the Minister of the Interior stated: 'The effect will be that the three districts for all practical purposes in connection with Asiatics will form a part of the Transvaal.'[15] In terms of the Act, a person registered as an Asiatic in the northern districts of Natal would have his or her provincial registration certificate issued by the person holding the appointment as the Registrar of Asiatics (Transvaal). In the nationalisation of the Asian population, the provincial boundaries could be made flexible.

Instead of adjusting the provincial boundaries, the Immigration (Amendment) Act 15 of 1931, together with the earlier Quota Act, continued the trend of centralising the registration of the Asian population. The 1931 Act addressed several issues of migration administration. It responded to the *Rashid Amod* judgment that distinguished between the right of domicile and the right of entry, bringing holders of TARC certificates into line with Indians living in the Cape and Natal. The Act also repealed large parts of Transvaal, Natal and Union laws governing Asiatic affairs.[16]

The integrated identification and migration function of the registration of the Asian population shifted from the provincial to the national level. This happened in two legal steps. The first was a nationalisation of the competence to regulate migration. The 1931 Act dropped the migration functions of the TARC and other certificates. In a display of tortuous legality, section 3 of Act 15 of 1931 did provide a further exemption (in terms of section 5 of the Immigrants' Regulation Act) for persons living in any province who were not otherwise exempted. Thus, the TARC would continue to have a vested but nationalised

---

14 Section 7(1) of Act 33 of 1927 (Union): 'Every adult Asiatic entering or residing in the northern districts shall upon demand made upon him by any European member of a police force lawfully established in the Union or any other European person authorised thereto by the Minister, produce the certificate of registration of which he is the lawful holder and supply such particulars and furnish such means of identification as may be prescribed by regulation.'
15 *Debates of House of Assembly (Hansard)* (23 June 1927) col 5668.
16 Bradlow, 1978: 171–176; Immigration (Amendment) Act 15 of 1931 (Union); sections 5–7 of Act 15 of 1931 (Union). See also Immigration Quota Act 8 of 1930 (Union) (the Quota Act).

migration function.[17] The old provincial certificates would also continue to source trading, voting and land-owning rights. However, these rights would no longer be linked to their holders' immigration status but rather to the persistence of this increasingly outdated provincial legislation. As opposition members of Parliament noted in protest, this change destroyed the value of the registration certificates and was 'an attack on the whole principle of the registration certificate'.[18]

The second legal step taken towards the nationalisation of registration by the 1931 Act was a combination of previously separate migration and identification functions. While section 25(2) of the Immigrants Regulation Act was not textually amended, the purpose of this section was effectively transformed.[19] As before, this Union certificate of identity would allow people to enter into and reside in the Union or any province. It would thus continue to function as an assurance of re-entry into the Union or any province. In addition, as a national registration document, the section 25(2) certificate would be able to take on an identification function in practice in addition to its migration function. By 1931, a system of national registration based on the section 25(2) certificate of identity was poised to replace the variety of provincial systems for the Asian population.

The paradoxical linking of restriction and nationalisation was pointedly demonstrated in the parliamentary debates around the draft Immigration (Amendment) Act of 1931. Here, some restrictionist European representatives took the rhetoric of nationalisation to its logical conclusion. These representatives came from Natal, where by far the majority of Indians in South Africa resided and where the ratio of Indians to Europeans was roughly one to one. To their parliamentary colleagues, these Natal representatives proposed *relaxing* the existing legislative restrictions on the movement of Asians between provinces.

---

17 Section 2(g) of Act 15 of 1931 (deleting section 4(2)(b) of Act 22 of 1913); see also section 2(h).
18 *Debates of House of Assembly (Hansard)* (2 March 1931) cols 998–1000, 1189–1191.
19 Section 2(h) of Act 15 of 1931 (inserting section 4(2A) which distinguishes between Immigrants Regulation Act section 25(2) certificates of identity and other documentation and certificates issued under other laws and vests capacity to enter and to reside only in the section 25(2) certificates).

Their motivation was to spread the Indian population across the nation, so that 'absorption' would reduce the 'menace'.[20] Some support for the proposal was also offered on the basis of the principle of freedom of movement for citizens.[21] Not surprisingly, Parliament rejected the Natal proposal, primarily on the basis that public opinion in the other provinces was not ready for such a move. Furthermore, some representatives argued that the 1927 Cape Town Agreement encouraging voluntary repatriation was a sufficient response to the Asian question and that it was not necessary to allow free inter-provincial movement.

As the counter-intuitive effort by the restrictionist Natal representatives underlines, the migration regulation of Asians demonstrated a series of paradoxical episodes. At the same time that the freedom of movement for Asians throughout the entire national territory and especially across provincial borders was being reduced, the nation increasingly treated Asians as nationals, as citizens belonging to the Union of South Africa rather than to any other political community. While the mobility of Asians within the national territory was being limited, the very mechanism of that limitation contributed to strengthening the identification of the Asian population with that of a broader South African political community. With the nationalisation and the centralisation of registration, Asians were increasingly accepted and registered by state officials as people with a national rather than a provincial identity.

---

20   *Debates of House of Assembly (Hansard)* (16 June 1927) col 5208.
21   Op cit: col 5776 ('I have always contended since 1913, when the Immigration Act came into existence, that it is an undoubted anomaly that there should be these provincial boundaries, and they not only apply to Asiatics, but in theory they apply to the European too. You have got the Union and yet each province is a self-contained country, as far as the immigration laws are concerned. It seems to me that so long as we are a Union there should be every opportunity to all citizens within the Union to stay in or migrate from one part to any other part, whether they be Europeans or non-Europeans. I do feel that now, 17 years after Union, some provision should be made whereby citizens whoever they may be, can pass from part to another part. To call this a Union and have four separate countries for immigration purposes is, I think, a grave anomaly.').

THE 1933 REPEAL OF THE CHINESE EXCLUSION ACT

The repeal of the provincial Chinese Exclusion Act in 1933 took place within these demonstrated trends of increasing restriction at the same time as increasing nationalisation of migration regulation. The duality of the process helps to explain the different perceptions of the same legal step. State officials and the Chinese community ended up agreeing on the repeal of legislation specifically regulating the Chinese community for diametrically opposed reasons.

The Chinese community in the Cape sought the repeal of the specific pre-Union provincial legislation, the Chinese Exclusion Act 37 of 1904, as a means to greater autonomy.[22] For many years, the Chinese Consul-General had made repeated requests to repeal this Act, and the issue had been examined by a select committee of the House of Assembly of the Cape Colony in 1908. However, these requests were largely ignored and regarded as outside the 'legitimate sphere' of the Consul-General and rather that of diplomatic and imperial channels.[23] The position of the Chinese Consul-General had its origin in the pre-Union labour migration to the mines in the Transvaal and the national government regarded the Consul-General's function as consistent with its origins — taking up individual cases of mine workers[24] but not issues of general policy.[25] The Chinese Consul-General's role was thus closer to that of the Portuguese Curator, who was concerned with the welfare of

---

22 Chinese Exclusion Act 37 of 1904 (Cape). See Chapter 3.
23 BNS 411, 55/74, vol 1: Governor-General to General Smuts (30 November 1910).
24 BNS 412, 55/74, vol 2: Principal Immigration Officer and Registrar of Asiatics to Secretary for the Interior (23 November 1925) (discussing letter seeking issue of a temporary permit for Mrs Wai Shee received from Chinese Consul-General). At this point, officialdom looked relatively favourably on the Chinese. The PIO's recommendation in this case was positive. This recommendation was forwarded to the Secretary by the Under Secretary with a handwritten notation: 'I think we should accept the PIO's recommendation. We do not have much trouble with Chinese.'
25 In this regard, the unsuccessful petition of the Chinese should be compared to the successful petition of the Turkish government on the topic of treatment of their nationals in terms of the Cape Immigration Act of 1906 and the Japanese government on the effect of legislation on its nationals. BNS 411, 55/74, vol 1: Private Secretary to Governor-General (23 November 1910).

individual Mozambican mine workers in South Africa, than to the role played by Indian government representatives.

In his campaign on behalf of the community, the Chinese Consul-General initially made the (historically accurate) point that the 1904 Exclusion Act was largely a response to the Chinese indentured labour system in the Transvaal. He argued that since the system had ended so too had the need for the Exclusion Act. Ironically, this assertion could also have implied the end of the need for a Chinese Consul-General.[26] In addition, the Chinese found the Act not only 'a great indignity but also a grievous injustice to the Chinese Nation'.[27] Particularly, the Consul-General complained that it was impossible for the remaining Chinese to obtain fresh permits to leave and re-enter the country and that some Chinese were deported for small offences such as gambling.[28]

For the Chinese community the most troubling issue was the authorities' interference with the immigration of the wives and children of Chinese residents. On this matter, the executive rather than the judicial organs of the state had long been the more progressive actors. By administrative order in 1914, the Minister of the Interior treated Chinese as Asiatics along with Indians and directed that no differentiation should be made between the two communities.[29] However, a few

---

[26] Governor-General Gladstone noted in November 1910 that the Consul 'was sent here by his govt to look after the Chinese coolies and ... now he is rather out of a job'. BNS 411, 55/74, vol 1.

[27] BNS 411, 55/74, vol 1: Acting Chinese Consul-General to Governor-General (12 November 1910).

[28] BNS 411, 55/74, vol 1: Acting Chinese Consul-General to Governor-General (12 November 1910); see also Acting Chinese Consul-General to Acting Secretary for the Interior (21 November 1910) ('If I am right in my assumption that the Act was passed to prevent the entrance of indentured labourers from the Transvaal into the Cape Colony, then the necessity for the Act has disappeared with the removal from the Transvaal of all indentured labourers; if I am wrong in my assumption I must confess that I am quite at a loss to understand why the Act was passed and why Chinese subjects should be singled out for special treatment as provided in the Act. The contention of my government is that Chinese subjects should be treated in exactly the same way as other Asiatics.' The Acting Consul-General notes several ways in which the legislative treatment of Chinese compared unfavourably with that of Asiatics.).

[29] CIA 34, M86: Under Secretary for the Interior to Principal Immigration Officer (Pretoria) (25 July 1914) ('I am directed to inform you that it is the wish of the Minister

years later, in the case of *Hoy Poy*, a Transvaal-based Supreme Court judge understood Chinese marriages to be polygamous.[30] Thus, the 1914 Indian Relief Act's provision allowing the entry of wives married monogamously (and minor children) was judged in law not applicable to the Chinese community.[31] Despite the judicially expressed view, the Union immigration bureaucracy continued with its practice of non-differentiation, on the strength of the Minister's discretion and written administrative order. Chinese persons were allowed to bring in wives and children upon proof of relationship and identity.[32] The Chinese also shared equally with Indians in later restrictions. With the restrictive amendment of the Immigrants Regulation Act in 1927 by the Immigration and Indian (Further Provision) Act 37 of 1927, the question again arose of whether the provision was to apply to the Chinese as to Indians. The Commissioner for Asiatic Affairs, HN Venn, decided that the Chinese would not be accorded any better treatment than the Indians.[33] These questions surfaced again immediately after the repeal of the Exclusion Act in 1933.[34]

---

that no differentiation should be made under the Immigration Laws between Indians and Chinese but that all Asiatics should be dealt with similarly in the future.').

30 *Hoy Poy v Principal Immigration Officer* 1916 (TPD). A Law Adviser's opinion on the case also concluded that the Chinese could not benefit from the exemption. CIA 34 M86: Memo to the Secretary of the Interior re *Hoy Poy v Principal Immigration Officer* (8 April 1918).

31 Section 3(2) of Act 22 of 1914 (amending the 1913 Act).

32 CIA 31, M31, vol 2: Principal Immigration Officer to Secretary for the Interior (1 October 1918) ('It is only an administrative order of the Minister which allows them to enter. The administrative order referred to is of course that which instructed Principal Immigration Officers to treat Chinese on the same lines as Indians. It follows therefore that no legal claim to enter the Transvaal can successfully be made by the Chinese in respect of their wives and children.').

33 CIA 31, M31, vol 1: Commissioner for Asiatic Affairs to Secretary for the Interior (23 August 1927)

34 In response to a long letter from the Principal Immigration Officer in Cape Town, the Commissioner effectively decreed that, whatever the legalities, Chinese marriages should 'now-a-days' be presumed monogamous and granted the same immigration benefits as such Indian marriages. See CIA 31, M31, vol 2: Principal Immigration Officer (Cape Town) to CIAA (18 July 1933); CIAA to Principal Immigration Officer (Cape Town) (7 October 1933) ('I must say that I am not quite sure that I understand why you consider it necessary to raise the question at all.').

The Chinese perceptions of interference were justified, as the CIAA continued the long-standing official focus of identification on the Chinese community. For instance, in 1929 the CIAA opposed the extension of temporary permits to two Chinese boys on the grounds of awaiting documents to prove that their mothers were either dead or in ill health. The CIAA stated:[35]

> [A]lmost every Chinese boy entering the Union for the first time submits a Chinese document certifying that his mother is dead. There are no means of having such documents confirmed as there does not appear to be any system of registration of births and deaths in China and I am convinced that the majority of the documents submitted are fraudulent.

In response to enquiries made by the Government of Australia in the same year, Commissioner Venn stated '[I]t is the practice of this Department to take finger prints for identification purposes of Chinese persons of ordinary standing admitted temporarily to the Union and of local residents granted permission to re-enter after temporary absence.'[36] At least until 1927, the demands of the Chinese Consul-General for repeal were refused by the Department of the Interior on the categorical grounds that the Act should remain 'so long as there are persons resident in the [Cape] province who are subject to its provision'.[37] However, realistic opportunities for the repeal of the Chinese Exclusion Act began to surface soon after the Commissioner's post was established in 1927.

In June 1928, a conference of principal immigration officers considered the question and recommended the repeal of the provincial legislation. The main reason given for repeal was that 'there should be as little distinction as possible between Chinamen and Indians'. In particular, the immigration officers noted that the Chinese were subject to slightly different provisions than the Indians: a higher age of admission of

---

35　BNS 412, 55/74, vol 3: CIAA to Secretary for the Interior (8 June 1929). This application had been supported by the Consul-General.
36　BNS 412, 55/74, vol 3: CIAA to Secretary for the Interior (14 June 1929).
37　BNS 411, 55/74, vol 1: Acting Secretary for the Interior to Chinese Consul-General (14 November 1910).

male minors; no defined period of absence from the Union; unembossed permits for visits abroad; and special liability to deportation.[38] Apart from the last provision (where the Immigrants Regulation Act deportation power was regarded as sufficient), these provisions were regarded by the principal immigration officers as placing the Chinese in a *better* situation than the Indian community. Placing the Chinese on the same basis as other Asiatics was thus regarded as reducing the advantages enjoyed by the Chinese community despite the fact that the community itself apparently viewed the repeal quite differently.

The repeal of the provincial Exclusion Act could also be regarded as simplifying the migration administration.[39] By 1928, several legal issues relating to matters arising as a result of the overlap of the provincial Chinese Exclusion Act and the national Immigrants Regulation Act had caused some confusion in migration administration.[40] While some of these issues led to a change or clarification in the administrative interpretation of the existing laws, most were disposed of on an individual ad hoc basis and could be repeated.[41] Repealing the Act would lead to consistency and presumably efficiency.

---

38 BNS 412, 55/74, vol 2: CIAA to Secretary for the Interior (30 July 1928).
39 BNS 412, 55/74, vol 2: CIAA to Secretary for the Interior (30 July 1928) ('It is therefore considered that the powers under the present Immigration Laws are sufficiently wide to meet all requirements and that the present elaborate machinery under the Chinese Exclusion Act may well be dispensed with ...'); see also BNS 412, 55/74, vol 3: Submission to the Secretary for the Interior (6 January 1932).
40 BNS 412, 55/74, vol 2: Secretary for the Interior to Commissioner for Asiatic Affairs (undated 1927) (confirming that section 25 of the Immigrants Regulation Act is not to be interpreted to override sections 3, 11, 20, 23 and 25 of the Exclusion Act); CIAA to Secretary for the Interior (25 July 1928) (implying that the Chinese may take either the Immigrants Regulation Act or the Exclusion Act but 'must take one Act in full'); but see Lawson Brown and Brown to Secretary for the Interior (20 November 1928) and Acting Under Secretary for the Interior to Lawson Brown and Brown (27 November 1928).
41 One case that led to a clarification in administrative interpretation was that of Joseph Leong Seng. BNS 412, 55/74, vol 2: CIAA to Secretary for the Interior (21 September 1928) (recommending rejection of the application); Under Secretary for the Interior to CIAA (3 October 1928); CIAA to Secretary for the Interior (23 October 1928) (Secretary for the Interior noting in handwriting that were the provisions of s 10 of Act 37 of 1927 (amending the Immigrants Regulation Act) applied to the case, domicile would not be lost); Under Secretary for Interior to CIAA (undated, 86/55/74); CIAA

The 1928 conference of immigration officers placed several conditions on their recommending the repeal of the Exclusion Act, primarily to retain the registration system with respect to the Chinese.[42] Following the conference, Commissioner Venn began to advocate repealing the Exclusion Act to the Secretary of the Interior. Also perceiving the repeal to place the Chinese on the same basis as Indians, the Secretary agreed to the repeal after ascertaining that the admission of wives and children of Chinese persons under the Exclusion Act was regulated on substantially the same basis as that of Indians under the Immigrants Regulation Act.[43]

Not only did the CIAA initiate the repeal, it implemented the drafting of the repealing legislation. With authority from the Secretary, Commissioner Venn first prepared a draft piece of legislation, the Cape Province Chinese Registration Bill of 1929. This Bill would have extended the registration provisions then applicable to Asians under the direct administration of the Commissioner to Chinese persons in the Cape Province. As the CIAA noted, this Bill 'follows closely the

---

to Secretary for the Interior (5 November 1928) (raising the policy issue of whether Chinese are to be given the benefit of section 10 of Act 37 of 1927); Secretary to Under Secretary (15 November 1928) ('Reply in affirmative, better that reply came forward for Secretary's signature.'); Secretary for the Interior to CIAA (21 November 1928) (confirming that Chinese should be given benefits of section 10 of Act 37 of 1927).

[42] BNS 412, 55/74, vol 2: CIAA to Secretary for the Interior (30 July 1928) (noting the following reservations of the Conference to the repeal of the Exclusion Act: '(1) The continued registration of all Chinamen. (2) The age when Chinese male children are to be registered. (3) The production by the holder on demand by an Immigration Officer or Police Officer of his Registration Certificate or Certificate of Exemption, failure to produce such certificate to be considered an offence. (4) Suitable penalties for failure to register.').

[43] BNS 412, 55/74, vol 2: Under Secretary to Secretary for the Interior (7 August 1928) ('I agree with C.I.A.A. Another point is that Chinese in the Cape can bring in a wife even though the applicant has offspring by another woman who is in the Union.'). The Secretary's response was 'We should apply the same principles, as in the case of Indians, when a Chinaman proposes to bring his *lawful* wife and legitimate children'. The Secretary requested a report on the procedures followed in respect of the admission of wives and children of Chinese persons. Secretary for the Interior to CIAA (15 August 1928); CIAA to Secretary for the Interior (24 August 1928) (reporting that procedures were nearly identical for those of Indians); Under Secretary for the Interior to CIAA (31 August 1928).

Transvaal and Northern Districts Registration Act ...'.[44] From the point of view of the CIAA, the repeal of the Exclusion Act was an opportunity to extend the system of national Asian registration to the Chinese population in the Cape Province.

In the end, the official demand for registration of the Chinese community would be met in another way. As discussed above, the section 25(2) certificate of identity originally intended for proof of re-entry had, by 1931, assumed an additional function as a national registration certificate for general use among the Asian population, following the same logic as the pass issued to uncovenanted Indians by Act 28 of 1897 (Natal) (see Chapter 3). With regard to the Chinese community in the Cape, such a generally available registration certificate at national level allowed for the repeal of the Exclusion Act in 1933 without the government having to pass separate registration legislation such as the CIAA had drafted in 1929.

Finally, the repeal of the Exclusion Act was also encouraged by a provision of the Immigration Quota Act 8 of 1930. From 1930, wives and minor children of Chinese residents were required to have immigration permits in terms of the nationally administered Quota Act in order to enter South Africa for permanent residence.[45] This led the Chinese Consul-General to point out that the Chinese now came under the administration of three separate immigration acts: the Immigrants Regulation Act 22 of 1913; the Immigration Quota Act of 1930; and the Chinese Exclusion Act:[46]

> *I venture to point out that the provisions contained in the Quota Act and the General Immigration Act and its Amendment in 1931 are very comprehensive and that the early repeal of the Cape Chinese Exclusion Act will not only do away with an Act which has long outrun its usefulness but it will also entail less work to the Immigration*

---

44 BNS 412, 55/74, vol 2: Acting CIAA to Secretary for Interior (10 January 1929). The sole purpose of the Act was stated to be 'to provide for the Registration of Chinese in the Province of the Cape of Good Hope'. See also Yapp and Man, 1996: 184.
45 BNS 412, 55/74, vol 3: Sekretaris van Binnelandse Sake to Ivan Wilke (29 April 1931).
46 BNS 412, 55/74, vol 3: Consul-General to Minister for the Interior (15 December 1931).

Department and ensure uniformity of Immigration matters as applying to Chinese.

With the continued support of the CIAA, the Minister gave his agreement in principle to the repeal of the Exclusion Act in 1932. A Bill to this effect was introduced in and passed by Parliament in the 1933 session. Act 19 of 1933 repealed the Chinese Exclusion Act of the Cape. In addition, sections 73 and 74 of the Indian Immigration Act of 1891 (Natal) were repealed at the request of the Indian community as relayed through the Protector of Immigrants. The repeal of these two sections brought the age of majority of Indian immigrants into line with the general South African law.[47] The parliamentary debate used the language of territorial control: 'Union legislation has been passed dealing with immigration as a whole. That legislation has been proved by actual experience to control quite adequately both the entrance into South Africa of Asiatics and also the registration and control of those already in the country.'[48] The benefits to both the community and the government were cited: '[I]t will be clear to the House that some of these provisions are unnecessarily vexatious to the Chinese. They lead to a good deal of extra labour from the official point of view … It is certainly unnecessary that we should maintain on our statute book more stringent provisions for controlling these 1 600 Chinese than are found to be necessary for the control of our 200 000 Indians in the Union as a whole.'[49]

The result of the repeal, as the CIAA noted, was that 'Chinese will, in future, be governed by the provisions of the Immigrants' Regulation Act No. 22 of 1913, as amended from time to time'. From 21 June 1933, magistrates in the Cape Province were directed to refer all Chinese applicants for 'Certificates, Permits, etc. to the local Immigration Officer, and, at other centres where there is no Immigration Officer, Magistrates will deal with Chinese in the same manner as Indians'.[50] Indeed, this

---

47 Section 2 of Act 19 of 1933; *Debates of the House of Assembly (Hansard)* (31 May 1933): col 128.
48 Op cit: col 129.
49 Op cit: col 129.
50 BNS 412, 56/74, vol 1: CIAA to Magistrates in the Cape Province (12 October 1933).

extra legislative responsibility was reflected later in the workload of immigration officers in cities such as Port Elizabeth.

CONCLUSION

The repeal of the Chinese Exclusion Act (Cape) was finally accomplished yet very much on the Commissioner's terms. The Chinese community gained parity of treatment with the Indian community but by being governed according to national migration legislation. As it did with the majority of the Indian community, this legislation presumptively regarded Chinese persons as prohibited immigrants rather than lawful residents. From this perspective, the repeal of the Exclusion Act was hardly a boon to the Chinese. Chinese residents in South Africa achieved the same paradoxical status as Asians, subject to increasing regulation and control yet also registered and treated as national citizens in terms of the Immigrants Regulation Act of 1913.

As detailed in this chapter, the bureaucracy of the CIAA expanded its power over the Asian population through paradoxical regulation, in the process adopting an increasingly legalistic style of decision-making. This simultaneously resulted in greater channels of national influence over the Asian population, as well as more restricted freedom of movement for that population within the nation. From a base in the Cape, the Chinese population was able to exploit the bureaucracy's desire for a set of uniform rules in order to repeal the discriminatory and politically odious provincial legislation, the Chinese Exclusion Act, in 1933. Increasingly regulated by a national rather than a provincial bureaucracy, the mobility of the Asian population was already entangled with that of the European population and would soon be conceptually linked with that of the African population as well, all under the aegis of the CIAA, the Commissioner of Immigration and Asiatic Affairs.

This memorandum also instructed that '[t]he Chinese registers and records of Chinese, in Magistrate's offices, should be retained by Magistrates'.

CHAPTER 8

One official South Africa

Beyond administering the national immigration policy for Europeans and Asians, the Commissioner of Immigration and Asiatic Affairs (CIAA) also negotiated a national policy on African migration regulation with the Native Affairs Department (NAD) in the decade from 1927. The relative success of this negotiation finally aligned the work of the national immigration bureaucracy with that of the South African state officials who were regulating the movement of the African population. The result was a 1931 deportation policy (revised in 1935) that treated the European and Asian populations together with Africans. For the first time, there was a single official view of South Africa as a combined albeit unequal population. Still, there was a major caveat. The CIAA and the NAD could not implement this policy effectively. By 1936, they acknowledged failing to deal with the problem of clandestine migration at which they had aimed their efforts. Nonetheless, this official and co-ordinated view of the national population had a lasting and constitutive impact. The following chapter shows that South Africa had become a territory over which migration control through populations could be exercised by an aligned bureaucracy.

This unified view finally emerges from the development of an official problem and an official solution regarding 'clandestine extra-Union natives'. In the late 1920s the state officials altered their understanding of the African population and began to distinguish between Union and extra-Union Africans — that is those from within South Africa and those from outside the country, and the latter became recognised as a policy problem. Although the CIAA and the NAD perceived this as a common problem in 1927, initially they proposed different solutions. The CIAA wanted to repatriate Africans only after they had been criminally convicted. The NAD envisioned a system of labour depots instead. After four years of negotiation and conflict, the two bureaucracies agreed in 1931 on a compromise: an employment-funded civil repatriation policy. This solution was closer to the CIAA proposal, which called for

Africans to be transported across national borders under civil rather than criminal law. The joint efforts of these departments to implement this policy soon ran into a series of problems in conception and practice, mostly because of funding and expense. Despite the authorities revising this policy in 1935 and providing better resources and co-ordination, and although the civil repatriation policy was not repudiated in principle, by the end of 1936 it was viewed as an official and expensive failure.

AN OFFICIAL PROBLEM BUT DIFFERING SOLUTIONS

The appointment of the Commissioner for Immigration and Asiatic Affairs catalysed the officials' perceptions of the problem of the regulation of African migration. By 1927, the immigration bureaucracy in the Union felt the need for an official response to the prevalence of clandestine extra-Union natives. In the view of the Principal Immigration Officer (Cape), 'the control of the entry of alien natives is extremely difficult and, in the absence of (1) a clearly defined policy, (2) consistency in dealing with them by the Native Affairs Department, and (3) Police action [the entry of alien natives] is not [a situation] which can possibl[y] be dealt with by the Immigration Department as at present constituted'.[1] In his analysis, the situation was 'the result of want of policy and lack of cohesion'.

Recognition of the problem in 1927 can be seen as a crystallisation of earlier developments. From the mid-1920s, police and immigration officers in the northern and western Transvaal frequently asked their superiors about the action they should take regarding non-Union Africans. At this time, these officers themselves were subject to varying lines of accounting to the police, NAD and the CIAA.[2] Understandably, this situation led to frustration and confusion among lower level

---

1 CIA 37, M130, vol 8: Principal Immigration Officer (Cape) to Secretary for the Interior (28 June 1927).
2 CIA 36, M130, vol 6: Statement by DJ Venter, Constable, South African Police (Zebediela) (22 February 1927); CIA 36, M130, vol 5: CH Kruger, Sergeant, South African Police (Duivelskloof) to Principal Immigration Officer (4 October 1926).

officials. For instance, the South African Police officer and appointed Immigration Officer in Messina wrote:[3]

> I shall be glad if you will define the action you require in respect of the thousands of illegal Native Immigrants that flood this district, from Nyasaland, etc., etc. I have searched this office's files without avail, yet it appears clear that some variation of the Law has been sanctioned, for hundreds of these natives receive passes from the S.N.C.'s office at Louis Trichardt. I have been instructed to ignore the law in respect of these natives in so far as Messina is concerned. As I receive my appointment from you, I consider that any variation of the Regulations, that you may allow, should more properly be communicated to me direct. At present, I feel that I am asked to make fish of one and flesh of another. Will you please instruct.

As the Messina officer pointed out, even where foreign Africans did report to an official as required, before 1927 police and other enforcement officials had no consistent or effective deportation or identification policies they could use to regulate the movement of these Africans. The articulated policy of the Department of Native Affairs was that foreign Africans were subject to the pass laws and were to be treated no differently from Union Africans.[4] Since the Pass Law Proclamation 18 of 1918 prescribed that every black person had to have a pass that should be endorsed upon entry, the proper response to reporting Rhodesian and Nyasaland Africans was technically criminal prosecution. Yet, as the NAD itself recognised, the prosecution of migrants who reported voluntarily was hardly a satisfactory long-term policy.[5]

---

[3] CIA 36, M130, vol 9: CIAA to Secretary for the Interior (18 October 1928) (joining minute received from Immigration Officer (Messina)).

[4] CIA 36, M130, vol 6: Secretary for Native Affairs to Secretary for the Interior (5 March 1927) (the issue of a section 25(1) permit does not exempt the bearer from the pass laws if he is otherwise subject to them).

[5] CIA 36, M130, vol 6: Statement by DJ Venter, Constable, South African Police (Zebediela) (22 February 1927) with annotation by CL Harries, Native Commissioner (23 February 1927). There is a clear expectation among the extant official correspondence that criminalisation is a mere holding action and that a general policy decision was expected. For instance, the Department of Native Affairs made ad hoc arrangements

Nonetheless, prior to 1927, criminalisation remained the only official response to clandestine entry. For instance, in 1926, the Secretary of the Interior's response to reports of the influx of Nyasaland and Rhodesian Africans had been to consult at ministerial level. He then assured the Principal Immigration Officer (Pretoria) that the Immigrants Regulation Act would be amended to provide for criminalisation of entry without notifying an immigration officer and for employing 'an illegal immigrant'. The immigration laws were indeed amended to provide for criminal sanctions in 1927.[6]

It was against this background that the newly established Commissioner held his first national conference of principal immigration officers in June 1927. While that conference was called primarily to implement the 1927 Indian Agreement, it included the matter of clandestine Rhodesian and Nyasaland Africans as well. Consideration of this matter yielded a formal policy. In consultation with the principal immigration officers, the CIAA adopted a national policy on deportations of these Africans, which was to continue the laissez-faire policy of not removing extra-Union natives unless they had criminal convictions.[7]

While such a policy might seem like little or no policy at all, the resolution was a significant step forward from the previous situation. As already noted, before 1927 immigration officers (who were often appointed additionally as police officers) could exercise discretion in dealing with people within the terms of the immigration laws. Besides instruction from the Principal Immigration Officer (Pretoria) in particular cases and general instructions to enforce the laws and pursue criminal prosecutions, these local officers had received little guidance

---

to allow Africans from adjacent districts to seek farm work. CIA 36, M130, vol 5: Under Secretary for the Interior to Principal Immigration Officer (Pretoria) (29 January 1926) (approving of such arrangements on the Bechuanaland border pending decision on general question of admission of natives from neighbouring territories).

6   CIA 36, M130, vol 6: Secretary for the Interior to Principal Immigration Officer (Pretoria) (2 December 1926); Secretary for the Interior to Principal Immigration Officer (Pretoria) (11 March 1927).

7   CIA 38, M130, vol 9: Principal Immigration Officer (Cape) to CIAA (17 September 1928) ('You will recollect that the decision arrived at was that such natives who were brought to, or reported at, this office were not to be interfered with, provided they were of good type and had no convictions recorded against them.').

on how their discretion should be exercised. For the first time, the 1927 laissez-faire policy offered them a coherent and consistent national plan of action, and added a second administrative response besides the earlier exclusive reliance on criminal penalties. Thus, the policy at the least formally unified the practices followed within the various components of the national immigration bureaucracy.

Within a year of adopting the Commissioner's laissez-faire policy on repatriations, the Department of Native Affairs adopted its own and different national policy with respect to extra-Union Africans. From 1 June 1928, the NAD policy was to apply self-funded repatriation to those extra-Union natives found in industrial areas who pleaded lack of funds to return home. Through their power to issue passes with specified conditions, NAD officials began to require that extra-Union Africans work to earn their costs of repatriation. As initially articulated by the Director of Native Labour, this policy did not commit his department to ultimately bearing the costs of repatriation. Instead, pass offices would record the employment details of extra-Union Africans who would be thus temporarily registered. At the end of their term of employment, the NAD official at the pass office was either to endorse the extra-Union African's service contract for his return home or hand him over to the immigration authorities as a prohibited immigrant.[8] It is significant that the Department of Native Affairs adopted this policy and thus set the repatriation of extra-Union Africans as an official goal.

In explaining the policy to officials of neighbouring territories, who were anxious about the repatriations, the Department of Native Affairs observed that the policy applied in practice mainly in towns and emphasised that it played a largely monitoring function. The response to

---

8   CIA 38, M130, vol 9: Circular of the Director of Native Labour re Extra Union Natives (1 June 1928) (Relaying the decision of the Secretary of Native Affairs, eg 'I have to inform you that indigent extra Union Natives should be permitted to take employment until they have earned sufficient to cover the expenses of their return home. Careful record should be maintained of such concessions in order that steps can be taken to enforce the condition'.) These instructions did not concern 'natives from the East Coast, Swaziland, Basutoland and Bechuanaland Protectorate'.

a query from the Nyasaland Protectorate Principal Immigration Officer by the Secretary for Native Affairs stated:[9]

> [S]uch unemployed alien Natives as fall within the class of prohibited immigrants and are unable to defray the cost of their return home should be permitted to engage themselves in service, preferably as agricultural labourers, for a limited period of time with a view to their acquiring sufficient means to enable their repatriation. Numbers of these Natives, however, drift into the towns and the practice has been adopted of endorsing their service contracts, to similar effect, where in default of their obtaining employment in agriculture, they have been permitted to work in urban areas. It is hoped by this means to keep at least some record of their movements which will be available should necessity arise.

The Native Affairs self-funded repatriation policy arose in part from concern for safeguarding the employment of Union Africans. The Secretary for Native Affairs informed the governments of Nyasaland and Rhodesia that, while a definitive policy was still under consideration, 'as far as possible the native population of the Union should have the first claim to employment within the Union'.[10] The same official argued to the immigration authorities in Bulawayo in Southern Rhodesia that 'while the influx of alien Natives congests the labour markets of the large towns, the Government has been called upon to provide large sums for famine relief for its own people who find themselves precluded from the opportunity of work by aliens'.[11]

---

9   CIA 38, M130, vol 9: Secretary of Native Affairs to Principal Immigration Officer (Limbe, Nyasaland Protectorate) (20 February 1929); Principal Immigration Officer (Limbe) to Principal Immigration Officer (Pretoria) (12 January 1929). The CIAA wrote on his copy of the Secretary's letter next to the sentence regarding the record of movements 'Yes, that is all that is likely to happen'.

10 CIA 38, M130, vol 9: Secretary for Native Affairs to Principal Immigration Officer (Limbe, Nyasaland Protectorate) (20 February 1929).

11 CIA 38, M130, vol 9: Secretary for Native Affairs to Chief Immigration Officer (Bulawayo) (14 January 1929).

The Native Affairs pay-so-you-can-go policy was reported in the Johannesburg daily newspaper *The Star* as a novel and troubling development.[12] The view of *The Star* was that:

> [h]owever desirable it may be to prevent the influx of natives from outside the Union, except under strict regulations of contract, as obtain in respect of the Mozambique natives labour employed on the mines, there appears to be an element of injustice about the expulsion of those who have worked in South Africa for a number of years and to whom there may be no objection on grounds of character and general conduct.

The Star further reported that:

> [m]any of those who are getting orders to leave are paying rent as well as supporting dependants, and while protesting against the present action, they argue that if they are to leave the country it will be necessary for the Government to provide them with the means of travel to their distant homes and with food for the journey.

The fact that the Commissioner for Immigration and Asiatic Affairs was unaware of the self-funding Native Affairs repatriation policy until it was reported in the newspapers demonstrated the lack of national co-ordination at this point. The CIAA took the side of the affected segment of the population and was concerned about the policy's harsh effects on foreign Africans as well as the cost of their deportation.[13] The Native

---

12   CIA 38, M130, vol 9: *The Star* (21 August 1928). 'The length of residence of such natives is not taken into consideration, unless they have been paying Union taxes, which few of them have done, their taxation payments being usually required to be made to their country of origin. Some natives who have had these orders to quit have married native women of South African origin, and have received instructions that when they leave they must take their families with them.'

13   CIA 38, M130, vol 9: CIAA to Secretary for the Interior (28 August 1928) ('The net result is that at the end of six months if the native has been in employment he is sent adrift and the last month's pay either forfeited or paid to him by the employer. In other cases, the native is unable to secure employment and as I found at Nelspruit merely wanders around begging for a living. We then have to step in and deport the native.').

CHAPTER 8 One official South Africa

Affairs policy both reduced employment opportunities and increased liability to deportation for extra-Union natives. Indeed, immigration officers received and considered requests to avoid repatriation from extra-Union natives with long periods of residence and employment.[14]

Nonetheless, a self-funding repatriation policy was not inconsistent with the CIAA's own laissez-faire policy, with one exception. The Commissioner's primary concern was that he be consulted, as his office was ultimately responsible for the costs of deporting extra-Union Africans who were caught up in this policy.[15] His position was that, where sufficient repatriation funds were available from outside his office, the Commissioner was willing to accept responsibility for the repatriation of extra-Union Africans.[16]

As subsequent newspaper reports had hinted, a variation in the Native Affairs' policy was soon to come. On 5 June 1929, the Minister of Native Affairs convened senior civil servants from several national departments to consider the issue of clandestine immigration of Africans from Rhodesia and Central Africa. This group (which included the Commissioner's superior but not the Commissioner) began from the

---

14 CIA 38, M130, vol 9: 'Blantyres without Job Living in Field' to Chief Immigration Officer (Pretoria) (8 November 1929): 'Sir, we are your dogs. Please throw us not aways. Kindly receive our cry. This punishment is too heavy for your dogs to carry. Please sir speak nicely to your officers here to make our punishment easy for us. We know the rule. But please let them make it as in Pretoria and in Johannesburg. Old boy must get a pass to look for work in farms or in cement work. But they write our pass home. How can we go home no money. We do not eat. No money. 12 died already walking on foot. No money no food; they died in October. It can be good for your officers to make passes to look for work not to put home we die of hunger. Yes, the rule stop new boys. But for Boys long ago here and pay tax please speak to your officers to allow looking for work. How can we go home. No money no food. A boy from Johannesburg Pretoria come here they write home. They give us no chance. Now we beg you our master. Please we die, we sleep in thorns, we don't eat drink but die we beg SIR. With tears your dogs. Blantyres without job Living in Field. Pp Cement cay Ltd. Slurry Transvaal.'
15 CIA 38, M130, vol 9: CIAA to Secretary for the Interior (28 August 1928).
16 CIA 38, M130, vol 9 CIAA to Principal Immigration Officer (Cape Town) (5 December 1928) ('It would however appear to require much more than one month's wages to defray the cost of returning a prohibited native to his home in Rhodesia.'); CIAA to Secretary for the Interior (18 October 1928) ('I suggest that it would be advisable to instruct ... that these natives should be dealt with in terms of Natives Affairs Circular Minute [laying out earn-your-repatriation-costs policy].').

frank premise that '[w]hile every endeavour has been made by means of the pass system to keep alien Natives out of the labour areas, the effort has been futile'. In their opinion, 'thousands' were in the Transvaal, 'a source of annoyance and irritation to local Natives whose women are molested and enticed away. They attract women from Swaziland and Basutoland, and generally, though on the whole good labourers, are most undesirable from a social, moral, and political points of view'. Still, one had to be realistic about the measures that could be taken.[17]

> It is accepted that no satisfactory means exist or can be devised to make prohibition of entry or deportation effective. Motives of humanity alone make it impossible to withhold entry from or deport bodies of Natives presenting themselves on the border wastes without food and in a semi starved condition after a journey on foot of hundreds of miles. Moreover, the heavy expenses involved and the impossibility of preventing re-entry at some other point on the exposed border make deportation of those found within the borders impracticable.

The solution arrived at by the senior civil servants at the 5 June 1929 Native Affairs meeting was to bend rather than to break and thus to channel rather than attempt to stop the migration flow.[18]

> We are of the opinion that we should concentrate on directing this traffic into channels where it could be controlled and disposed of to the best advantage. If we are to be compelled to admit it to our markets, then we should lay down in what market and for what period it should be employed. The obligation to afford protection and just and equitable treatment on the part of employers is, of course, assumed.

---

17   CIA 38, M130, vol 9: To Minister of Native Affairs (17 June 1929) (no author). The meeting consisted of the Commissioner of Police, the Secretary of the Interior, the Under Secretary for Justice, the Director of Native Labour and the Secretary for Native Affairs.
18   CIA 38, M130, vol 9: To Minister of Native Affairs (17 June 1929) (no author). Duncan argues that many officials in the Native Affairs Department found farm labour conditions morally offensive. (Duncan, 1995: 31).

The resulting proposal of this group of senior civil servants was far-reaching in its attempts to channel extra-Union African migration. The starting point was evidently apparent: 'Obviously, they should be employed in districts adjacent to the border and the period of employment should not exceed twelve months upon expiration of which they should be required to return home.' The group of senior civil servants further proposed that the authorities should closely observe this employment to 'secure their departure'; that 'alien Native labour should find no place' in 'the industrial areas where the white labour policy operates against our own Natives'; and that, owing to the scarcity of farm labour, 'alien labour should be afforded the opportunity of employment in agriculture in border districts, the area being extended inwards as the supply exceeds requirements'. The group did not recommend any disturbance to existing contracts in the industrial areas.

The major recommendation of the June 1929 working group was a system of labour depots linked to the immigration laws and the extensive use of policing powers. 'To bring clandestine immigrants under control' the group recommended increasing the number of reception depots to three, two to be established on the north-western border in addition to the one barely operating at Louis Trichardt. Combined with policing, these depots would 'enable us to exercise the necessary control upon the movements of the Natives after entry and to prevent their permanent residence'. The police would arrest 'any Native reasonably suspected of being a prohibited immigrant' and provide him with a pass to the nearest depot.[19] At the depot, an immigration officer would give the person a notice of declaration as a prohibited immigrant and at the same time issue a temporary permit for 12 months' employment.[20] An immigrant already employed would have to pay a fee of 10 shillings for this permit, while employers engaging a new labourer needed to pay only the per head engagement fee to the depot. In sum, foreign Africans were to be simultaneously declared prohibited yet also put to work. As the civil servants recognised, this scheme depended on 'control over prohibited

---

19 This arrest would be authorised by section 27(1) of Natives Act 31 of 1917 (Union).
20 The prohibition notice would be in terms of section 2(5) of the Immigrants Regulation Act 22 of 1913 (Union) and the temporary permit in terms of GN 1055 of 29 June 1928.

immigrants employed in the Union to secure their repatriation at the expiration of period of employment' and the 'immediate prosecution and repatriation of such Natives as have completed a contract of service [in agriculture in the border districts], have returned to their homes, and are subsequently found in the Union'. The June 1929 proposed policy was thus essentially self-funding repatriation bolstered by a system of labour depots.

This policy was translated into a proposed circular to be issued by the Secretary for Native Affairs.[21] The theme of injury to the South African indigenous population was prominent in the circular,[22] but in general the proposed circular reflected the policy of the 5 June 1929 group of senior civil servants. Within months, the CIAA discussed the matter with the Secretary for Native Affairs and the Commissioner was asked to comment on the proposal of the senior civil servants.

The Commissioner's comments proposed several significant modifications to the scheme.[23] First, the CIAA clarified that the circular did not apply to people from Swaziland, Basutoland and British Bechuanaland. Second, the Commissioner also proposed that the term 'peace officer' be used regarding the arrest of Africans so that immigration and pass offices would also be able to exercise such powers along with police officers. Third, ever mindful of departmental costs, the CIAA confirmed that the proposed labour depots would be staffed by Native Affairs and not by immigration officials. Finally, the Commissioner pointed out the obvious flaw in the scheme — that black immigrants would be more likely to abscond rather than work for the final two months of their contract to pay their repatriation costs. To solve

---

21 CIA 38, M130, vol 9: Secretary for the Interior to CIAA (12 September 1929) (enclosing circular on 'Native Immigrants from the Rhodesias, Nyasaland and Tropical Africa').
22 The draft circular began: 'Notwithstanding the provisions of the Immigrants Regulation Act No. 22 of 1913, it has not been found possible to prevent the entry into the Union of the above class of native aliens, yet their presence constitutes a serious injustice to the indigenous population which, *pro tanto*, loses the natural market for its labour'.
23 CIA 38, M130, vol 9: Handwritten annotations on draft circular; handwritten sheet of notes; CIAA to Secretary of the Interior (23 September 1929).

this problem he proposed that a proportion of the relevant labourers' wages be withheld each month.

Significantly, the Commissioner also argued strongly for dignified terminology with respect to foreign Africans: 'I would at the outset like to state that the terms "native aliens", "aliens" and "alien natives" are scarcely applicable as the natives concerned are British subjects. I have to suggest that the term "extra-territorial natives" or "non-Union natives" would be more suitable and that the interpretation of the term be given in the Circular.' The Chief Clerk of the CIAA continued this effort in later comments on draft administrative documents. These comments expunged the term 'alien'; replaced the terms 'immigrants' and 'alien labour' with 'natives'; used the criteria of birth to make 'alien tropical natives' rather 'non-Union natives born in the above Territories' and 'alien Natives' into 'Natives born outside the Union' or 'non-Union natives'; and specified that the term 'native' or 'natives' as used in the circular meant 'any Native born in the Rhodesias, Nyasaland and Central Africa'.[24]

While the Department of the Interior discussed the Native Affairs proposed circular regarding clandestine immigrants, it continued to apply its own laissez-faire regularisation and policy of deporting only after criminal conviction. Furthermore, the CIAA affirmed the policy of allowing Africans born in the Union to re-enter the territory.[25] Thus, the practice was 'not to interfere with such Natives who are in employment and do not come into the hands of the Police'.[26] For instance, where commissioners referred foreign Africans to the Principal Immigration Officer, as in Natal, they could be given a special temporary permit (without fee or deposit) as was the case with Africans from Mozambique.[27]

As the Depression began to take effect, these two proposed policies remained on the table. The policy conflict between the two

---

24 CIA 38, M130, vol 10: Handwritten annotations to Draft Union Circular No. ___ of 1931 enclosed in Secretary of Native Affairs to CIAA (7 April 1931); Chief Clerk to CIAA (18 April 1931).
25 CIA 38, M130, vol 9: CIAA to Immigration Officer (Mafeking) (19 December 1929).
26 CIA 38, M130, vol 9: CIAA to Principal Immigration Officer (Natal) (5 June 1930).
27 CIA 38, M130, vol 9: Principal Immigration Officer (Natal) to CIAA (26 May 1930).

FROM PROHIBITED IMMIGRANTS TO CITIZENS

departments persisted throughout 1930. Native Affairs continued to express concern about the large number of extra-Union natives without passes in Johannesburg. For instance, in October 1930, 172 of the 247 total extra-Union natives registering at pass offices had no passes. Of the remaining 75, 13 received temporary passes from police stations in the northern Transvaal, 36 had Rhodesian registration certificates, 25 had service contracts and one a six-day permit issued in Pretoria.[28] The Commissioner stuck with his own policy, however, arguing that it[29]

> would be a waste of money to attempt a general repatriation of Rhodesian and other natives from tropical areas as they would return to the Union soon after they were put over the border. Further, the repatriation of all such natives would ruin many farmers and industrial concerns in the Transvaal. In my opinion the only natives (other than Portuguese natives) who should be dealt with under the Immigration law are those illicit entrants who are unemployed or who show criminal tendencies.

The CIAA added that the planned immigration office at Beitbridge would reduce (but not eliminate) the influx of foreign Africans.

Although there was no common solution yet, what had developed by 1929 and 1930 was a common official recognition of a problem. Extra-Union natives now loomed large in the official mind of the Department of Native Affairs and the Commissioner of Immigration and Asiatic Affairs.

AN OFFICIAL SOLUTION

The Depression heightened the appreciation of the distinction between Union and non-Union Africans. As policy proposals were being considered, groups of extra-Union natives were wandering around the northern Transvaal, looking for work and competing with local

---

28 CIA 38, M130, vol 9: Director of Native Labour to Secretary for Native Affairs (11 November 1930); Acting Pass Officer Johannesburg to Director of Native Labour (5 November 1930).
29 CIA 38, M130, vol 9: CIAA to Secretary for the Interior (4 December 1930).

Africans. In March 1932, the Rustenburg Platinum Mine was planning to shut operations within a month or two, and discharge 1 200 Rhodesian and Nyasaland Africans. Faced with this prospect, Native Affairs was concerned that the Department of the Interior deport these extra-Union Africans 'in view of the prevailing unemployment amongst Union natives'. It decided to act, which included serving prohibition notices and taking fingerprints for these Africans.[30] In the view of many Native Affairs officials the problem had come to be defined as one of migration status and nationality. Writing to the Native Affairs Committee, a Cape Town superintendent stated:[31]

> *I beg to draw the attention of the Committee to the considerable influx of ex Union Natives, **who are really prohibited immigrants**, and I consider that something should be done in the matter. I would suggest that in view of the numbers of **our own people** who are unemployed, the question be gone into with the Native Affairs Department, as the position, in my opinion, is serious and unfair to **our natives**.*

The official resolution of the policy conflict between the CIAA and the Department of Native Affairs that had surfaced in 1929 came in 1931. It turned on the terms of the already existing Mozambique Convention model, which exempted first-time Mozambican entrants from the criminal penalties of the immigration laws provided that the employer would fund repatriation. This Convention did not provide for labour depots. The resolution of the Native Affairs–CIAA policy conflict in 1931 was prefigured by skirmishing over a similar issue in 1929. At that time, the mining industry had been pushing for a labour depot to be established at Graskop in rural eastern Transvaal to facilitate receiving clandestine Mozambican Africans.[32] At the same time, the mines

---

30 CIA 38, M130, vol 11: Secretary for Native Affairs to Secretary for the Interior (18 February 1932); Secretary for Native Affairs to Secretary for the Interior (4 March 1932). CIAA to Secretary for the Interior (9 March 1932).
31 CIA 38, M130, vol 11: Superintendent of Natives (Ndabeni Location) to Chairman and Members of the Native Affairs Committee (15 March 1932) (emphases added).
32 CIA 38, M130, vol 9: Director of Native Labour to Portuguese Curator (20 June 1929); Secretary for Native Affairs to Director of Native Labour (6 July 1929); General

were pushing the NAD to relax the ban on in-Union recruitment of Mozambicans. The Minister of Native Affairs was agreeable provided any concerns of the Portuguese Curator were met. The Curator, in turn, agreed on condition that clandestine Mozambicans would have the choice to either work on the mines or be repatriated.

The CIAA, however, strongly opposed establishing a labour depot at Graskop. In his view, the mines' proposed depot was special pleading at its barest:[33]

> *The proposals submitted by the Native Affairs Department simply mean that the Mines are to receive all the advantages to be obtained from the illicit entry of Portuguese natives at the expense of the Union Government, farmers and other employers. The Government would not only lose thousands of pounds in fees for Temporary Permits but would be involved in heavy expenditure. Farmers especially in the Northern and Eastern districts of the Transvaal would lose practically all their native labour and consequently be faced with ruin.*

One should note that an earlier informal policy of the Minister of Justice and the South African Police had favoured farmers by allowing police officers to issue passes to Mozambicans seeking work after serving 14 days of detention, a practice which persisted at least in the Kruger National Park till 1933.[34]

In 1929, asserting the Department of the Interior's formal jurisdiction over clandestine entrants, the Secretary of Interior forwarded an alternative proposal: that the draft policy regarding employer repatriation deposits for clandestine immigrants from Rhodesia and Nyasaland be applied to such immigrants from Mozambique to South Africa's rural areas. Writing to the Portuguese Curator, the Secretary stated:[35]

Manager Witwatersrand Native Labour Association to Director of Native Labour (20 August 1929).

33   CIA 38, M130, vol 9: CIAA to Secretary for the Interior (10 October 1929).
34   CIA 38, M130, vol 11: CIAA handwritten memorandum (27 January 1934).
35   CIA 38, M130, vol 9: Secretary for the Interior to the Curator of Portuguese Natives (27 September 1929).

It is confidently anticipated that this procedure will act as a deterrent to further or repeated illicit immigration as the Native will have to pay for the privilege of remaining in the Union, will have to perform arduous physical labour, will be debarred from entering the towns and industrial areas, and finally will have to bear the expense of his repatriation.

Neither the original proposal for the Graskop labour depot nor the counter-proposal was adopted.

This internal government discussion demonstrated that a policy designed and proposed for Rhodesian and Nyasaland Africans could be extended to Africans from Mozambique, as well as the reverse. In 1931, it was the formal easy regularisation policy already applied by immigration officials to clandestine Mozambicans (except in cases of criminal conviction) that would be extended to those black immigrants from Rhodesia, Nyasaland and elsewhere.[36] In 1931, the Secretary of the Interior proposed to Native Affairs that the system adopted in regard to Portuguese natives who fell within the terms of Article XVI of the Union–Portuguese Convention be extended to 'Rhodesian, Nyasaland and other tropical natives who have illegally entered the Union'.[37] In this way, the policy conflict would be resolved within the framework of the

---

[36] CIA 38, M130, vol 10: CIAA to Hartshorne (8 April 1931) (requesting files of non-Union natives and of Portuguese natives coming under Article XVI of the Convention).

[37] CIA 38, M130, vol 10: Secretary for the Interior to Secretary for Native Affairs (6 February 1931). Article XVI provided: 'Except upon production of a written authority from the Portuguese Curator, no pass shall be issued by an official of the Transvaal government (a) to clandestine immigrants who, being in possession of a Portuguese pass or passport, desire to be employed otherwise than in the mining industries; (b) to natives who desire to work for an employer and who did not enter the Transvaal after executing a contract in accordance with law in the Province, or who desire to work with a new employer. Whenever a Portuguese native is authorised to work for any person (not being the employer by whom he was originally engaged in accordance with law in the Province), or whenever a native is authorised to work for a new employer, the Portuguese Curator shall receive from the employer or native a registration fee of ten shillings. When the engagement of native labourers is made by an agency which is authorised to recruit on behalf of several employers, such labourers shall be regarded for the purposes of this article has having been originally engaged for any of such employers.' *1919 Year Book of the Union*: 659.

immigration laws.

Begun initially in 1897, the Mozambique Convention itself encapsulated a relatively stable labour migration policy from the 1920s. Talks to revise the Convention broke down in 1922 over South African insistence on controlling the administration of the port of Lourenço Marques (present-day Maputo).[38] The result was a suspension of the railway and customs agreement. However, the labour recruitment provisions — contained in Article XVI — were continued. As Katzenellenbogen points out, 'recruiting was not an operation that was amenable to sudden changes. If the number of recruits accepted were to be reduced abruptly, it could take months to recover the numbers lost when it once again became possible, or necessary, to recruit more men'.[39]

The provisions of Article XVI were themselves substantially revised in 1928. Beyond introducing deferred pay, this revision of the Convention made clandestine immigration from Mozambique more difficult. Mozambicans who did not return from South Africa after their contracts had ended would be dealt with in terms of the Immigrants Regulation Act and could be excluded — that is, declared prohibited immigrants and repatriated. However, upon payment of a fee, the Portuguese Curator could issue clandestine immigrants with migration documentation to seek work in the Union.[40]

Labour recruitment in terms of the Mozambique Convention was only nominally under the authority of the Department of Interior. Despite that department's formal authority, the implementing department for Article XVI itself was the Department of Native Affairs. Furthermore, in practice, the scheme was administered nearly entirely by the mining industry itself, through the Witwatersrand Native Labour Association (WNLA) (see Chapter 2).[41]

The Mozambican system had one fundamental difference from the Native Affairs scheme under discussion in 1929: there was no labour

---

[38] Katzenellenbogen, 1982: 120–140.
[39] Op cit: 136–138.
[40] Op cit: 153.
[41] WNLA (see Chapter 2). The Native Recruiting Corporation was established in 1912 to govern recruiting within the Union and the protectorates. Jeeves, 1985: 121–152, 187–220.

depot system to channel clandestine extra-Union labour. Instead, status was easily granted in terms of the Immigrants Regulation Act for those Africans who found work (except for clandestine immigrants with criminal records). As under Article XVI, a 10 shilling fee would be paid to the Rhodesian or Nyasaland authorities' representative in the Union for clandestine immigrants engaged by labour recruiters. The extension of the Mozambican system could be put into effect by simply extending the responsibility of NAD officials already appointed as immigration officers.

By April 1931, the CIAA's proposed policy to extend the Mozambican system was adopted. The draft circular compiled by Native Affairs and directed at Africans from Rhodesia and Nyasaland embodied the Mozambican system of employer-funded repatriations rather than the earlier labour depots proposal of 5 June 1929. Migration status within the Union would be granted to those with clean records. While it was not precisely clear who would bear the costs of repatriation, Native Affairs adopted the CIAA's proposal of monthly deductions from the employee's wages. Where the withheld funds were insufficient, the Department of the Interior would bear the final cost of repatriation.

Since Native Affairs officials did not wish to deal with extra-Union Africans without specific instructions, the Commissioner was again asked to comment on the draft policy with respect to such people, as well as to propose an additional paragraph to the necessary administrative circular.[42] In response, the CIAA produced numerous modifications and five pages of additions.[43] The effect of these modifications and suggestions was to bring the policy with respect to extra-Union Africans more clearly under the framework of the immigration laws administered by the Commissioner rather than under the pass laws administered by Native Affairs. These modifications also modelled the policy on immigration procedures rather than on pass laws and labour recruitment in a number of respects. For instance, the Commissioner suggested that immigration officers rather than employers hold the repatriation deposits. The CIAA also proposed that the repatriation

---

42   CIA 38, M130, vol 10: CC Re Attached letter from the Police (10 April 1931).
43   CIA 38, M130, vol 10: Secretary for Native Affairs (Herbst) to CIAA (7 April 1931).

amount be calculated in order to include children if they 'deserve to leave the Union'. The Commissioner also clarified and confirmed that the criminal prosecutions policy would only come into effect once a 'native has actually been deported and has illegally returned'. The Commissioner suggested procedures including requirements for taking fingerprints from prohibited immigrants; detaining prohibited immigrants in gaols; ordering removal; and escorting deportees during their transportation by train. The CIAA also noted that a definite policy might be adopted for wives and children of deportees.[44]

Modelling the policy for extra-Union natives on immigration procedures, the Commissioner proposed an additional procedure that drew heavily on his existing application of the Immigrants Regulation Act — the ability to read and write a European language. One of the principles of the new policy was that an African from Southern Rhodesia, Northern Rhodesia, Nyasaland and Central Africa 'who is *unable* to read *and* write an European language to the satisfaction of an Immigration Officer, found in employment shall be formally declared to be a prohibited immigrant by such officer ...'.[45] An echo of the Natal clause, this gave Africans an opportunity to demonstrate this ability and thus avoid deportation. The CIAA also proposed an opportunity

---

44   CIA 38, M130, vol 10: Hartshorne to CIAA (11 April 1937) (making an additional set of comments, including that the opportunity be taken to get a definite ruling on the question of deporting wives and children together with the deportee; also expressing here a classic trusteeship argument: 'There may be hundreds of these alien natives residing in the Union married to Protectorate and Union women who have proved that they are desirable inhabitants. It would, then be a very great hardship to force repatriation on them, inasmuch, as they entered the Union under a false sense of security. Where repatriation is being forced on such a native who has entered subsequent to 1921, the question arises would it be fair to expect him to have to pay for the repatriation of his wife and family say to NYASALAND, and further, would it not be the duty of the Government to pay for the repatriation of his wife and family, and for that matter his own repatriation, seeing that it has been a forced repatriation. (HERE IT MUST BE REMEMBERED THAT ALLOWANCE MUST BE MADE FOR IGNORANCE OF IMMIGRATION RULES WHEN NATIVE ENTERED THE UNION). The native is not like the White man, and an allowance of some kind must be made.' (Upper case in the original.)

45   CIA 38, M130, vol 10: Under Secretary for the Interior to CIAA (7 August 1931). (Emphasis in the original.)

for exemption of natives of long residence by reducing the threshold from 15 years to 10. Furthermore, the CIAA added notification and appeal procedures for prospective prohibited immigrants. Indeed, the CIAA was clearly concerned with the legality of process, noting that '[t]he Courts of the Union lean on the side of prohibited immigrants and it is very essential therefore that the prohibition notice and the removal order should be most carefully completed'. Despite an objection from the police regarding the workload placed on them by the proposed policy circular,[46] this circular was finalised with all the changes made by the Commissioner accepted. With textual revisions, it was sent to the Minister of the Interior in August 1931.[47] Estimating 'conservatively' that 10 000 Rhodesian and 12 000 Nyasaland black immigrants were subject to the policy, the employment-funded repatriation element of the policy was justified to the Minister by comparison with that of 'summary' removal through the usual criminal processes of the immigration laws.[48] That 'summary' procedure would cost £100 000 compared to the then-current budget of £2 500. The Minister did not object to the broadened exceptions to the strict operation of the immigration laws.

The resulting official policy applied to extra-Union Africans from Mozambique, Rhodesia and Nyasaland. It was based on the supposition that repatriation would not be preceded by criminal conviction and its operation would be funded through employment deposits. Its legal force depended more on the Immigration Act than on the pass laws. Yet its implementation depended on the police and the bureaucracy of Native Affairs more than on the immigration bureaucracy. It would soon become an expensive and failed policy.

---

46 CIA 38, M130, vol 10: Commissioner of Police to Secretary for Native Affairs (16 July 1931).
47 CIA 38, M130, vol 10: Under Secretary for the Interior to CIAA (7 August 1931); CIAA to Secretary for Native Affairs (10 August 1931).
48 CIA 38, M130, vol 10: Secretary for the Interior to Minister for Native Affairs (4 September 1931).

AN OFFICIAL FAILURE

Implementation of the 1931 repatriation policy initially had encouraging results. In Pretoria, the new policy was put into practice to some degree in 1932. On 4 January 1933, the police reported that 'the Urban Area of Pretoria has now, to a large extent, been cleared of undesirable extra-Union Natives'.[49] Yet at least one underlying problem with the deposit-funded repatriation policy was already apparent: extra-Union Africans who had managed to find work and who were issued with temporary permits had failed to pay the monthly deposits towards their repatriation fees. As the Commissioner had warned, they did not readily buy into the employee-funded repatriation element of the policy.[50]

As repatriation under the new policy began to take place during the early 1930s, the home governments of extra-Union Africans noted other problems. Meeting with their black countrymen in Johannesburg and Pretoria in January 1933, Nyasaland government representatives reported three prominent hardships: the deportation of Nyasaland Africans long resident in South Africa and with families; the common feature of deportees '[having] been given insufficient time in which to dispose of their belongings, e.g. their houses and cattle, which on their departure have been seized by local Natives without payment'; and deportation only as far as Rhodesia, rather than the full distance to Nyasaland, leaving the deportee 'stranded to make his way home on foot'.[51]

---

[49] CIA 38, M130, vol 11: Deputy Commissioner to CIAA (4 January 1933); Hartshorne to Commissioner (2 February 1933) (suggesting that the police and Native Affairs officials be instructed to deal in terms of the immigration laws only 'with Extra-Union Natives whose bad conduct bring them to their notice'). 'There are many thousands of Extra-Union Natives in the Transvaal, and many in Pretoria who do not come to the notice of the Police, and I am told that the attitude of those who are prohibited is one of protest against being singled out and dealt with in this way.')

[50] CIA 38, M130, vol 12B: South African Police (Komatipoort) to District Commandant (Ermelo) (17 May 1935) (noting practice not to pay deposits causing 'heavy loss of revenue'.).

[51] CIA 38, M130, vol 11: Chief Secretary to the Government to Secretary for Native Affairs (21 January 1933); Secretary for the Interior to CIAA (2 June 1933) (instructing CIAA to make the necessary enquiries and ensure that the deportees were given sufficient time to dispose of their belongings and did not become stranded).

The issue of the belongings of deportees was a prosaic but problematic one. Where, for instance, Africans to be deported wished to bring along bicycles, it added substantially to the costs of repatriation.[52] The Commissioner essentially claimed that this issue was a problem for the police and accepted that the police took sufficient care.[53] People deported from Beitbridge would at times hide their belongings in the Union before deportation and retrieve them after deportation (by illegal re-entry) prior to either returning home or going on further in the Union.[54] This new practice also spawned other logistical problems, resulting often in excessive periods of detention for deportees.[55] Across the board, these civil deportations demanded other administrative innovations, such as a new set of immigration forms.[56]

Another set of problems lay at a deeper level. These civil repatriations on the basis of prohibited immigrant status differed from all previous deportations in South Africa, except those of Mozambicans under the Mozambique Convention (which had been administered by the Department of Native Affairs and the police). Previous deportations

---

52 CIA 38, M130, vol 11: CIAA to Commissioner of Police (Pretoria) (13 October 1933) (advising disposal of 'cycles' unless the deportee pays the cost of transport).
53 CIA 38, M130, vol 11: CIAA to Secretary for the Interior (c. November/December 1933).
54 CIA 38, M130, vol 12A: Deputy Commissioner of Police (Transvaal) to Commissioner of Police (7 July 1933).
55 CIA 38, M130, vol 12A: Commissioner of Police to Director of Prisons (22 February 1934) (arguing against the fixing of a limit to detention pending removal); Director of Prisons to CIAA (7 March 1934) (enclosing legal ruling of Law Advisers) (reporting situation of woman convicted under section 6 of Act 22 of 1913; distinguishing section 6 of Act 22 of 1913 as criminal and section 21 as administrative; 'it seems to us that it would be advisable to lay down a maximum period of detention under order by an Immigration Officer, so as to avoid the complaints which are being made as to unduly long detention: 14 days should surely be ample time in which to arrange for deportation, whether under sections 21 or 22, particularly in the case of residents in Basutoland or other neighbouring Territories.'). A handwritten notation of the CIAA states: 'It also seems nec. [necessary] to take steps to give effect to the LA's [Law Advisers'] recommendation ...'.
56 CIA 38, M130, vol 12A: D.I. 38 'Removal of Prohibited Immigrant in Terms of Act No. 22 of 1913' (with left and right thumb impressions and grounds of prohibition under s 4(1); for return to Commissioner of Police and transmission to CIAA), D.I. 37 CIAA to Commissioner of Police (Pretoria) (form letter).

had been of convicted criminals — people, who even if not serving a sentence, would have gone through a criminal trial and been convicted of a crime. Such a crime might have been an immigration-related offence, but it was not entering or being present in the territory without status that would trigger deportation. No longer based on criminal status, repatriations in the early 1930s were now based on civil status, on being identified as a non-Union African. Instead of deporting criminals, the Union was now repatriating people on the basis of civil violations of the immigration law.

However, the line between criminal and civil in immigration enforcement was never fixed, as the practice of removals at Mafeking illustrates. Here, people would be prosecuted and convicted locally for violation of section 3 of Act 22 of 1867 (Cape). This violation was then treated as a deportable offence and a removal order was often requested and, when received from Pretoria after a delay of about two months, executed. When authority was given to grant removal orders locally, it was pointed out that section 3 violations were not deportable and thus section 4(1)(b) or (c) needed to be used as well.[57]

The civil nature of the new repatriation policy was strongly resisted in the neighbouring territories, particularly the protectorates. For instance, the Government of Swaziland initially insisted that the usual extensive accompanying documents (a description of the person, a copy of fingerprints and a list of criminal convictions) for criminal deportations be continued even with civil repatriations.[58] Officials would not accept deportees from South Africa without full identification. The usual

---

57   CIA 38, M130, vol 12A: Immigration Officer (Mafeking) to CIAA (21 May 1934), CIAA to Immigration Officer (Mafeking) (in reply). Reflecting the changing practices at this time, the terms used continued to be a mix between 'repatriation', 'deportation' and 'removal'.

58   CIA 38, M130, vol 12A: Office of the Government Secretary (Mbabane) (25 January 1934), Government Secretary (13 February 1934) ('You will observe that it is stated in the letter [accompanying a deportee, Sam Magagula] that he has been declared a Prohibited Immigrant, but no reason is given for such declaration. Is it to be assumed that this native had been deported to Swaziland previously as a criminal deportee and that on being discovered again in the Transvaal, he was declared a Prohibited Immigrant? I can trace no record here of Sam Magagula having been deported to Swaziland as a Criminal Deportee.').

procedure was to send a copy of fingerprints only, but the South African Police (managing the deportations) were willing to order a copy of the criminal record, if any, as well as particulars of origin to accompany administrative deportations.[59] Indeed, the resistance of officials of neighbouring countries often manifested itself as concern regarding the identification of the deportee. If there was any question of identity, the Union immigration authorities did not aggressively push repatriation.[60] The difficulty of identification also undermined the ability of the mines to support repatriation efforts, with these institutions claiming not to have the capacity to identify prohibited immigrants among the thousands of labourers they engaged. The most that would happen was that the immigrant would be liable to the provisions of section 6 of the Immigrants Regulation Act should he come to the attention of the police or other authorities.[61]

In another limitation to its scope, the new policy on clandestine immigrants did not propose to deal with black immigrants from Bechuanaland. They had been allowed to enter South Africa with a travelling pass from their home authorities since 1922. Even though this document did not appear to conform to the immigration laws after

---

[59] CIA 38, M130, vol 12A: Inspector Walters to Government Secretary (Mbabane) (27 March 1934) (pointing out that this would obviate the necessity of the Swaziland officials corresponding with the Criminal Bureau); CIA 38, M130, vol 12B: Chief Deputy Commissioner of Police to Government Secretary (Mbabane) (5 February 1935), Commissioner of Police to CIAA (20 November 1935) (complaining regarding a proposal by the Swaziland government that people scheduled for deportation be held in detention until their identity was established); CIAA to Government Secretary (Mbabane) (30 November 1935) ('I would stress the difference between criminal deportees and prohibited immigrants.') (noting also that similar arrangements were accepted by the authorities of the other neighbouring territories: Basutoland, the Bechuanaland Protectorate, Southern and Northern Rhodesia and Portuguese East Africa), Government Secretary to CIAA (5 December 1935) (agreeing to continue present system).

[60] CIA 38, M130, vol 11: CIAA to Secretary of Interior (c. November/December 1933) ('Further, apart from the injustice to the Native, it would be uneconomical to incur deportation expenses when any doubt exists as to the acceptance of the deportee on arrival at his destination, and this fact is borne in mind when his statements are under investigation.')

[61] CIA 38, M130, vol 11: CIAA to Secretaries, Transvaal Chamber of Mines (11 November 1933), Secretaries to CIAA (15 November 1933).

their amendment in 1930, the Secretary agreed with the Commissioner that 'we need not worry about natives from Bechuanaland Protectorate. The existing arrangements [e.g. criminal deportation] will suffice for purposes of section 6 of the Act 8/1930'.[62]

The South African officials charged with implementing the repatriation policy soon recognised it as ineffective at reducing clandestine entry. One aspect of this was the lack of identification, particularly prevalent around Messina.[63]

> *The N.C.O. in charge of Police, Messina, reports that natives arriving at Messina from Rhodesia and adjacent territories, are passless, thus enabling them to assume entirely different names to those by which they are known in the country of origin. Even natives previously deported from the Union, can under the same conditions, and provided they are not known to the Police, obtain employment with the Messina (Tvl) Development Co.*

In the months from January to September 1933, 1 084 extra-Union Africans 'entered' Johannesburg according to officials of the NAD.[64] Regarding the entry of Rhodesian and Nyasaland Africans, establishing an immigration office at Beitbridge did not have the desired effect. The South African Police at the bridge reported experiencing resistance to arrests.[65] Furthermore, as the officer there reported:[66]

---

62   CIA 38, M130, vol 10: CC to CIAA (22 April 1931) (handwritten annotation of CIAA). CIA 38, M130, vol 12B: Secretary for Native Affairs to Secretary for the Interior (25 March 1935) (asking whether the entry policy for Bechuanaland natives of 25 September 1925 still holds).
63   CIA 38, M130, vol 12A: Sub-Inspector Prinsloo to Commissioner of Police (26 July 1933).
64   CIA 38, M130, vol 11: Secretary for the Interior to CIAA (20 October 1933).
65   CIA 38, M130, vol 12A: Deputy Commissioner of Police (Transvaal) to Commissioner of Police (7 July 1933) (discussing the deportation procedure at Beitbridge and conveying the report that '[t]here appears to be a growing contempt of the present deportation system among the Rhodesian and other Extra-Union natives which is becoming reflected in the ordinary contact of the Police with the native population of Messina, as witness the fact that two natives have been convicted for resisting arrest and another for assaulting Police during the current month.').
66   CIA 38, M130, vol 11: Immigration Officer (Beitbridge) to CIAA (25 June 1933).

> *I beg to inform you that I have discovered that there is a steady influx into the Union of alien natives. How this is to be remedied is very difficult to suggest. The river is so low that it can be traversed at any spot and therefore no need for the natives to cross by the bridge ... The natives don't come near my office as they are being advised by their associates not to do so, because they will only be served with a prohibition order and their finger prints taken. I shall be glad to have your instructions as to how this can be prevented.*

The availability of farm labour, however, was also a factor to be considered:[67]

> *In view of the serious unemployment problem amongst Union natives, I think it is high time that drastic action was taken to deport these prohibited immigrants so as to make room for our own natives to get work. I would, however, make an exception in regard to that portion of this District which lies to the North of the Zoutpansberg range. The natives of this District have always had a rooted objection to working on the farms north of the mountain, and the unemployment which exists here has made little or no difference in this respect, and without the natives from the north many farmers would find it very difficult to carry on.*

Officials even questioned the efficacy of deporting to Basutoland criminals who had served their sentences.[68] Only when prohibited immigrants were transported far from the Union border, as with deportations through Mafeking to Bulawayo, was there some feeling

---

67 Additional Native Commissioner (Louis Trichardt) to Secretary for Native Affairs (29 March 1934). See also CIA 38, M130, vol 12A 'Many Prohibited Immigrants; Union Swamped with Foreign Natives; Police Powerless to Stop Them', *Cape Times*, 5 April 1934.
68 CIA 38, M130, vol 11: Magistrate (Smithfield) to Secretary for Native Affairs (9 November 1933) (noting that constables upon arrest often enter assumed information (eg Basutoland birthplace) and that without appropriate legal machinery 'so the error is perpetuated and the Native driven from pillar to post'); CIAA to Secretary for the Interior (c. November/December 1933).

of effectiveness.[69] Many officials valued the policy only for its symbolic effects,[70] the Justice of the Peace in Zebediela (in the northern Transvaal) presenting an extreme case of giving up:[71]

> *I beg to advise you that all instructions, at one time issued by this office to foreign natives within a stipulated time, have been, as far as can be ascertained, ignored. Under the circumstances I have for some time refrained from attempting to influence the foreign element to leave the Union as I am convinced that thereby official authority would merely be brought into disrepute.*

The government began to review the self-funding civil repatriation policy in 1934. Around May 1934, in response to the reported situation that a large percentage of foreign Africans (two-thirds of those reporting to the pass offices) had no documentation at all,[72] the Minister of Native Affairs issued an internal instruction that 'extra-Union natives' found in the Union and criminally convicted for being without passes should be removed from the Union.[73] However, the police resisted and refused to comply with this instruction.[74] The fact that the Minister issued this instruction indicated that within the national government the

---

69 CIA 38, M130, vol 12A: Deputy Commission of Police (Transvaal) to Commissioner of Police (7 July 1933).
70 Deterrence depended upon such performances. CIA 38, M130, vol 11: Principal Immigration Officer (Cape) to CIAA (10 November 1933) handwritten annotation to Commissioner ('In my opinion we should prosecute and deport some of these extra-Union natives occasionally if only to advertise the fact amongst their compatriots that they are not allowed in.').
71 CIA 38, M130, vol 11: Special Justice of the Peace to Native Commissioner (Potgietersrust) (25 March 1933).
72 CIA 38, M130, vol 12B: Director of Native Labour to Secretary for Native Affairs (15th June 1935) (from 5 December 1934 to 25 February 1935, 1 000 Africans from the tropics entered without passes and 452 had Rhodesian registration certificates).
73 CIA 38, M130, vol 12A: CIAA to Commissioner of Police (n.d. c May 1934) (proposing to extend the system already in use for Natives prohibited under section 4(1)(b) and (f)), CIAA Telegram Reference Minister's Instructions Removal Extra-Union Natives (25 April 1934).
74 CIA 38, M130, vol 12A: CIAA to Secretary (16 May 1934), Commissioner of Police to CIAA (11 May 1934).

repatriation deposit policy was regarded as ineffective.

Soon after issuing his 1934 instruction, the Minister of Native Affairs appointed a multi-departmental committee to investigate 'the question of the entry into the Union of Natives resident outside the borders thereof in contravention of the Immigrants Regulation Act of 1913 and who have taken up their abode in urban areas, and to recommend what steps should be taken to repatriate such natives'.[75] The Minister thus (again) charged an inter-departmental committee with finding a more effective repatriation policy for black migrants. These 1934 terms of reference were notable both for their dependence on the immigration laws and for their urban focus.

One set of interests the review committee needed to consider was that of the mining industry, which was based on a low-wage system that depended on the exploitation of ever new sources of labour prepared to accept the mines' wages and the dangerous work.[76] According to Crush, Jeeves and Yudelman, '[t]he constant ability to expand the geographic pool from which the migrants came enabled employers to keep blacks' wages low and almost static in real terms between 1897 and 1970'. Throughout the 1920s, the mines were able to expand through the strategy of more fully exploiting their existing sources of labour in the Union, the protectorates and Mozambique. But from the late 1920s, the mines began to take steps through WNLA to exploit the labour pool of black Africans from the tropics, those residing north of latitude 22°S.[77]

The efforts of the mining industry to expand their labour pool intensified in the 1930s. From 1932, WNLA and its director, William Gemmill, engaged in a series of initiatives to restore access to northern labour markets.[78] Having sent a senior official on a scouting trip as early as 1928, Gemmill began first with Southern Rhodesia, but moved later to focus on recruitment in Northern Rhodesia and Nyasaland. With the power of the mining industry behind him, Gemmill conducted direct negotiations with these regional governments on a quasi-diplomatic

---

75 CIA 38, M130, vol 12A: Secretary for Native Affairs to CIAA (September 1934) (requesting Mr Kincaid's presence to give evidence on 25 September 1934).
76 Crush, Jeeves and Yudelman, 1991: 3.
77 Op cit: 33–54; Jeeves, 1986: 73–92.
78 Jeeves, 1985.

basis. In this sense, WNLA was the successor to Cecil Rhodes's British South Africa Company. Gemmill began in the mid-1930s with small consignments of first 2 000 and then 5 000 black Africans from the tropics on an experimental basis to demonstrate that earlier health concerns about tropical labour had been met.

South African farmers who had enjoyed largely undisturbed access to the clandestine tropical African labour market from 1913 opposed WNLA's plans. However, the mining industry was able to argue that access to the northern labour market was an investment in its future. Ultimately, these experimental schemes also raised the need to work out procedures for complying with the Immigrants Regulation Act with the Commissioner.

The Commissioner for Immigration and Asiatic Affairs was a key player in this 1934 policy review committee. He presented evidence to the committee regarding deportations under the policies to date, showing the growing numbers and focusing on the matter of increasing costs, as the Department of Interior was the funder of last resort of the civil repatriations. During the financial year 1932–1933 (from 1 April 1932 to 31 March 1933), 2 362 foreign Africans were deported from the Transvaal.[79] In the financial year 1933–1934, 2 807 'Natives' were deported.[80] The costs for the first year were £3 530 and for the second £9 000. These figures appear to tally roughly with the numbers of black migrants from the tropics endorsed out of the Johannesburg area in a similar period. In March, April and May of 1935, 1 360 tropical Africans were compulsorily endorsed out.[81]

The CIAA also suggested amending the Immigrants Regulation

---

[79] CIA 38, M130, vol 12A: 725 were deported to Basutoland, 134 to Swaziland, 69 to Northern Rhodesia, 302 to Southern Rhodesia, 207 to Nyasaland, 117 to the Bechuanaland Protectorate and 808 to Portuguese East Africa.

[80] CIA 38, M130, vol 12A: 1 058 were deported to Basutoland, 144 to Swaziland, 61 to Northern Rhodesia, 379 to Southern Rhodesia, 247 to Nyasaland, 162 to the Bechuanaland Protectorate, 755 to Portuguese East Africa and one to South West Africa.

[81] CIA 38, M130, vol 12B: Director of Native Labour to Secretary for Native Affairs (15 June 1935) (noting also that 'Several cases have occurred recently in which Tropical Natives have passed themselves off as Portuguese Natives in order to secure work on mines.').

Act with respect to the exemption process to streamline immigration procedures for people recruited to the mines.[82] Other evidence placed before the committee was even more critical of the repatriation policy. Reverting to earlier suggestions, a Cape Town Native Affairs' superintendent noted that civil repatriations were perhaps too expensive and suggested that the Natives (Urban Areas) Act be amended simply to prevent employment of ex-Union natives in Cape Town. This idea met with opposition on the grounds that some of those affected were already registered voters, while the Transvaal Native Congress, opposing the deportation of those from Nyasaland, expressed the view that one year's residence should qualify such immigrants for naturalisation.[83]

The Native Affairs committee continued to consult into 1935 as the policy of the repatriation of Africans continued to be implemented. By May 1935, the committee had reported to Cabinet. Initially viewing the problem as one of resources, Cabinet approved of the principle of civil repatriation and decided to intensify the existing policy, a move noted by some in South Africa's official history. As the Froneman Commission states: 'Before 1934 foreign Bantu found in the Republic were dealt with on a very loose footing, but in 1934/35 it was decided to enforce the provisions of the Immigrants Regulation Act more strictly ...'.[84]

The intensified policy meant greater coordination between the CIAA and the Native Affairs Department. The CIAA's suggestion for improving compliance with the immigration laws on the mines was adopted and regulations made in terms of the Immigrants Regulation Act 22 of 1913 were amended to introduce a six-month temporary permit system.[85] The Minister of the Interior also began to appoint officers of the Native Affairs Department as passport control or immigration

---

[82] CIA 38, M130, vol 12B: CIAA to Secretary for the Interior (29 October 1935).
[83] CIA 38, M130, vol 12B: Report of the Superintendent of Natives Dated 11th April and Submitted to the Native Affairs Committee on the 15/4/35. Indeed, there is a surprising degree of elite African support for foreign Africans. See eg CIA 38, M130, vol 12B: Secretary for Native Affairs to CIAA (23 May 1935).
[84] Froneman Commission Report, 1962: para 100.
[85] CIA 38, M130, vol 12B: CIAA to Secretary for the Interior (18 May 1935). These regulations were published in the *Government Gazette* of 23 September 1935. The Cabinet decision was also implemented by means of Interior Circular of 16 September 1935.

officers.[86] For instance, magistrates and native commissioners in Natal and Zululand who were not yet immigration officers were appointed as such.[87] Other aspects of the migration administration were also tightened. In May 1935, the CIAA formalised government procedures for dealing with Mozambican clandestine entrants.[88] Mozambicans were to be presumptively prohibited in terms of section 4(1)(b) and (c) of the Immigration Act but those found within the Union would nonetheless be allowed to regularise their South African status: in terms of the immigration laws, they either could have a temporary permit (for a fee) if they had a passport or other registration documents from a Portuguese official, the Curator. If they had no money, they would be allowed to seek work and then pay the fee for a temporary permit. Those without Curator documents would be repatriated as would those who, according to their fingerprints, had been deported from the Union previously.

With greater resources and coordination of efforts devoted to the problem, the earlier repatriation efforts involving the Commissioner for Immigration and Asiatic Affairs were thus continued under the intensified policy through 1936. In the financial year 1934–1935, 2 396 black Africans were deported to Rhodesia, Nyasaland, Mozambique, Bechuanaland, Swaziland and Lesotho.[89] In 1937, it was reported in Parliament that at least 3 000 were deported in 1936 at a cost of around £15 000.[90]

Despite the devotion of increased resources and greater coordination, the results remained disappointing. By the end of 1936, the expense and the extent of the policy failure were manifest. As the Froneman Commission later put it, after detailing some of the implementation problems: 'The expense incurred (R58 000.00 to repatriate 4 000 Bantu)

---

86 Froneman Commission Report, 1962: para 68 (noting this practice in terms of section 30 of Act 22 of 1913); see also para 103.
87 CIA 38, M130, vol 12B: CIAA to Secretary for the Interior (c August 1935).
88 CIA 38, M130, vol 12B: CIAA to Commissioner of Police (c. May 1935) (enclosing Instructions for Immigration Officers appointed to deal with Portuguese Natives under Article XVI of the Mozambique Convention).
89 Report of the Controller and Auditor-General for Financial Year 1934–1935 (U.G. 39 of 1935): 175.
90 *Debates of House of Assembly (Hansard)* (31 March 1937) col 4009.

was consequently not justified.'[91] Helen Bradford vividly describes the operation of the policy: 'From 1930 to 1936, vast sums were spent in an effort to export thousands of unemployed black aliens back to their peripheries. Many were wrenched from their families and force-marched to trains; some died on the journey to the nearest dumping spot; others were seized by wild animals when ditched on the road.'[92]

From the point of view of the Department of the Interior, the 'experiment' of repatriation was a failure. The Minister of the Interior admitted in Parliament that 'we cannot control the situation'.[93] In 1936, the commitment of the Department of the Interior to fund repatriation was thus suspended.

CONCLUSION

As detailed here and in the previous chapter, over a 10-year period the Commissioner for Immigration and Asiatic Affairs led two separate processes of nationalisation: one for the Asian population and one for the black population. By different methods and with starkly different degrees of administration, the regimes regulating the mobility of both populations were nationalised by 1937. While he was from the start charged with Asian affairs, the Commissioner used his power over legal interpretation and the constitutional competence of immigration to expand his influence over the officials within the Native Affairs Department. Indeed, he did so at the very time that the Department was itself exercising greater power over the mobility of the African population. This process was aided by the increasing significance of the mobility of problematic 'clandestine extra-Union Africans'. Under the trying circumstances of the Depression, white political elites and state officials began to articulate and exercise an option in favour of black residents. The Commissioner succeeded in setting the terms in which the problem of 'extra-Union Africans was defined, even within the understanding of the Native Affairs' Department. By these means, the Commissioner subverted the policy solution of the labour depots

---

91 Froneman Commission Report, 1962: para 101.
92 Bradford, 1993: 105.
93 *Debates of House of Assembly (Hansard)* (19 April 1937) col 5077.

initially favoured by the Native Affairs Department and successfully put into place the solution of civil deportations of extra-Union Africans in terms of the immigration laws. This dramatically expanded the influence of the Commissioner's office through the projection of its power onto the black population. For the first time, a single public official held significant influence — albeit through separate bureaucracies and differentiated populations — over a conceptually unified regime of migration regulation of the entire South African population.

CHAPTER 9

Enacting nationality, 1927–1937

The developments reflected and promoted by the establishment of the Commissioner for Immigration and Asiatic Affairs (CIAA) were consolidated in three important series of legislative enactments, which are covered in this chapter: one around 1927, another from 1930–1931, and the last in 1937. These laws entrenched population regulation, with control over mobility to be exercised both at internal and external borders. The civil repatriation policy negotiated by the Commissioner for Immigration and Asiatic Affairs with the Department for Native Affairs (NAD) was taken from the level of bureaucratic instruction and legislated into the Union statute book, despite its expense. Just as significantly, these laws also completed the formal transition from prohibited person status to citizenship. Reflecting and confirming existing bureaucratic practice, they gave substance to the status of Union nationality, thus consolidating the status of South African citizenship.

The first set of laws comprised the British Nationality in the Union and Naturalisation and Status of Aliens Act 18 of 1926 and the Union Nationality and Flags Act 40 of 1927. These laws introduced the formal concept of Union nationality, in section 1(a) of the little-discussed 1927 Act.

The second series of laws consisted of the Immigration Quota Act 8 of 1930 and the Immigration Amendment Act 15 of 1931. These laws entrenched the change in the conceptual structure of migration regulation that had occurred during the bureaucratic negotiations between 1927 and 1932. They fundamentally modified the vision of the Immigrants Regulation Act 22 of 1913. That Act had not itself prohibited physical entry to South Africa. It had regulated immigrants, not migration. Under these two Acts of 1930 and 1931, national migration regulation for the entire population, including the European population, became enforced through a dominant concept of border control.

The final series of laws consisted of the Aliens Act 1 of 1937, the Immigration Amendment Act 27 of 1937 and the Natives (Urban Areas)

Act 46 of 1937. These three Acts built upon and consolidated the conceptual structure of migration regulation put into place by the earlier series of laws in 1930 and 1931. The Aliens Act restricted permanent residence. The Immigration Amendment Act repealed the ban on recruitment of black Africans from the tropics, instituting instead a regime for regulating extra-territorial recruitment of foreign labour. The Natives (Urban Areas) Act introduced a national strategy of control over the black population that increasingly focused on the urban boundary. One effect of this series of laws was to extend to the black population the conceptual structure of the original 1913 Act and its view of residence-based citizenship.

This final series of laws also built on the earlier ones to put into law a substantive concept of South African citizenship, one derived from migration regulation. When introduced to the statute books in 1926 and 1927, Union nationality was initially merely a formal status. While it depended on migration status, it had no content — no rights or powers were linked to it. It fulfilled an external function but had no domestic ones. Nationality may be defined as the status of belonging to a state, a primarily legal term.[1] The most conspicuous international function of the nationality concept is the right of a state to extend protection to its nationals abroad.[2]

However, in the series of laws passed in 1930–1931 and 1937, Union nationality began to perform substantive work in migration regulation both internal and external to South Africa's borders. It also began to play an important role in the regulation of permanent residence, the status at the centre of South African citizenship. The increasingly significant role played by national status in the regulation of national permanent residence rights occurred at the same time that the distinction between foreign and national black residents in urban areas and at the borders was legally entrenched.

Citizenship in modern usage 'is not a synonym of nationality or a term generally used for the status of belonging to a state, but means specifically the possession by the person under consideration, of the

---

1   Koessler, 1946: 58–76, 61–63.
2   Op cit: 70.

highest or at least of a certain higher category of political rights and (or) duties, established by the nation's or state's constitution'.[3] The South African citizenship that was consolidated in these laws of course did not follow that modern usage — it permitted structural racial inequality and did not extend the highest category of political rights to the entire population. Significantly, South Africa's leading international lawyer has recognised that 'South African legislation in particular is guilty of failing to draw a clear distinction between the two concepts [of citizenship and nationality]'.[4]

This interpretation of these 1930s laws as the culmination of four decades of bureaucratic development consolidating a warped and unequal form of citizenship derived from migration regulation must be seen together with the dominant body of research on these laws, which has emphasised their racially discriminatory nature through attention in particular to discrimination against Jews within the European population. The 1930 Quota Act, the first legislative entrenchment of this period, is notorious for its numerical limits on immigrants. Together with the Aliens Act, the Quota Act is often in particular identified as the racist root of subsequent South African migration policy and usually explained as being driven by the desire to limit Jewish immigration to South Africa.[5]

The 1930 Quota Act did indeed introduce a discriminatory pre-entry visa requirement for people from territories with high rates of Jewish emigration. It also introduced a new Immigrants Selection Board, which restricted immigration and became engaged in significant ongoing conflict with the South African Jewish community over its operation. Jewish immigration was also the subject of parliamentary attention in 1933, when legislation that had sheltered semi-skilled Europeans from being prohibited immigrants was reversed.[6] A further significant influence on the 1937 Aliens Act was a response to the increasing Jewish

---

3   Op cit: 63.
4   Dugard, 1994: 208–209.
5   Peberdy, 2009: 59–83.
6   Section 3 of Immigration (Amendment) Act 19 of 1933 (deleting section 5(h) of Act 22 of 1913).

immigration from the 'scheduled' country of pre-Nazi Germany.[7] (Scheduled countries were those, such as European countries and the United States, that were seen as desirable by white elites.) However, these two Acts and related legislation were by no means solely responsive to anti-Jewish sentiment within the European population. A perspective that places them in the broader dynamics of migration regulation over the Asian and African populations and within developments in the nationalised immigration bureaucracy reveals the deeper reading, context and consequences of these laws.

THE INAUGURATION OF UNION NATIONALITY

Union nationality is the direct legal predecessor to contemporary South African citizenship expressed first in the Citizenship Act of 1949 and then in its successor legislation in the era of constitutional democracy in 1995.[8] One might draw an unbroken legal thread to connect Union nationality to the contemporary framework that governs citizenship in post-apartheid South Africa. One place to source the beginning of that thread, as Chapter 4 did, is with the relatively scant attention paid to questions of nationality at the time of Union. The Naturalisation of Aliens Act of 1910 operated against a background of imperial rules of nationality and adopted the Cape model of the facially neutral acquisition of citizenship at the Union level.[9] Indeed, it was uncontroversial that the legal position of nationality, determined and understood as subjecthood within the British Empire, would continue past Union. Significantly, naturalisation after Union within any of the constituent provinces would not be specific to any one province and would also count as naturalisation throughout the Union.[10]

The term 'British subject' was understood with much more clarity throughout the Empire than was the term 'citizen'. To be a British subject meant to be under the British flag, owing allegiance to the crown. The status was a homogenous one with a relatively stable and uniform

---

7 Peberdy, 2009: 65–70.
8 Klaaren, 2000: 221–252; Klaaren, 2001: 304–325; Klaaren, 2010: 94–110.
9 Klotz, 2013: 118–122. Klotz describes the imperial developments in nationality law and policy from 1905 to the 1920s.
10 See Chapter 4.

understanding. 'All under the British flag, whether in London or Lagos, were technically subjects, all owing allegiance to the crown.'[11] By contrast, imperial citizenship was heterogeneous, due in part to the lack of a written constitution for Britain. 'Thus [the] unofficial, rhetorical, and localized nature of citizenship gave rise to great discrepancies among imperial subjects in rights, benefits, and duties.'[12] In this world, the starkest divide in citizenship status was between the subjects of the United Kingdom and the dominions on the one hand and the subjects of the dependent Empire.[13]

The superficial development regarding South African nationality was taken significantly further and deeper in the decade roughly from 1926 to 1937. As a formal concept, Union nationality was introduced to the statute book by the Union Nationality and Flags Act 40 of 1927, a law that is best understood together with its own predecessor, the British Nationality in the Union and Naturalisation and Status of Aliens Act 18 of 1926. The changes in South Africa regarding nationality took place simultaneously with similar processes in other dominions and colonies: Australia, Canada, India, Ireland and New Zealand.[14]

The difference between the 1926 Act and the following year's successor law on nationality may be understood as the difference between asserting a power and actually exercising it. The 1926 British Nationality in the Union Act implied assumption by the Union of the authority (the legal competence) to define a specific category of nationality, with the members of that category being considered holders of the equivalent in terms of rights and privileges to those enjoyed by natural-born British subjects.[15] Within the imperial legal context, the Act asserted that a particular dominion, South Africa, had the legal competence to define natural-born British subjects. The Minister of Interior used this language in introducing the Bill, stating:[16]

---

11   Gorman, 2006: 19.
12   Klotz, 2013: 20.
13   Ibid.
14   McIntyre, 1999: 193–212.
15   Section 1(1) provided: 'The following persons shall in the Union be deemed to be natural-born British subjects, namely ...'
16   *Debates of the House of Assembly (Hansard)* (31 March 1926) col 2159.

> *This Bill deals with British nationality and British subjects. It assumes, taken together with the other Bill which I intend introducing, that we have a South African citizenship, but the South African citizenship again assumes that every South African citizen is also a British subject. Therefore this Bill deals with both South African citizenship and British nationality.*

This is an explicit and official statement of South African citizenship, albeit one that is officially consistent with prior policy and indeed with nationality within the British Empire.

Working within the conceptual framework of the British Empire, the 1926 Act made few changes to pre-existing South African policies. The Act essentially followed imperial rules of citizenship and subjecthood, codifying those rules (for instance spelling out under what circumstances nationality would be lost) and extending them so that they had effect throughout the British Empire and the rest of the world.[17] During this period, British citizenship laws themselves were moving from employing the principles of *jus soli* (the right of soil, or territory) to determine subjecthood to using those of *jus sanguinis* (the right of blood, of descent).[18]

Two specific changes made to the naturalisation policy by the 1926 Act demonstrated the increasing autonomy enjoyed by the South African polity within the Empire. The 1926 Act amended the 1910 naturalisation legislation (as discussed in Chapter 2).[19] In terms of the 1910 Act, the

---

17 *Debates of the House of Assembly (Hansard)* (31 March 1926) cols 2160–2161 ('The chief defect of the 1910 Act which is to be replaced by the present Bill is that no provision is made in the old Act for recognition of our nationality in other countries of the world, nor even in other parts of the British empire. If a foreigner comes to South Africa and we naturalise him, so that under our law he becomes a British subject, it avails him nothing if he lives outside of South Africa. As soon as he gets three miles from the coast outside the territorial waters his British citizenship lapses. In the first place, that is not consistent with the dignity and constitutional status we have attained.'). See also col 2164.

18 Lee, 2014: 99, 101.

19 The Act also covered registration. Section 9 allowed for certificates granted by other dominion governments to have effect in the Union. Section 9: 'A certificate of naturalisation granted by the Secretary of State having charge of the administration

residency requirement had been Empire residency during two of the five years preceding application. The 1926 Act extended the requirement of Empire residency to five of the eight years preceding application with an additional year of local residence in the Union. The final decision was at the absolute discretion of the Minister. The second modification was more substantive — adding a more localised eligibility requirement. According to section 2(1)(b), an applicant for naturalisation needed to satisfy the Minister 'that he is of good character and is able to read and write either of the official languages of the Union to the satisfaction of the Minister'.

The parliamentary debate around this clause demonstrated that the understanding of the South African lawmakers of this incipient nationality legislation depended on their own 1913 Immigrants Regulation Act. One member objected to the initial formulation of the language requirement for naturalisation which used the term 'adequate knowledge' on the grounds that the phrase lacked precision. In defending the clause and its formulation, the Minister of the Interior responded that the intention was to parallel the education test of section 4(b) of the Immigration Act: 'The provision is necessary and we cannot do better than make a provision of the same nature as exists in the Immigration Act.'[20] In 1926, the substantive policy written into the provisions of the nationality law flowed directly from immigration regulation.

The other Bill referred to in the 1926 debate was what turned into the 1927 Act. What was implicit in the 1926 legislation — South Africa's power to define its own nationals — was made explicit in the 1927 Union Nationality and Flags Act.[21] Passed with very little debate in Parliament, this law defined the status of Union nationality.

---

of the British Act or by the Government of any British Possession shall, in the Union, have the same force and effect as a certificate of naturalisation granted in pursuance of this Chapter.'

[20] *Debates of the House of Assembly (Hansard)* (12 April 1926) col 2219. See also cols 2610–2611 ('I am putting in wording similar to those in the immigration laws. It will make it more precise and we know what it will mean.' This extract shows that the lawmakers wanted to put words from the immigration context into the nationality statute to ensure that the nationality statute followed and was consistent with the immigration statute.)

[21] Union Nationality and Flags Act 40 of 1927.

Significantly, the 1927 Act defined Union nationality in such a way as to be completely dependent on two prior legal concepts: status as a subject of the British Empire and status as not a prohibited immigrant in South Africa. While the first reflected the conceptual background of Empire, the second — not being a 'prohibited immigrant' — was distinctively South African. Section 1(a) of the 1927 Act provided: 'The following persons shall be Union nationals — (a) a person born in any part of South Africa included in the Union who is not an alien or a prohibited immigrant under any law relating to immigration.' Other sections of the Union national definition (section 1(b) and (c)) included British subjects with two years' lawful domicile and Union-naturalised British subjects with three years of domicile as well as those persons born to Union national fathers outside the Union (section 1(d)). Section 1(b) and (c) used concepts of birth and period of domicile to qualify a British nationality as Union nationality, while (section 1(d)) adopted the prevailing rule of paternal transmission of nationality. All British subjects in South Africa who were not prohibited immigrants became Union nationals.

An alien was defined as a person who was not a British subject. A prohibited immigrant was defined 'under any law relating to immigration', meaning the Immigrants Regulation Act of 1913. Indeed, prohibited immigrant status was a legal status entirely under the control of the South African government. From its introduction in 1927, the concept of Union nationality depended on the migration concept of a prohibited immigrant.

Because of its dependence on the Immigrants Regulation Act and its character of duality with British nationality, Union nationality was initially inaccessible to individuals. Derived from one's status as a British national and one's status as a prohibited immigrant, Union national status was not itself subject to individual application, although there was an individualised renunciation procedure.[22] One could naturalise as a British national, but not as a Union national. In 1927, a person might be born or deemed to be a Union national but one could not apply to become a Union national. Conceptually, one could also become a Union

---

22   Sections 5 and 6 of Act 40 of 1927.

national by escaping from the status of a prohibited person in terms of the Immigration Regulation Act of 1913.

In 1927, Union nationality was thus a legal status with no immediate practical consequence.[23] Conceived in these terms, the status of Union nationality was empty of substantive rights at its birth. For instance, Union nationality did not entail the exercise of the franchise even for white persons.[24] Nor would it be understood to include the right to own land. In fact, with regard to land ownership, in 1910 General Smuts had rejected a proposed amendment to the Naturalisation of Aliens Bill partly by noting that Roman-Dutch Law contained no bar to alien property ownership. However, such a rule could be (and had been in several provinces) altered by statute.[25]

From the point of view of migration regulation, the additional category of Union nationality also changed nothing at the time of its introduction. As before, aliens were able to migrate to South Africa and to be naturalised as British nationals in the Union. Indeed, in 1962 the Froneman Commission noted that black immigrants from Southern Rhodesia had continued this practice from 1923 through to 1947.[26] As before, British nationals were able to migrate to South Africa, subject only to the inspection regime of the Immigrants Regulation Act 22 of 1913. A later statute, however, did provide for the naturalisation of former burghers of the Transvaal and the Orange Free State and for amnesty for people involved in the Witwatersrand labour unrest of 1922.[27]

Until 1927 and indeed to a significant degree until 1937, the legislated regime of migration regulation operated with little if any reference to a concept of South African nationality. It is worth noting, however, that in terms of section 9 of the Quota Act, Union nationality exempted a

---

23 For an account of related symbolic legislation, see Saker, 1980.
24 In 1923, Smuts defended the exclusion of Indians from the franchise by noting that an Australian coming to South Africa (in the context, a white Australian) would not automatically enjoy the franchise on the basis that he was a British subject. Pachai, 1971: 103.
25 *Debates of the House of Assembly (Hansard)* (21 November 1910) cols 192 and 193.
26 Froneman Commission Report, 1962: para 173.
27 Nationalization and Amnesty Act 14 of 1932 (Union).

person from the restriction on entry and permanent residence as well as from being deemed a prohibited person in terms of section 5 of that Act. Whether people without South African domicile were British nationals or not, intending immigrants were subject to the Immigrants Regulation Act 22 of 1913.

As we have seen, the organisational developments detailed in the previous two chapters led to a conceptual unity regarding the regulation of the mobility of the Union population, reflecting in particular a distinction between foreign Africans and Union Africans.

Returning to the formal introduction of Union nationality in 1927, the new policy use of nationality was entrenched in legislation in the final series of migration regulation laws passed in 1937. However, before examining these enactments, this text first considers the important developments associated with the second series of parliamentary laws in this period of consolidating South African citizenship — the notorious 1930 Quota Act and its amendment.

THE ACTS OF 1930-1931 AND POPULATION REGULATION

The Quota Act did not introduce numerical quotas for all people entering South Africa — only for those intending to reside permanently and furthermore only for some of those. The Act distinguished between people emigrating for permanent residence from scheduled and unscheduled countries. Those from the scheduled countries, that is people seen as desirable immigrants by the ruling elite, were able to immigrate to South Africa as they always had done — within the framework of the Immigrants Regulation Act of 1913.[28] Immigrants from these countries were thus subject only to the minimal health and morals provisions of the 1913 Act as applied by the immigration officers at the port of entry and as many people as wished could immigrate from these countries. Conceptually, and in fact, 'non-white' people from a scheduled country could immigrate and receive permanent residence. For instance, India was a member of the Commonwealth and was

---

28 The schedule included 'Territories comprised within the British Commonwealth of Nations', Austria, Belgium, Denmark, France, Germany, Holland, Italy, Norway, Portugal, Spain, Sweden, Switzerland and the United States of America.

treated as a country of unrestricted immigration. In 1931, 829 Indians emigrated from India to South Africa. Likewise, 'non-white' people from an unscheduled country could also immigrate and receive permanent residence. In 1931, 39 Chinese immigrants came to South Africa.[29] However, for people coming from the unscheduled countries, there was an additional restrictive requirement — the 1930 Quota Act placed a maximum quota of 50 persons per year on immigration.

For immigrants from some countries of origin, the Quota Act supplemented the Immigrants Regulation Act 22 of 1913, enacted 17 years earlier.[30] The application of both these pieces of legislation meant that immigrants from these countries had to fulfil three additional substantive conditions for entry beyond the minimal health and morals criteria of the 1913 Act. Quota immigrants needed to be 'of good character'; to be 'likely to become readily assimilated with the inhabitants of the Union and to become a desirable citizen within a reasonable period'; and not to be pursuing a profession or trade in which a sufficient number of people in the Union were already engaged. The assimilation clause of the 1930 Quota Act was an innovation compared with the 1913 Act. It was a facially neutral provision. Quota permits were indeed granted to at least some Chinese people.[31]

The Quota Act also significantly changed the institutional structure of the 1913 Immigrants Act by setting up a new institution, the Immigrants Selection Board, to implement the quota criteria and to supervise the processing of applications by immigrants.[32] This Board differed completely in institutional form and function from the still-existing Immigrants Appeal Boards set up in terms of the Immigrants Regulation Act of 1913. The Immigrants Selection Board was centralised whereas the Immigrants Appeal Boards were decentralised; the former consisted of five members, appointed by the Governor-General; it limited itself to applications for permanent residence and did not

---

29 *1931–1932 Year Book*: 842.
30 Section 10. This same relationship to the principal Act was apparently followed by the Aliens Act 1 of 1937.
31 See CIA, M31, vol 2: CIAA to Principal Immigration Officer (7 October 1933) (detailing practice of allotting quota permits to Chinese wives).
32 Section 2.

constitute a more general internal appeal structure. Section 2(1) of Act 8 of 1930 states that the Board is established 'for the purpose of selecting immigrants for entry into the Union ...'.[33]

The most significant change made by the Quota Act, however, was none of these innovations. Instead it was the shift for the entire population to the territorial border control concept developed through regulating the Asian and African populations. As shown in Chapter 4, the Immigrants Regulation Act 22 of 1913 had not prohibited physical entry to South Africa. It was a law regulating immigrants, not migrants. Instead of prohibiting entry, the 1913 Act deemed several categories of people (in particular Asians) to be prohibited immigrants and then directed that immigration officers were to remove such persons from the Union. The legal baseline of the 1913 Act was thus one of prohibited immigration rather than one of prohibited entry. This allowed for persons exempted from the 1913 Act as a class, such as black Africans (whether South African or not), to escape regulation in terms of the Act in their movement across both provincial and national borders, although they were subject to other migration regulations, such as the pass laws. Also of note is the exemption of section 5(d) of the 1913 Act, which stated that persons governed by 'any law' or convention with an adjacent state would be exempt from the Immigrants Regulation Act. Because of the Mozambique Convention, the entry of unskilled black labourers, from Portuguese East Africa could be regarded as legal after they had been issued with proper documentation. Likewise, the movement of black Africans across provincial boundaries would be allowed in terms of the Immigrants Regulation Act.

The Quota Act supplemented the 1913 Act in a way that changed the fundamental structure of the 1913 Act. The first section of the 1930 Act placed a blanket prohibition on entry from non-scheduled (undesirable) countries, unless such entry had been approved by regulation and the entering person was in possession of written authority.[34] This new legal baseline reflected the growing influence, jurisdiction and power of the CIAA. The prohibition on entry was now operative as a rule to be applied

---

33 Section 2(1).
34 Section 1(1).

on a territorial basis rather than only at ports of entry for immigrants. It was to be applied to all people of all populations, no longer only to certain persons as immigrants. Later in the Immigration Amendment Act 15 of 1931, the section of Act 22 of 1913 dealing with prohibited immigration was also amended. The phrases 'is found within' and 'is found in' were replaced with the phrase 'has entered'. The process of territorialisation is evident in this shift from an emphasis on personal to territorial jurisdiction.[35] The regulation of the movement of people was itself now coordinated from one legal instrument, the nationally applicable 1930 Quota Act, administered by the CIAA and politically responsible through the Minister of the Interior.

This territorial border control aspect can also be seen with the Immigration Amendment Act 15 of 1931. To this point, the 1913 Act authorised the recovery of costs of repatriation only in connection with return sea passages. In an important attempt to set up adequate funding for the civil repatriation policy, the 1931 amendment allowed for cost recovery for removals carried out more generally.[36] Indeed, the Minister's introduction of this change in Parliament elicited surprise that this had not been accomplished in law previously:[37]

> *According to the existing law, an immigrant who arrived by sea and is declared to be a prohibited immigrant can appeal to the Appeal Board, and if necessary can get a temporary permit to remain in the Union, but he must make a certain monetary deposit. Strange to say, we have got no similar provision for prohibited immigrants over the land borders ... What is proposed here is to put the prohibited immigrant coming over the land borders on the same footings as a prohibited immigrant entering through a seaport.*

The passing of the Quota Act and the 1931 Act affected all population groups — European, Asian and African. For one, documented migration status began to have as great a significance among the

---

35 Section 2(a) of Act 15 of 1931 (amending section 4(1) of Act 22 of 1913).
36 Section 1 of Act 15 of 1931 (amending section 2(7) of Act 22 of 1913).
37 *Debates of the House of Assembly (Hansard)* (2 March 1931) col 996.

European population as it had for the Asian population. The 1930 Act mandated that persons over 16 years of age needed a passport to enter the country, with the exception of those born in the Union. This passport requirement could not be satisfied by a passport provided by the Portuguese Curator to Mozambicans in terms of the Mozambique Convention.[38] The increased documentation demands were in line with the greater 'paperisation' of control over the land borders of the territory.[39] Coming barely three years after the establishment of the CIAA, the Immigration Quota Act was an important if temporary step in establishing a territorial control concept of migration regulation.

One of the significant ways in which the Quota Act and the 1931 Amendment Act entrenched a territorial view of South Africa was by using the concept of Union nationality. As already noted, this concept was articulated in 1927 at the conclusion of a significant struggle with Asians over their place in the Empire and the South African political community. It was expressed in terms of migration status and the accompanying concepts. Three years later, the Quota Act put the concept of Union nationality to work in migration regulation for the first time, a relatively small but significant step. Union nationality became a defence against prohibited immigrant status. Section 9 of the 1930 Quota Act exempts Union nationals from being declared prohibited immigrants in terms of section 5, while section 1 of the 1927 Union Nationality Act defines Union nationals in terms of those who are not prohibited immigrants. One may debate which Act holds, but legally the earlier definition would prevail.[40] However, assertion and proof of status as a Union national would prevent one being treated (and potentially removed) as a prohibited immigrant, even if otherwise one may be declared such. While this status was not the same as an affirmative right of permanent residence, the protection it could afford against prohibited immigrant status would still be a powerful defence against bureaucratic discretion threatening the exercise of an individual's rights to residence and mobility.

---

38   Section 6; Froneman Commission Report. 1962: paras 70 and 77.
39   MacDonald, 2014: 154–177.
40   Section 9.

Indeed, the prohibited immigrant concept itself played an additional role in this system, one of bolstering the power of border control. While the Quota Act did not directly preclude prohibited immigrants from entering the country, nevertheless by providing the conditions for entry, it indirectly enabled officials to deny prohibited immigrants permission to enter. The 1930 Act significantly expanded the categories of people who were prohibited immigrants in terms of the 1913 Act. The Quota Act declared that every person who was born in an unscheduled (ie undesirable) country was presumptively a prohibited immigrant. As ever, there were some exceptions: the Immigrants Selection Board could decide differently and one could be covered by a regulation as well.[41] Nevertheless, this presumptive prohibited immigrant status would be understood in a bureaucratic context as a marker of unlawful migration status. Thus it became potentially more significant that the status of being a prohibited immigrant could be avoided (defended against) by Union national status.

The 1931 Immigration Amendment Act added two further sources of prohibited immigrant status: any person who had been removed from the Union,[42] as well as any person convicted of an offence and consequently deemed undesirable by the Minister. The Act also expanded the list of criminal offences that could result in administrative removal on the grounds of being an undesirable person.[43] Parliamentary debate focused on the breadth of these provisions in the light of the severity of deportation.[44]

THE ACTS OF 1937 AND POPULATION REGULATION

In this final series of laws — those of 1937 — Union nationality became even more prominent, again even as border control became more entrenched. The 1937 Aliens Act, which, like the Quota Act, was

---

[41] Section 5.
[42] Section 2(e) of Act 15 of 1931 (inserting paragraphs (i) and (j) in section 4(1) of Act 22 of 1913).
[43] Section 4 of Act 15 of 1931.
[44] *Debates of the House of Assembly (Hansard)* (2 March 1931) cols 1012–1014, 1032–1034; *Debates of the House of Assembly (Hansard)* (4 March 1931) cols 1116–1117, 1122; *Debates of the House of Assembly (Hansard)* (5 March 1931) cols 1179, 1186.

supplemental to the Immigration Regulation Act 22 of 1913,[45] entrenched and deepened the restrictions of the earlier Quota Act. The system for granting permanent residence introduced by the Aliens Act differed significantly from the border inspection plus quota regime of the Quota Act. The 1937 Act instituted a separate and substantive pre-entry measure, an embarkation permit. A reconstituted and centralised Immigrants Selection Board would issue the embarkation permits. This Selection Board was additionally given the task of adjudicating all applications for permanent residence in South Africa. It should be noted that many people with the right of permanent residence apparently did not apply for British nationality. Moving from being a permanent residence permit holder to a British national would require applying for a certificate of naturalisation in terms of the British Nationality in the Union and Naturalisation and Status of Aliens Act 18 of 1926 (Union). The usual term of residence would be five years. There was little incentive to acquire British nationality other than to gain the right to movement within the Commonwealth. Furthermore, an applicant for permanent residence needed to be of good character, not engaged in a competing trade or occupation, and needed to be 'likely to become readily assimilated with the European inhabitants of the Union'.[46] By comparison with section 3(1) of the Quota Act, the Aliens Act formulation differed in specifying 'European inhabitants' rather than 'inhabitants'. The explicit European racial filter had passed from being an exemption to the grounds of prohibition in 1930 to being a necessary condition to apply for permanent residence in 1937.[47]

As significant as these changes were to the system of permanent residence, the 1937 Aliens Act also importantly formalised a national temporary residence system. For the first time, an alien from any country entering the Union for temporary or permanent residence needed to be in possession of a permit issued in terms of the Immigration Act. Section 2 put into place this restriction on alien immigration.

---

[45] Section 6 of the 1937 Act makes this explicit.
[46] Section 4(3) of Act 1 of 1937.
[47] As discussed above, section 5(h) of the principal Act was repealed in Act 19 of 1933. *Debates of the House of Assembly (Hansard)* (31 May 1933) cols 130, 132–133.

Section 2(a) covered entrance for permanent residence; section 2(b) covered entrance for temporary residence. With respect to unscheduled countries, the blanket prohibition on entry had been first placed into law in the 1930 Quota Act (section 1(1)) and implemented through the prohibited immigrant concept.

This 1937 provision had the effect of reversing the exemption of the black population from the 1913 Act and thus effectively overriding the policy of the pass laws at the territorial borders. This legislative development was foreshadowed by the development of a unified policy between the CIAA and the Department of Native Affairs (NAD) around the problem of non-Union Africans. In terms of immediate impact, this meant a liberalisation of access to lawful status for both foreign Africans and protectorate Africans as this series of laws repealed the long-standing ban on recruitment of black labour from tropical countries. This legislative repeal followed a concerted and successful effort by the mining industry during this period (see Chapter 7).[48] Black migrants crossing the national border were able to regularise their status within the Union in terms of the Immigrants Regulation Act through the officers of the CIAA. They were able to regularise their presence upon payment of 50 cents for an immigration temporary permit.[49]

The other two laws of this 1937 series fit into this new framework of the Aliens Act. The second statute specifically applied to the black population in the urban areas and set up a removal process, albeit one that operated within the South African national territory. The Native Laws Amendment Act 46 of 1937 (also known as the Natives (Urban Areas) Act) afforded greater power to the Minister of Native Affairs to remove black residents from an urban area, where they were 'redundant' or deemed surplus to labour requirements, to rural areas. It also raised barriers to access by women and work-seekers.[50] Upon declaration by the Minister, the notice to leave would be served on the person by the municipality. In terms of the Act, the state could enforce the notice

---

48 See also the Immigration Amendment Act of 1937.
49 Froneman Commission Report, 1962: para 101 (Protectorate Africans were paying R2).
50 Maylam, 2001: 161.

through removal beyond the bounds of the urban areas to rural areas but not beyond the territory of South Africa. These removal provisions particularly served the interests of white commercial agriculture rather than the growing industrial sector.[51] The law thus stayed within the framework of an internal control over movement and residence. Employers in these urban areas also bore the financial responsibility of returning workers home after a contract.

The forerunner of the more repressive 1950s and 1960s legislation, this 1937 Act is rightly regarded as the significant threshold in the implementation of influx control.[52] The 1937 law for the first time allowed local authorities to declare a total ban on entry by black migrants. It also restricted the freedom of movement and residence of black labourers by restricting permit holders to one particular district or part thereof. The Act provided for a co-ordinated local and national response to migration by Africans.[53] It further allowed for the central government to force local authorities to implement the influx controls it provided. After its enactment, the central government implemented this provision and the number of implementing local authorities increased dramatically from 12 to 143 in one year — 1938. Hindson notes that 'convictions under the pass laws increased sharply' between 1924 and 1940.[54]

In the consolidation of 1937, the most direct amendments to the 1913 Immigrants Regulation Act itself came via the third statute, the Immigration Amendment Act 27 of 1937. The changes to the 1913 Act were as a result of the Aliens Act formalising a national system of temporary residence permits. The Immigration Amendment Act formalised the entry inspection system itself, requiring a passport or other document of identity. This document needed to contain a description of the person, a photograph, the name of country and date of birth. It also had to have a visa or endorsement. The principal Act, that of 1913, was also amended to allow provisional permits to be issued

---

[51] Hindson, 1987: 45–46; Posel, 1991: 43.
[52] Maylam, 2001: 161.
[53] Jeeves, 1986: 73–92, 78.
[54] Hindson, 1987: 45.

to people suspected of being prohibited immigrants. These permits were valid for up to two years and were issued by the immigration officers, who, during this period, were to decide whether the person was or was not a prohibited immigrant.[55] In addition, the Act allowed for the arrest or removal of a person who had not reported to an immigration officer upon entry.[56] These amendments moved the innovation of the prohibition on entry of the Quota Act directly into the operation of the 1913 Immigrants Regulation Act. Furthermore, the amendment expanded the concept of prohibited immigrant status. Unskilled Africans born outside the Union and repeat offenders (against both the civil and criminal laws) became two new categories of prohibited immigrants.

Taken as a package or individually, this series of 1937 laws increased the prominence of the concept of Union nationality within South Africa's system of migration regulation, paradoxically alongside its explicit violation of the freedom of movement of the national black population. The place of Union nationality in the 1937 Aliens Act lay both in the Act's scope and in its regulation of permanent residence. As the name implied, by definition the Aliens Act applied only to aliens. It did not define certain people as prohibited immigrants, as the 1930 Act had done. Under the 1913 and 1930 Acts, the prohibited immigrant category was clearly a dominant category: the world was split into prohibited immigrants and all others. With the introduction of the alien category in 1937, the prohibited immigrant category was no longer clearly a master category, even though it remained implicit in the concept of Union nationality. For instance, the blanket designation of all people from unscheduled countries as prohibited immigrants, section 5 of the Quota Act, was repealed by the Aliens Act 1 of 1937.

Section 1 of the Act defined 'alien' as 'a person who is not a natural born British subject or a Union national'. In using the distinction between aliens and non-aliens rather than that between prohibited immigrants and non-prohibited immigrants, the 1937 Act reflected the developments of the previous decade. Legislating to regulate aliens

---

[55] Section 3 of Act 27 of 1937; section 2 of Act 27 of 1937.
[56] Section 2(2) of Act 27 of 1937 (substituting section 19(3) of Act 22 of 1913).

implied that non-aliens were the preferred members of the political community. In the 1937 Act, those preferred members fell into two separate categories: British subjects and Union nationals.

As for permanent residence, by the terms of the Aliens Act, Union nationals — although they did not need to apply for a specific permit — enjoyed the same rights of permanent residence as natural-born British subjects. Even though excused from the requirement of having a permanent residence permit, both categories still needed to fulfil the substantive criteria (ie not be a prohibited immigrant) of the Immigrants Regulation Act when being inspected at the border.

However, the real significance of Union nationality status now lay in its providing an alternative route to acquisition of the right of permanent residence. In 1937, Union naturalisation for British subjects (whether they were natural-born British subjects or naturalised British subjects) required two years of domicile (as opposed to lawful residence) and was automatic.[57] As an alternative to the Aliens Act process of applying to the Immigrants Selection Board for an embarkation permit and so on, a British subject could simply lawfully enter the Union and, once two years of domicile were concluded, have status as a Union national. As a Union national, such a person would be exempt from the Aliens Act and would enjoy the right of permanent residence. Thus, with the operation of the Aliens Act, Union nationality had become an integral part of the migration regulation regime and had moved beyond its initial solely symbolic status.

Given the European assimilation clause in the Immigrants Selection Board process, Union nationality was of greater significance for some population groups than for others. The Union nationality route to permanent residence was open to both Europeans and to non-Europeans, although a later piece of legislation in 1937 partly closed this door to the latter. Nor could time spent in the Union with a recruitment scheme count towards establishing a Union domicile (and thus Union nationality).[58] Hence, since Asians and Africans were unable to access

---

[57] Section 1(b) of the Union Nationality and Flags Act 40 of 1927 (Union).
[58] Section 1(2) of the Immigration Amendment Act 27 of 1937 amended section 5(d) of Act 22 of 1913.

CHAPTER 9 Enacting nationality, 1927–1937

the Immigrants Selection Board, the status of Union national was of greater significance for them than it was for Europeans. Likewise, the formalisation of the temporary permit system within the national structure of the Immigration Act was of particular benefit for Asians and Africans who depended on lawful status in order to gain the right of permanent residence through Union nationality.[59]

Union nationality also played a significant role in the 1937 revision of the Natives (Urban Areas) Amendment Act. This Act was not a simple strengthening of a pre-existing municipal-based strategy to regulate access to a space defined as urban. Rather its restrictions on movement in urban areas should be viewed within the framework of migration regulation. In particular, that framework works well to explain the place of extra-Union Africans within the Natives (Urban Areas) Act. In terms of the 1937 Act, foreign Africans were generally treated like Union nationals or Africans from the protectorates. All three categories of Africans could be removed from urban areas to rural areas within the South African territory. Section 21 of the Act did, however, distinguish between 'a native lawfully domiciled in the Union' and one not 'lawfully domiciled in the Union', but allowed the Minister to determine arrangements with respect to both classes similarly and therefore to treat Africans without domicile like those with domicile.[60] However, the 1937 Natives (Urban Areas) Act did initiate at least one crucial distinction among these three black populations: a prohibition on the employment of foreign Africans in urban areas.[61] Foreign Africans were thus unable to enter urban areas and thereby gain residence rights, while Union and protectorate Africans in principle could. The 1937 Act thus legislatively entrenched the distinction between Union and non-Union Africans developed through bureaucratic negotiation between the CIAA and the Department of Native Affairs since 1929.

Both the content and the terms of debate around the 1937 Immigration Amendment Act also demonstrate the increasing

---

59 Section 5 of the Aliens Act.
60 Section 21 of the Native (Urban Areas) Act 46 of 1937 inserting section 16ter in Act 21 of 1923.
61 Section 5quater of Act 21 of 1923 as amended by Natives (Urban Areas) Act 46 of 1937.

significance of nationality in migration regulation. The Act repealed the 'tropical native' labour recruitment ban contained in the Immigrants Regulation Act. The parliamentary debate was conducted in language that reflected the conceptual territorialisation of the black population with, for instance, members on both sides of the debates asserting the interests of 'our own South Africans'. Corroboration of this stance followed when, subsequent to the CIAA's suggestion, the Act was amended to streamline the exemption for foreign Africans recruited for the mines and other schemes. Such people would no longer need an immigration permit or any travel documents.[62] In supporting the repeal, the Minister pointed out that the scheme was no different in principle from the Mozambique Convention, while the Acting Minister stressed that permission to import foreign labour would be subject to repatriation being at the expense of the mining industry. Deserters from the mines would become prohibited immigrants, this status being based either on the literacy or public charge requirement.[63] Referring to the line of 22°S, the Acting Minister viewed lifting the recruitment ban as simply getting rid of 'what has come to be an illogical geographical barrier'.[64] Opponents attacked the scheme on the grounds that the mines wanted only foreign labour because such employment entailed fewer social responsibilities and was cheaper than South African labour.[65] In their view, such labour recruitment was little better than slave labour.[66]

---

62 *Debates of the House of Assembly (Hansard)* (22 March 1937) col 3591. *Debates of the House of Assembly (Hansard)* (31 March 1937) cols 3994, 5777.
63 *Debates of the House of Assembly (Hansard)* (19 April 1937) col 5076 ('The scheme must provide not only for recruitment but also for repatriation. That is an essential part of the scheme.'); Froneman Commission Report, 1962: para 20. The Commission went on to note: 'If such Bantu do not comply with their contracts of service and desert, or on the expiration of their periods of contract, they of course automatically become prohibited immigrants in South Africa.'
64 *Debates of the House of Assembly (Hansard)* (19 April 1937) col 5078; *Debates of the House of Assembly (Hansard)* (6 April 1937) col 4311.
65 Op cit: col 4307 ('The South African native, unfortunately for them, cannot be sent away as soon as his employment ceases.'). Further, the proponents were the servants of the mining industry. *Debates of the House of Assembly (Hansard)* (31 March 1937) cols 3993, 4313 (Mr Kentridge).
66 Op cit: cols 3986, 4307.

A consistent theme in this debate was a concern with identifying black workers. The Aliens Act introduced a rudimentary form of identification regulation that prohibited a person from changing his or her surname without the permission of the Governor-General. This was to avoid people assuming another identity, describing themselves differently or passing with a different surname. People wishing to change their name could do so only after giving notice, investigation by the resident magistrate and approval from the Governor-General. While such legislation was of doubtful efficacy, it established the principle of national competence over a register of permanent identification.[67] Opponents harkened back to the experience with the Chinese migrant labourers: 'The Chinese were bad enough but the Chinese at all events could be identified. Can the Minister guarantee for one moment that anything other will result from this importation than has resulted from the importation of natives from other parts of Africa in the past? How are you going to identify a tropical native if he escapes and finds it preferable to live in this country than to return home?'[68] The Minister's response was that the scheme would be 'nearly 100 percent effective'.[69] In light of the failed repatriation effort of 1936, the Minister also ingeniously argued that the repeal of the ban on recruitment would at least provide some control over and repatriation potential with respect to extra-Union Africans in the Union.[70]

The debate around the repeal of the recruitment ban overlapped to some extent with the parliamentary debate on the 1937 Urban Areas legislation. Indeed, one member pointed out the seeming contradiction between the expansion of recruitment and the simultaneous imposition of influx control: '[A]t times I feel that we in this House are taking part in a mad hatter's party ... On the one hand we want to get these tropical natives into the Union, and on the other hand we have apparently so many thousands of natives running about the towns unemployed,

---

67 Section 9(1) of the Aliens Act. Section 9(2) (providing exceptions for women and children); Scott, 1999: 64–71. James Scott suggests that the invention of permanent inherited patronyms is one of the necessary preconditions of modern statecraft.
68 *Debates of the House of Assembly (Hansard)* (19 April 1937) cols 5019, 5048.
69 Op cit: col 5077.
70 Op cit: cols 5077–5078.

getting into all sorts of mischief and obviously annoying the Minister of Native Affairs, that it is necessary to pass a law to deport these natives into some kind of concentration camp in the country districts.'[71]

As noted above, at its inception Union nationality was a formal legal status, bringing no substantive legal consequences yet soon playing a significant role in South Africa's migration regime recently focusing on controlling borders. A similar shift towards significance was taking place in the self-identification of the national population, at least as measured by the official census. In the 1921 census, only 1.6 per cent of the European population was recorded with a nationality anything other than British.[72] In the 1926 census, 46 per cent of the population identified as South African and 52 per cent as British. By the 1936 census, 98 per cent were indicating a South African nationality.[73] The shift in the statistics for the coloured population (in a different census but with the same question as the white population) was from 99.8 per cent British in 1921 to 99.7 per cent South African in 1936. The black population was covered but was not asked its nationality at all in these Union censuses. In 1921, the Indian population was asked for its 'original nationality' and responded with a 97 per cent identification as 'Indian'. In 1936, nationality was requested in the census for this part of the population and resulted in 82 per cent 'Indian (South African)' and 17 per cent 'Indian (British)'.[74] Even discounting for official bias and differential implementation, a clear shift to South African nationality had taken place across the national population by 1936–1937.

CONCLUSION

The three series of statutes considered in this chapter put into place a system of migration regulation based on border control for the entire South African population. It may come as no surprise or mere coincidence that the first physical fences on the international border of South Africa — along the Lebombo ridge — appeared at the end

---

[71] Op cit: cols 4305–4306.
[72] Christopher, 2009: 101–109, 105.
[73] Op cit 105.
[74] Ibid.

of these three series of statutes in 1937.[75] In particular, the enactment of the final series of laws in 1937, in spite of the official failure of the policy of civil repatriation described in the previous chapter, shows how much a matter of 'common sense' the concept that South Africa had a single population over which a single official could exercise a significant amount of control (in terms of migration regulation) had become.

The enactment of nationality legislation and the growing policy significance of Union nationality within the system of migration regulation was also arguably due as much to the practices of the now nationalised immigration bureaucracy as it was to the desires of the political elite for national autonomy. Union nationality initially developed in line with imperial trends and was first legislated in South Africa in 1927 as a purely formal legal status. By 1937, the status was put to use as a small but significant instrument within the now conceptually unified nationalised migration bureaucracy and the status itself had become a marker of the legal cultural concept of South African citizenship. It would take more than half a century for the racial inequality structured within this concept to be legally eradicated by the 1993 Interim Constitution and for the South African movement from prohibited immigrants to citizens to be formally complete.

---

75 MacDonald, 2014: 177.

CHAPTER 10

South African citizenship and the way forward

> *There is a misconception that immigrants have a constitutional right to progress towards residency or citizenship status. A sovereign state has the prerogative to determine who enters its territory and to enact laws accordingly. States also have the right to protect themselves from risks, such as the entry and stay of fugitives from justice who are linked to organised crime.[1]*
>
> Green Paper on International Migration, Department of Home Affairs, June 2016

> *The story of South Africa is of a country perpetually eluding and escaping our grasp and fixation. A country forever on the move. What remains as a constant is the realisation that the story of modern-day South Africa is also the story of the perennial search in our hearts for a place called home.[2]*
>
> Bongani Madondo, *Sunday Times*, 18 December 2016.

This book has explicated the development of South African citizenship from 1897 to 1937. The legal cultural concept of South African citizenship developed from the official practices regulating the mobility of different populations of subjects of the British Empire. These were begun in the colonies that would form the Union. By 1927, South Africans of all races were formal legal nationals of their own country, even if their rights of citizenship were sharply limited and differentiated by population. For instance, under the influence of India, many members

---

1   Department of Home Affairs, 2017.
2   Madondo, 2016.

of the Asian population were officially acknowledged as permanent residents, even if generally denied political rights. By 1937, with the move to territorial border control as the country's migration regime, South Africans of all races had become subject to one conceptually unified official bureaucracy regulating their mobility. It would take more than half a century for the racial inequality structured within South African citizenship to be legally eradicated by the 1993–1994 Interim Constitution and for the movement from prohibited persons to constitutional citizens to be formally complete.

In such a historical overview, the period covered in the preceding chapters could be termed the first of three epochs of South African citizenship. A second epoch would of course be the apartheid story told from a migration, nationality and citizenship perspective. This epoch would cover from 1937 through to the inauguration of constitutional citizenship in 1993–1994. The story of that epoch would put at the centre how apartheid made foreigners of black persons in South Africa, but would also need to attend to the place of non-South African Africans and Asians without permanent residence.[3] As with the story told in the preceding chapters, it is one of political repression, official contradictions and popular struggles.[4]

In this schema, a third epoch of South African citizenship would then be the one from the advent of constitutional democracy to the present day. This is the post-apartheid national story of which the ending has yet to be written. Challenges here include those of the provision of socio-economic rights,[5] as well as those of democracy and countering xenophobia.[6]

It is enough for one book to tackle one such epoch. This concluding chapter aims to relate some of the themes and the principal arguments developed in the preceding chapters to events in present-day post-apartheid South Africa. To do so, this chapter first explores a debate that has developed in South Africa's post-apartheid constitutional democracy

---

[3] Klotz, 2013: 113–169.
[4] Shapiro, 2016: 763–781.
[5] Langford et al, 2013.
[6] Klotz, 2016: 180–194.

in the Constitutional Court over citizenship; next the chapter notes a disturbing potential development in South Africa's official citizenship policy; and finally concludes by putting South Africa's contemporary citizenship debate where it has always been — in a global context.

POST-APARTHEID CONTESTATIONS OF SOUTH AFRICAN CITIZENSHIP

In the judicial branch of today's South African state, hidden beneath the dry and often lengthy prose of Constitutional Court judgments, is a significant tussle between two competing ideas of citizenship. This is a debate ultimately of what it means to be a South African. In what one may term the preamble view, to be a South African is to live in the given territory. In what one may term the new republican view, to be a South African is to have and enjoy the formal legal status of South African nationality.

Two Constitutional Court cases decided within five months of each other in 2004 show the two poles of this debate, with the respective positions able to be identified with two leading and respected former Justices of the Court (the second a former Chief Justice): Justice Yvonne Mokgoro and Justice Sandile Ngcobo. In *Khosa v Minister of Social Development*,[7] the Court upheld the rights of permanent residents to social security. In the later case of *Kaunda v President of the Republic of South Africa*,[8] the Court refused to order protection for citizens outside South African borders potentially, although not imminently, faced with violations of human rights including arguably the potential imposition of the death penalty. In both cases, the judges of the Court grappled with some of the difficult debates concerning the conceptual character of South African citizenship.

The *Khosa* case concerned Mozambican nationals with South African permanent residence applying for social welfare benefits from the South

---

[7] *Khosa and Others v Minister of Social Development and Others, Mahlaule and Another v Minister of Social Development* (CCT 13/03, CCT 12/03) [2004] ZACC 11 (4 March 2004); 2004 (6) SA 505 (CC); 2004 (6) BCLR 569 (CC), accessed 3 September, 2014.

[8] *Kaunda and Others v President of the Republic of South Africa* (CCT 23/04) [2004] ZACC 5 (4 August 2004); 2005 (4) SA 235 (CC); 2004 (10) BCLR 1009 (CC), accessed 3 September 2014.

African state. These foreign nationals had been granted South African permanent residence in December 1996 after having fled the civil war in Mozambique over the previous years. Some of the applicants in *Khosa* were destitute and would have qualified for old-age grants but for their Mozambican nationality. The applicants had also presented applications for child-support and care-dependency grants. The proceedings of the case — the matter actually consisted of two joined cases — were themselves somewhat chaotic. The government's lawyers initially requested an extension of time. When this was denied, the government simply conceded some elements of the applicants' legal argument at the next hearing. Pertinently, the evidence showed that the regional office of the Department of Social Development had initially supported the applicants' entitlement to social grants. It was at the national level that it had been decided to oppose the Constitutional Court relief sought by the applicants. This background of bureaucratic contestation may be read to indicate the unsettled state of the executive branch of the state with respect to a contemporary understanding of South African citizenship.

The *Khosa* applicants wanted to have the Social Assistance Act, 1992, the statute disqualifying persons who are not South African citizens from receiving welfare grants, declared unconstitutional.[9] The applicants were indigent residents living in the poor Limpopo province, the present-day South African province bordering on Mozambique and Zimbabwe. This area has long been one where people with links to both Mozambique and South Africa have lived.[10] The applicants asserted their constitutional right of social security, a socio-economic right found in section 27(1) of the South African Constitution and guaranteed to 'everyone', unlike a smaller set of rights such as the right to vote.[11] While the applicants were unopposed in the lower court, the national government later argued justifiable limitation in front of the

---

9 The Social Assistance Act 59 of 1992.
10 *Khosa and Others v Minister of Social Development and Others, Mahlaule and Another v Minister of Social Development* (CCT 13/03, CCT 12/03) [2004] ZACC 11 (4 March 2004); 2004 (6) SA 505 (CC); 2004 (6) BCLR 569 (CC) para 2.
11 Section 27, Constitution of the Republic of South Africa Act 108 of 1996: 'Everyone has the right to ... social security, including, if they are unable to support themselves and their dependants, appropriate social assistance.'

Constitutional Court. On 4 March 2004, the Constitutional Court granted the application and struck down the statutory provisions excluding permanent residents from the socio-economic right of social assistance.

Judge Yvonne Mokgoro wrote the majority judgment in *Khosa*.[12] In her view, the proper legal doctrine to frame this case was the socio-economic right to social security rather than the right to equality. As with other socio-economic rights, the ambit of the right to social security in South Africa should be determined with reference to the reasonableness of the measures adopted to fulfil the obligation. In two paragraphs that contrasted everyone's right to social security with the right of access to land granted in section 25(5) only to citizens, Mokgoro J confirmed that 'everyone' in the context of section 27 (and seemingly section 26) would apply to non-citizens.[13] In supporting the application of these socio-economic rights in this case, she explicitly cited the residence-based nature of the Bill of Rights. Indeed, her use of the Bill of Rights with respect to the claims went beyond the category of socio-economic rights: Mokgoro J noted, '[t]he rights to life and dignity, which are intertwined in our Constitution (*S v Makwanyane*), are [also] implicated in the claims made by the applicants'.[14]

The textual interpretation of the socio-economic right to appropriate social assistance did not end the enquiry. The Court still needed to specifically consider that the applicants here were non-citizens. In addition to life and dignity, the social security scheme put in place by the state raised an equality issue. In restricting the availability of social assistance to otherwise eligible South African permanent residents on the basis of their foreign nationality, the scheme arguably violated the Constitution's prohibition in section 9 (the right to equality) against

---

12 Mokgoro J (Chaskalson, Langa, Goldstone, Moseneke, O'Regan, and Yacoob JJ concurring). Mokgoro J was also the author of an earlier Constitutional Court case, finding the right to equality protected against discrimination on the grounds of nationality; Klaaren, 1998: 286–295.
13 *Khosa and Others v Minister of Social Development and Others, Mahlaule and Another v Minister of Social Development* (CCT 13/03, CCT 12/03) [2004] ZACC 11 (4 March 2004); 2004 (6) SA 505 (CC); 2004 (6) BCLR 569 (CC) paras 46–47.
14 Op cit: para 41.

unfair discrimination.[15] Mokgoro J thus delved back into equality jurisprudence and considered the reasonableness of citizenship as a criterion of differentiation in this context.[16] She concluded that there was indeed a potential violation of the equality right: '[E]ven when the state may be able to justify not paying benefits to everyone who is entitled to those benefits under section 27 on the grounds that to do so would be unaffordable, the criteria on which they choose to limit the payment of those benefits (in this case citizenship) must be consistent with the Bill of Rights as a whole.'[17] At the time of this case, permanent residents could apply for naturalisation after five years of that status. However, Mokgoro reasoned that this was not within the control of the applicant and, moreover, there was no justification offered for the bar to social security benefits during this period. Mokgoro J rejected the argument that the scheme provided an incentive to naturalise, reasoning in part from the provision of equality within the Immigration Act, 2002.[18] The state did not argue that the limitation was either a temporary measure or one designed as part of a strategy of the progressive realisation of rights.[19] Mokgoro J also rejected some American jurisprudence that found discrimination against legal permanent residents to be justified constitutionally, even against a challenge based on the right of equality. This equality finding allowed Mokgoro J to decide the case on her initial argument, that the case was a socio-economic rights case set firmly with the Bill of Rights protecting the residents of South Africa.

Judge Sandile Ngcobo wrote a cogently argued minority judgment in *Khosa*.[20] He accepted for purposes of argument that the right of social security was available to everyone and that the case could be decided in that light.[21] However, he focused on the government's claim to be justifiably restricting this right through the limitations clause, section 36 of the Bill of Rights. In applying this analysis, Ngcobo J

---

15 Op cit: para 44.
16 Op cit: paras 53–57.
17 Op cit: para 45.
18 Op cit: paras 56–57.
19 Op cit: para 50.
20 Op cit: paras 99–140. Madala J concurred in the judgment of Ngcobo J.
21 Op cit: para 111.

differed significantly from the majority. In his view, the applicants' lack of South African citizenship was a temporary condition. It would exist for a five-year waiting period, should the applicants choose to apply for citizenship. Further, there were legislative provisions to grant social grants in exceptional circumstances and even to extend the definition of citizens.[22] Ngcobo J judged successful the state's arguments in favour of limiting social assistance in these instances to South African citizens and not permanent residents. The state had raised justification arguments that included controlling the rising costs of the social assistance system, reducing the incentive for foreign nationals to immigrate to South Africa, and promoting the need for resident immigrants to be self-sufficient.[23] In addition, the social assistance limitation effectively provided an incentive for such permanent residents to naturalise (to turn their permanent residence into citizenship) — a powerful reason in the argument of Ngcobo J.[24] 'The unequivocal declaration of loyalty and commitment that an alien can give to a country is through naturalisation and taking the oath of allegiance. After this a permanent resident becomes a citizen and thus qualifies for social security benefits.'[25] Ngcobo J thus would have found the limitation on the section 27 right to be reasonable and would have decided the case differently from the majority.[26]

The difference in approach between the majority and the minority judgments in *Khosa* should not be overstated. Still, the animating spirit for Ngcobo J's opinion is that of citizenship as an exclusive membership community with relatively sharply defined boundaries and envisioning full political participation in a Republic, whereas the spirit of the majority is the less sharply defined South African tradition of citizenship as lawful residence, mixed together with elements of a post-nationalist universal human rights culture. It is also worth mentioning that the

---

[22] Op cit: paras 116–118.
[23] Op cit: para 126.
[24] Op cit: para 130.
[25] Ibid.
[26] Op cit: paras 134–135. Ngcobo J's reasoning was limited in this respect and did not extend to the claims for dependency and child support grants where he noted that the discrimination hits the dependant through the primary caregiver.

underlying vision of neither Justice appears to draw significantly on a view of citizenship as membership in a cultural bloc.[27]

The tension apparent in *Khosa* between Mokgoro's lawful residence concept of citizenship and Ngcobo's more republican vision may also arguably be seen in the later Constitutional Court case of *Kaunda*. In a matter concerning South African citizens engaging in reprehensible mercenary activity but left stranded in Equatorial Guinea, the majority judgment delivered on 4 August 2004 and penned by Chaskalson CJ arguably broke new ground in international law and articulated an extra-territorial state duty of diplomatic protection of nationals. This duty was both based in and contrasted with the duty that the state owed to its residents within the territory.[28] Chaskalson CJ noted that foreigners lost their rights to protection by the South African government of life and dignity and not to be punished in a cruel and unusual way when they were outside the territory of South Africa. His question was whether section 7(2) gave citizens more rights.[29] The strong emphasis here on territoriality and extra-territoriality reflects the lawful residence character of South African citizenship. This aspect was combined with the reasoning where citizenship (given in section 3 of the Constitution), and thereby nearly always nationality, entitled the citizen to request diplomatic protection as a benefit of citizenship.[30] Chaskalson's majority judgment quoted and used the language in section 7(1): 'This Bill of Rights is a cornerstone of democracy in South Africa. It enshrines the rights of all people in our country and affirms the democratic values of human dignity, equality and freedom.'[31] This clause and particularly the first part of the second sentence — 'It enshrines the rights of all people in our country' — seems destined to be the cornerstone of the understanding of the lawful residence character of citizenship in South

---

27 Klaaren, 2000: 221–252; Klaaren, 2001: 304–325.
28 *Kaunda and Others v President of the Republic of South Africa* (CCT 23/04) [2004] ZACC 5 (4 August 2004); 2005 (4) SA 235 (CC); 2004 (10) BCLR 1009 (CC) para 1–145. Five other judges joined in this judgment: Langa, Moseneke, Yacoob, Van der Westhuizen and Skweyiya JJ.
29 Op cit: para 36.
30 Op cit: para 63.
31 Op cit: para 37.

Africa.[32] It also resonates with the fifth line of the Preamble to the Constitution, stating that the people of South Africa 'believe that South Africa belongs to all who live in it, united in our diversity'.[33]

The *Kaunda* majority contrasts with a concurrence by Ngcobo J as well as a dissent by O'Regan J. Ngcobo J's concurrence clearly understands South African citizenship rights to be consistent with a republican notion of the citizen. Ngcobo noted the positive duty of the state to protect its citizens within its border and wished the right of citizenship to be construed purposively 'so as to give it content and meaning'. He decides diplomatic protection is at least a benefit if not a right of citizenship.[34] In a somewhat similar approach, the dissent of O'Regan J (who would have granted further relief to the mercenaries than did the majority) likewise explored the degree of necessity of giving extra-territorial rights to South African citizens although perhaps only to avoid giving no meaning to this constitutional concept. At least within the confines of the *Kaunda* case, the concurrence and the dissent both extend and uphold diplomatic protection to be enjoyed by citizens and not by permanent residents. In this, they contrast with the conceptual understanding underlying the majority refusal to extend relief (at least in the circumstances presented to the Court in that case) to these citizens outside South African borders.

A specific future case in the Constitutional Court may well resolve some or all of the formal doctrinal aspects of these debates. But the broader social debate over the meaning of citizenship in post-apartheid South Africa cannot be decided in a court, even by a majority vote of the judges of the Constitutional Court. That debate happens in society more widely and crucially in South African society within the arena of immigration politics.

---

32 Klaaren, 2008: 60-1-16.
33 Constitution of the Republic of South Africa, 1996.
34 *Kaunda and Others v President of the Republic of South Africa* (CCT 23/04) [2004] ZACC 5 (4 August 2004); 2005 (4) SA 235 (CC); 2004 (10) BCLR 1009 (CC) para 180.

CONTEMPORARY SOUTH AFRICAN CITIZENSHIP POLICY

The contemporary Department of Home Affairs is very different from its direct ancestor, the Commissioner of Asiatic and Immigration Affairs, and just as different from the fragmented departments of apartheid South Africa. But it is still at the heart of significant administrative contestation over the meaning of citizenship in South Africa. The Green Paper on International Migration released in 2016 presents an initiative to delink residency from citizenship — albeit confined at the present to the policy issues of asylum-seekers and refugees. This initiative can be seen as part of the development of a type of republican citizenship that is distinct from and arguably at odds with the tradition of residence-based citizenship that developed in South Africa from 1897 to 1937.

The Green Paper's initiative can also be understood as aligned with what is termed the new politics of immigration worldwide — a politics which leaves behind the immigration-friendly (if also racist) identities of settler societies. Instead of aiming to facilitate immigration this new politics intends to prevent it.[35]

The Green Paper's targeting of the refugee population is no accident. While recognised refugees are only a small proportion of the South African population — in the order of 0.2 per cent — the issue is significant not only for the refugee population but also for South Africa's self-understanding.[36] People seeking refuge in South Africa occupy the same liminal space in the politics of South African citizenship today as did Asians and extra-Union Africans in the past. This drive to delink residency and citizenship for long-term refugees in South Africa presents yet another instance of the ongoing contestation of democracy and citizenship. South Africans concerned to fulfil the Constitution's ever-changing promise of transformation should resist the invitation to allow most refugees a second-class citizenship only and should instead explore diverse ways to include refugees in this open and democratic society at the southern end of Africa.

On 24 June 2016, the Department of Home Affairs published for discussion and comment its draft policy on international migration. The

---

35   Dauvergne, 2016.
36   Klotz, 2016: 170–229.

Green Paper presents an overview of international migration in South Africa, summarises the evolution of the international migration policy and presents statistical profiles of contemporary international migrants. Migrants from Africa and Asia are prominent in the Green Paper. To take one example, the Green Paper notes that '[t]he highest number of applications for permanent residence [are] from Zimbabwean nationals followed by foreign nationals from China, India, Nigeria and Pakistan. [These] five countries accounted for 68% of all applications'.[37] As one would expect of a policy document in the twenty-first century, the Green Paper calls for a new international migration policy for South Africa which 'embrace[s] global opportunities while safeguarding our sovereignty and ensuring public safety and national security'.[38] Still, the distinct impression is that of old wine in new bottles, albeit better managed ones. The limits to change are clear and at times even frankly acknowledged:[39]

> *National thinking and attitudes to international migration are currently influenced by an unproductive debate between those who call for stricter immigration controls and those who call for controls to be relaxed ... SA has not yet built a consensus at policy, legislative and strategic levels on how to manage international migration for development. What is proposed in the Green Paper is that by adopting a managed migration approach we can work together to achieve common goals.*

On the whole, the Green Paper seems to validate Audie Klotz's claim that South Africa has so far failed to build a strong enough rights-markets coalition to overcome its new economic nationalism.[40] It also would appear to validate Catherine Dauvergne's claim that the collision of economic and human rights discourses has resulted in a paralysis of policy globally — a trend of which South Africa may have been a

---

[37] Department of Home Affairs, 2016: 28.
[38] Op cit: 9.
[39] Ibid.
[40] Klotz, 2016: 215–227.

harbinger.[41] Mercifully, it does not partake of the worst of global efforts to isolate Africa[42] — instead at the least embracing an African rhetoric.

While there is much to explore, discuss and debate in the Green Paper and the policy proposals it contains, its most relevant section for current purposes is the three-page section on the management of residency and naturalisation.[43] This small section contains a distinct and two-fold change to current policy. After presenting an analysis of the situation, this section of the Green Paper proposes and details an ongoing intervention that is titled simply and revealingly 'Delinking of residency from citizenship', an intervention which largely would be played out with respect to refugees. It is worth quoting in full the four key paragraphs of this section under the above title. According to the Green Paper,

> [t]here should be no automatic progression or right to permanent residency or citizenship in law or in practice; and the granting of permanent residency and citizenship should be delinked. For reasons given above, refugees should not be allowed to apply for permanent residence on the grounds of the number of years spent in the country. Refugees may still qualify under the Immigration Act to apply for permanent residence on other grounds, such as meeting skills and investment requirements.

The Green Paper goes on to argue that the 'granting of citizenship should be considered as being exceptional'.[44]

It should be clearly noted that it is asylum-seekers and refugees who are most prominent in this discussion. The immediate example and implication (and one quite clearly spelled out) of the delinking of residency and citizenship is to sharply reduce the opportunities for recognised refugees to become either permanent residents or South African nationals. Currently, section 27(d) of the Immigration Act

---

41 Dauvergne, 2016: 196, 204–208.
42 Landau, 2017.
43 Department of Home Affairs, 2016: 39–41.
44 Op cit: 54–56.

authorises the granting of permanent residence to recognised refugees.[45] And refugees admitted for permanent residence may apply for naturalisation as citizens in terms of section 5 of the Citizenship Act.[46]

It would be a mistake to see this proposal as the mere momentary policy fad of anonymous Green Paper authors. This proposal for delinking must be recognised as a subtle yet significant development in line with other developments. As the previous chapters have demonstrated, development and change in the legal culture of citizenship — in the self-understanding of a nation — is of long and by no means determined trajectory. This means that the effects of the migration-derived and migration-filled concept of South African citizenship persist to the present day. Nonetheless, some of the currents in contemporary South African politics push hard against the tradition of a residence-based citizenship. This is the context in which we must understand the Green Paper's call to reduce avenues to citizenship for current refugees.

REFLECTIONS ON THE NEW SOUTH AFRICAN IMMIGRATION POLITICS: TOWARDS AFROPOLITAN DENIZENSHIP?

As has been shown above there is a contemporary call for sharply limiting integration of even recognised refugees into South African society. Such a call is in fact consistent with one pole of an important debate over the meaning of citizenship in one of the crucial institutions at the heart of the South African constitutional democracy, the Constitutional Court. How did we get to this point? In great part the weakness of South Africa's tradition of residence-based citizenship is of course the legacy of apartheid. The tradition was never allowed to develop to its full potential; citizenship and nationality were formal for most of the population rather than substantive. In the real sense entailed by the term 'belonging', South Africa did not belong to all who lived within it until 1994. Not only political participation and the right to vote but economic opportunities and cultural attachment to the nation were curtailed through white privilege and power. The negative and limiting

---

[45] Immigration Act 13 of 2002, section 27(d).
[46] South African Citizenship Act 88 of 1995, section 5.

effects of apartheid radiated throughout society and continue through to the present.

It did not have to be this way. Despite its introduction as an empty status at its origins, the concept of Union nationality could have been developed in order to fashion a substantive concept of South African citizenship. Most obviously, nationality and the franchise could have been linked together. Or Union nationality could have been used as a category in the policies related to land ownership or job reservations. Such substantive use would not necessarily have entailed an expansion of the rights of non-Europeans; it could well have entailed their restriction. Indeed, the criteria for Union nationality could have been amended to provide for an explicitly racial citizenship. Nationality policy could have used the same sort of explicit filtering mechanisms already at work in immigration laws towards the same end.

But it is this way. These political possibilities and potential formal legal developments are counterfactual ones. Except through the perverse avenue of the homelands regime in the apartheid epoch of citizenship,[47] South African nationality policy was not used in an innovative or even halting or grudging way as a tool for substantively addressing the pressing national problems of the day. Instead, these questions were addressed in significant part through more informal control over movement, through influx control, apartheid planning and a policy of mass deportations. Insofar as Union nationality achieved salience, it did so firmly within the migration policy context rather than as an independent concept.

This history of the control of mobility has brought those living in South Africa to the current place and moment. As shown above, a principled argument has now emerged — having nothing to do with apartheid — against the tradition of South Africa belonging to all who live within it. The new republican line of thought argues cogently and within a rights-based framework for reserving the primary benefits of inclusion in the South African polity to those with formal status as South African citizens. While this line of argument is muted, it is significant, arguably ascendant, and surfaces in numerous documents in the public sphere.

---

47   Klotz, 2016: 113–169.

The rise of this new republican line of thought coincides with the argument raised by some scholars of immigration and citizenship that a new politics of immigration is emerging globally and that settler societies form no exception. Catherine Dauvergne has argued that political traditions — whether for good or for ill — rooted in the practices and traditions of settler societies have lost their salience and potency in the beginning of the twenty-first century. In part due to this decline, a new set of 'mean-spirited' political discourses and practices of immigration have emerged globally. This new politics of immigration may be seen in discourses of fortress Europe and newly protectionist America.[48] As she puts it: 'Freed from settlement, society and colonial linkages, the new politics of immigration is grounded in sharp distinctions between sought-after highly mobile individuals on the one hand and illegal migrants on the other.'[49] The rights of refugees are both caught within and contribute to this global current and are increasingly precarious, with the 'asylum crisis' deriving in part from the open-ended nature of refugee law and its variable implementation by receiving states.[50]

Some forward-looking scholars of citizenship have argued for radical doctrinal changes in order to provide for more flexible conceptions of sovereignty and citizenship. For instance, the American constitutional scholar Alex Aleinikoff has urged the US federal government to negotiate First Nations compacts with people and US nationals in the American overseas territories in the Pacific and the Atlantic in order to affirm through such compacts more durable forms of self-government. In this sort of imagined future path, citizenship should be 'decentred', and understood as a commitment to an inter-generational national project, not as a basis for denying rights to immigrants, foreigners or non-nationals.[51] Others have called for the telling of persuasive and compelling stories at the level of the individual with the potential for disrupting the new politics of immigration.[52]

---

[48] Dauvergne, 2016.
[49] Ibid, 8.
[50] Op cit: 39–61.
[51] Aleinikoff, 2009.
[52] Dauvergne, 2016: 212.

What might a commitment to an inter-generational national project mean for South Africa? What might such compelling and disruptive personal stories be? What is the way forward after expunging internal colonialism?[53] If those who perceive an ascendant racial nationalism are correct, how can the agency and voice in politics of all South Africans be protected? Consistent with the call for a plurality of notions of democracy and citizenship, I will conclude here by sketching some currently live forms of democracy and citizenship. Elements from these constellations might be combined (and left out) in various permutations.

One such form of democracy and citizenship might fire up its imagination with a democratically informed understanding of a people. This form might be understood as exemplified in South Africa's cities.[54] Understand this as a reassertion of the rights of those who are living in South Africa, a re-reading of the preamble view of citizenship identified above with Justice Mokgoro. Ivor Chipkin, for instance, explicitly links his political philosophy with the preamble view of citizenship. He states: '[t]he South African people as a unified concept is composed of those individuals *living* in the territory of South Africa.'[55] The emphasis is in the original. For Chipkin, the proper limit for a people as a democracy may be specified. Such a boundary 'encloses citizens who share a special solidarity produced in and through democratic encounters'. South Africa meets his definition, though it cannot rest easy. As he states,[56]

> [e]very state is in itself cosmopolitan, indistinct and contingent because its borders never coincide with any one ethnic or cultural or religious group, and because its particular social character is not the expression of some or other pre-given identity. Yet we must struggle for this basic fact to become part of the democratic imaginary itself.

---

53   Steinmetz 2014: 84. Steinmetz argues that '[t]he idea of internal colonialism seems to make a useful distinction only where the ancestors of current ruling elites arrived as colonial conquerors and where the internal colony is descended from the natives conquered by the original colonizers'.
54   Madondo, 2016; Nuttall and Mbembe, 2008.
55   Chipkin, 2007: 186.
56   Op cit: 218

The South African Constitution itself provides resources and platforms for such efforts, including further rights charters.[57]

Another form of decentred democracy and citizenship based in South Africa might take participation in the political project of the nation as its starting point. Call this the ascendant democratic tradition of those who are voting now in South Africa, a reinterpretation of the new republican view of citizenship identified above with Justice Ngcobo. Something along these lines is offered in words by Rev Frank Chikane, reflecting on his years in government service as Director-General of the Presidency during the Mbeki years:[58]

> *In my opinion, the greatest risk this country faces is the danger of compromised (and corrupt) leaders who not only serve their own interests but also those of the people who compromised them — be these individual business people, foreign and intelligence entities, or even countries. This is a force capable of negating our strategic objectives of ending poverty and changing the quality of lives of all South Africans. It is this threat that we must fight by all means to ensure that we achieve the strategic objectives of the N[ational] D[emocratic] R[evolution].*

Chikane's church in Soweto has been publicly linked to a model of community action combining an anti-poverty strategy with the anti-xenophobia campaign — one based on 'a place based approach, one family at a time and one community a time'.[59]

Another form of democracy and citizenship based in Africa would be at the same time territorial (indeed continental, African that is) yet also universal. Such a vision might start from a number of places including blackness,[60] the Carribean,[61] a historical understanding of cultural

---

57 Klaaren, 2009: 82–90.
58 Chikane, 2013: 341.
59 The SACC Update on the Xenophobic Challenges in South Africa|The Methodist Church of Southern Africa.
60 *openDemocracy*, 2016; Pierre, 2013.
61 Collis-Buthelezi, 2015: 37–54.

citizenship,[62] or exploring the reinvention of pan-Africanism in an age of xenophobia. Indeed, there appears to be no constitutional bar in South Africa to giving people with African Union citizenship local voting rights. In an essay entitled 'Scrap the borders that divide Africans', Achille Mbembe has argued that[63]

> ours is ... an era of planetary entanglement ... The capacity to decide who can move and who can settle, where and under what conditions, will be at the core of the political struggle over sovereignty. The right of non-citizens to cross national borders and enter a host country may not have been formally abolished yet. But, as shown by countless ongoing incidents, it is becoming increasingly procedural and can be suspended or revoked at any time and under any pretext ... Within the continent itself, postcolonial states have failed to articulate a common legislative framework and policy initiatives in relation to border management, the upgrading of civil registries, visa liberalisation, or the treatment of third-country nationals residing legally in member states ... The fetishisation of the nation-state has done untold damage to Africa's destiny in the world. The human, economic, cultural and intellectual cost of the existing border regime in the continent has been colossal. It is time to bring it to closure.

Mbembe offers a vision of a way forward:[64]

> To become a vast area of freedom of movement is arguably the biggest challenge Africa faces in the 21st century ... The continent must open itself to itself. It must be turned into a vast space of circulation. This is the only way for it to become its own center in a multipolar world ... The next phase of Africa's decolonisation is about granting mobility to all her people and reshaping the terms of membership in a political and cultural ensemble that is not confined to the nation-state.

---

62 Obarrio, 2014.
63 Mbembe, 2017.
64 Ibid.

This is a call which recognises that much of South Africa's history is a history of movement, of circulation — that is how we have built our cities. In this view we need to move from a citizenship based on attachment to territory to one based on attachment to a pluralist world. We should push for a vision that does not conflate the *demos* with *ethnos* — the accident of birth. Social movements and civil society ought to put pressure on states for an overarching framework on rights which will have political membership in this sense.

One might term this vision one of Afropolitan denizenship. Contained within the historical development of South African citizenship — but yet also something new — may lie the seeds of a completely new concept driving citizenship globally, that of denizenship. This concept is usually defined as granting membership in a community on the basis of residence rather than nationality. Denizenship is a contemporary concept with global as well as local import, since it represents one of the directions in which citizenship may move (in part through increasing its attention to inter-generational equity in addition to the bare notion of lawful residence).[55]

Within each of these constellations of democracy and citizenship there are words and notions that are compelling and potentially disruptive. South Africa is an important place from which to start thinking the new politics of immigration — what some have called apartheid without apartheid — anew. To engage in this conversation would turn against the proposed policy of strictly separating residency and citizenship from refugee status and would turn towards exploring new forms of citizenship for the twenty-first century. While one can easily overstate the exemplary character of its polity, South Africa may still offer a guide to the future direction of the content of citizenship. Exploring these possibilities points to the expansion of social justice not through an increase in rights, but through a change in the right to bear rights. South African legal developments not only draw upon but contribute to global ones.[66]

---

65   Aleinikoff, 2009.
66   Klug, 2000.

Bibliography

Primary sources
Annual Reports
1911 Natal Annual Report
1912 Natal Annual Report
1916 Natal Annual Report
1919 Annual Report
1925 Annual Report
1926 Natal Annual Report

Year Books
1917–1921 *Year Books*
1917 *Year Book*
1919 *Year Book of the Union*
1921 *Year Book*
1923 *Year Book*
1924 *Year Book*
1926 *Year Book*
1931–1932 *Year Book*

CIA – the archives of the Commissioner of Immigration and Asiatic Affairs, held in the National Archives, Pretoria.

Secondary sources
Aleinikoff, T A. 2009. *Semblances of sovereignty: The constitution, the state, and American citizenship.* Cambridge: Harvard University Press.
Baldoz, R. 2011. 'The strange career of the Filipino "national": Empire, citizenship, and racial statecraft', in *The third Asiatic invasion: Migration and empire in Filipino America, 1898–1946.* New York: New York University Press.

Barnes, T. 1997. '"Am I a man?": Gender and the pass laws in urban colonial Zimbabwe, 1930–80'. *African Studies Review*, 40(1): 59–81.

Beinart, W. 2001. *Twentieth-century South Africa*. Oxford: Oxford University Press.

Bhana, S. 1991. 'Indentured Indian emigrants to Natal, 1860–1902: A study based on ships' lists'. http://repository.tufs.ac.jp/handle/10108/59960 (Accessed 22 June 2016).

Bhana, S and Brain, JB. 1990. *Setting down roots: Indian migrants in South Africa, 1860–1911*. Johannesburg: Witwatersrand University Press.

Bradford, H. 1993. 'Getting away with murder: "Mealie kings", the state and foreigners', in *Apartheid's genesis, 1935–1962*, edited by P L Bonner, P Delius and D Posel. Johannesburg: Ravan Press.

Bradlow, E. 1978. 'Immigration into the Union 1910–1948: Policies and attitudes'. PhD dissertation. Cape Town: University of Cape Town.

Breckenridge, K. 1998. 'The rise and fall of a public sphere on the South African gold mines, 1920 to 1931'. *Comparative Studies in Society and History*, 40(1): 71–108.

Breckenridge, K. 2014. 'Flesh made words: Fingerprinting and the fantasy of documentary panopticism, 1900–1930'. Occasional papers of Roskilde University, International Development Studies, 23: 76–96.

Budlender, G. 1985. 'Incorporation and exclusion: Recent developments in labour law and influx control'. *South African Journal on Human Rights*, 1: 3–9.

Cape Times (5 April 1934) (Chap 8).

Chanock, M. 1977. *Unconsummated union: Britain, Rhodesia and South Africa, 1900–45*. Manchester: Manchester University Press.

Chanock, M. 2001. *The making of South African legal culture 1902–1936: Fear, favour and prejudice*. Cambridge: Cambridge University Press.

Chikane, F. 2013. *The things that could not be said: From A(IDS) to Z(imbabwe)*. 1st edition. Johannesburg: Picador, Africa.

Chin, GJ. 2002. 'Regulating race: Asian exclusion and the administrative state'. *Harvard Civil Rights-Civil Liberties Law Review*, 37.

Chipkin, I. 2007. *Do South Africans exist?: Nationalism, democracy and the identity of the people*. Johannesburg: Wits University Press.

Christopher, AJ. 2009. 'Delineating the nation: South African censuses 1865–2007'. *Political Geography*, 28 (2): 101–109.

Christopher J. 2014. *Unreasonable histories: Nativism, multiracial lives, and the genealogical imagination in British Africa.* Durham: Duke University Press.

Collis-Buthelezi, VJ. 2015. 'Caribbean regionalism, South Africa, and mapping new world studies'. *Small Axe,* 19 (1 46): 37–54.

Constitution of the Republic of South Africa, Act 108 of 1996. http://www.constitutionalcourt.org.za/site/theconstitution/english-2013.pdf (Accessed 27 November 2013).

Corder, H. 1984. *Judges at work: The role and attitudes of the South African Appellate Judiciary, 1910–1950.* Cape Town: Juta & Company.

Cott, NF. 1998. 'Marriage and women's citizenship in the United States, 1830–1934'. *The American Historical Review,* 103 (5): 1440–1474.

Crush, JS, Jeeves, A and Yudelman, D. 1991. *South Africa's labor empire: A history of black migrancy to the gold mines.* Boulder: Westview Press.

Dauvergne, C. 2005. *Humanitarianism, identity, and nation: Migration laws in Canada and Australia.* Vancouver: UBC Press.

Dauvergne, C. 2016. *The new politics of immigration and the end of settler societies.* Cambridge: Cambridge University Press.

Department of Home Affairs. 2016. Green paper on international migration. http://www.gov.za/sites/files/40088-;on738.pdf

Desai, A and Vahed, GH. 2010. *Inside Indian Indenture: A South African Story, 1860–1914.* Pretoria: HSRC Press.

Dhupelia-Mesthrie, U. 2007. 'The place of India in South African history: Academic scholarship, past, present and future'. *African Studies,* 57 (1): 12–34.

Dhupelia-Mesthrie, U. 2009. 'The passenger Indian as worker: Indian immigrants in Cape Town in the early twentieth century'. *African Studies.* 68 (1): 111–134.

Dubow, S. 1989. *Racial segregation and the origins of apartheid in South Africa, 1919–36.* Berlin: Springer.

Dubow, S. 2006. *A commonwealth of knowledge: Science, sensibility, and white South Africa 1820–2000.* Oxford: Oxford University Press.

Dugard, J. 1994. *International law: A South African perspective.* Cape Town: Juta & Company.

Duncan, D. 1995. *The mills of God: The state and African labour in South Africa, 1918–1948.* Johannesburg: Witwatersrand University Press.

Evans, I. 1997. *Bureaucracy and race: Native administration in South Africa*. Oakland: University of California Press.

Evans, J and Philips, D. 2001. '"When there's no safety in numbers": Fear and the franchise in South Africa — the case of Natal', in *Law, history, colonialism: The reach of empire*, edited by D E Kirkby and C Coleborne. Manchester: Manchester University Press: 91–105.

Foster, H, Berger, BL and Buck, AR. 2009. *The grand experiment: Law and legal culture in British settler societies*. Vancouver: UBC Press.

Gilroy, P. 2016. '[I]n search of a not necessarily safe starting point ...', *openDemocracy*, April 30, 2016, https://www.opendemocracy.net/paul-gilroy-rosemary-bechler/paul-gilroy-in-search-of-not-very-safe-starting-point. (Accessed 10 May 2016).

Gorman, D. 2006. *Imperial citizenship: Empire and the question of belonging*. Manchester: Manchester University Press.

Harries, P. 1994. *Work, culture, and identity: Migrant laborers in Mozambique and South Africa, C. 1860–1910*. Cape Town: Pearson Education.

Hassim, A. 2002. *The lotus people*. Johannesburg: Real African Publishers.

Hattersley, AF. 1950. *The British settlement of Natal: A study in imperial migration*. New York: Cambridge University Press.

Hellmann, E. 1948. *Rooiyard: A sociological survey of an urban native slum yard*. Manchester: Manchester University Press.

Hindson, D. 1987. *Pass controls and the urban African proletariat in South Africa*. Athens: Ohio University Press.

Hulsebosch, DJ. 2003. 'The ancient constitution and the expanding empire: Sir Edward Coke's British jurisprudence'. *Law and History Review* 21(3): 439–482.

Huttenback, RA. 1976. *Racism and empire: White settlers and colored immigrants in the British self-governing colonies, 1830–1910*. Ithaca: Cornell University Press.

Indian Opinion (16 August 1913)

Indian Opinion (23 August 1913)

Jeeves, A. 1985. *Migrant labour in South Africa's mining economy: The struggle for the gold mines' labour supply, 1890–1920*. Montreal: McGill-Queen's University Press.

Jeeves, A. 1986. 'Migrant labour and South African expansion, 1920–1950'. *South African Historical Journal*, 18(1): 73–92.

Kahn, E. 1949. 'The pass laws', in *Handbook on Race Relations in South Africa*, edited by E Hellmann and L Abrahams. Aldershot and Burlington: Octagon Books.

Katzenellenbogen, SE. 1982. *South Africa and southern Mozambique: Labour, railways, and trade in the making of a relationship*. Manchester: Manchester University Press.

Kennedy, WPM and Schlosberg, HJ. 1935. The *law and custom of the South African Constitution: A treatise on the constitutional and administrative law of the Union of South Africa, the mandated territory of South-West Africa, and the South African crown territories*. London: Oxford University Press.

Kirkby, DE and Coleborne, C. 2001. *Law, history, colonialism: The reach of empire*. Manchester: Manchester University Press.

Klaaren, J. 1998. 'Non-citizens and constitutional equality — Larbi-Odam v. The Member of the Executive Council for Education (North-West Province) 1998'. *South African Journal on Human Rights*', 14: 286–295.

Klaaren, J. 2000. 'Post-apartheid citizenship in South Africa', in *From migrants to citizens: membership in a changing world*, edited by DB Klusmeyer and TA Aleinikoff. Washington, DC: Carnegie endowment for international peace: 221–252.

Klaaren, J. 2001. 'Contested citizenship in South Africa', in *The post-apartheid constitutions: Perspectives on South Africa's basic law*, edited by P Andrews and S Ellmann. Johannesburg: Witwatersrand University Press: 304–325.

Klaaren, J. 2008. 'Citizenship', in *Constitutional Law of South Africa*, edited by S Woolman, 2nd revised and enlarged edition. Kenwyn: Juta and Company: 60: 1–16.

Klaaren, J. 2009. 'Human rights protection of foreign nationals'. *Industrial Law Journal* 30: 82–90.

Klaaren, J. 2010. 'Constitutional citizenship in South Africa'. *International Journal of Constitutional Law*, 8: 94–110.

Klotz, A. 2013. *Migration and national identity in South Africa, 1860–2010*. Cape Town: Cambridge University Press.

Klotz, A. 2016. 'Borders and the roots of xenophobia in South Africa'. *South African Historical Journal*, 68(2): 180–194.

Klug, H. 2000. *Constituting democracy: Law, globalism and South Africa's political reconstruction*. Cape Town: Cambridge University Press.

Klug, H. 2013. 'Constitutionalism, democracy and denial in post-apartheid South Africa', in *Demokratie-Perspektiven: Festschrift Für Brun-Otto Bryde Zum 70. Geburtstag*, edited by M Bäuerle, P Dann and A Wallrabenstein. Heidelberg: Mohr Siebeck.

Koessler, M. 1946. '"Subject," "Citizen," "National," and "Permanent Allegiance"', *Yale Law Journal*, 56: 58–76, 61–63.

Lambert, J. 2000. 'South African British? Or dominion South Africans? The evolution of an identity in the 1910s and 1920s'. *South African Historical Journal*, 43: 197–222.

Lambert, J. 2005. 'An identity threatened: White English-speaking South Africans, Britishness and dominion South Africanism, 1934–1939'. *Kleio*, 37(1): 50–70.

Landau, L. 2017. 'The containment chronotope: The European refugee "crisis" and shifting sovereignties in sub-Saharan Africa'. https://gallery.mailchimp.com/ebf39baff4da9ed51c02e6754/files/2880b840-773f-44f3-8089-c4357de85dba/LandauFloridaDraft.pdf. (Accessed 29 March 2017).

Langford, M, Cousins, B, Dugard, J and Madlingozu, T. 2013. *Socio-economic rights in South Africa: Symbols or substance?* Cape Town: Cambridge University Press.

Lee, C. 2014. *Unreasonable histories of Nativism, multi racial lines, and the genealogical immigration in British Africa*. Durham: Duke University Press.

Lourie, A. 1927. 'Administrative law in South Africa'. *South African Law Journal*, 44: 10–23.

Loveland, I. 1999. *By due process of law? Racial discrimination and the right to vote in South Africa, 1855–1960*. Oxford: Hart Publishing.

MacDonald, A. 2014. 'Forging the frontiers: Travellers and documents on the South Africa–Mozambique border, 1890s–1940s'. *Kronos*, 40:154–177.

Madondo, B. 2016. 'Searching in our hearts for a special place called home', *Sunday Times*, 18 December, http://www.timeslive.co.za/

sundaytimes/opinion/2016/12/18/Searching-in-our-hearts-for-a-special-place-called-home. (Accessed 7 April 2017).

Mamdani, M. 1996. *Citizen and subject: Contemporary Africa and the legacy of late colonialism*. Princeton: Princeton University Press.

Maylam, P. 2001. *South Africa's racial past: The history and historiography of racism, segregation, and apartheid*. Aldershot: Ashgate Publishing Company.

Mbembe A. 2001. *On the postcolony*. Oakland: University of California Press.

Mbembe A. 2017. 'Scrap the borders that divide Africans'. *The M&G Online*. https://mg.co.za/article/2017-03-17-00-scrap-the-borders-that-divide-africans/. (Accessed 22 March 2017).

Mbembé, JA. 2000. 'At the edge of the world: Boundaries, territoriality, and sovereignty in Africa'. *Public Culture*, 12(1): 259–284.

McIntyre, WD. 1999. 'The strange death of dominion status'. *Journal of Imperial Commonwealth History*, 27: 193–212.

McKeown, AM. 2008. *Melancholy order: Asian migration and the globalization of borders*. New York: Columbia University Press.

Nuttall, S and Mbembe, A. 2008. *Johannesburg: The elusive metropolis*. Durham: Duke University Press.

Obarrio, J. 2014. *The spirit of the laws in Mozambique*. Chicago: University of Chicago Press.

Pachai, B. 1971. *The international aspects of the South African Indian question, 1860–1971*. Cape Town: C Struik.

Parker, K. 2015. *Making foreigners*. Cambridge: Cambridge University Press.

Peberdy, S. 2009. *Selecting immigrants: National identity and South Africa's immigration policies, 1910–2008*. Johannesburg: Wits University Press.

Pierre, J. 2013. *The predicament of blackness: Postcolonial Ghana and the politics of race*. Chicago: University of Chicago Press.

Posel, D. 1991. *The making of apartheid, 1948-1961: Conflict and compromise*. Oxford: Clarendon Press.

Posel, D. 2000. 'A mania for measurement: Statistics and statecraft in the transition to apartheid', in *Science and Society in Southern Africa*, edited by S Dubow. Manchester: Manchester University Press: 116–142.

Posel, D. 2001. 'Race as common sense: Racial classification in twentieth-century South Africa'. *African Studies Review*, 44(2): 87–114.

Richardson, P. 1982. *Chinese mine labour in the Transvaal*. London: MacMillan Publishers Limited.

Rogers M. 1997. *Civic ideals: Conflicting visions of citizenship in Amerian history*. New Haven: Yale University Press.

Rogers M. 2001. 'Citizenship and the politics of people-building'. *Citizenship Studies*, 5(1): 73–96.

Saker, H. 1980. *The South African Flag Controversy, 1925-1928*. Cape Town: Oxford University Press.

Salyer, LE. 1995. *Laws harsh as tigers: Chinese immigrants and the shaping of modern immigration law*. Chapel Hill: University of North Carolina Press.

Scott, JC. 1999. *Seeing like a state: How certain schemes to improve the human condition have failed*. New Haven: Yale University Press.

Shapiro, KA. 2016. 'No exit? Emigration policy and the consolidation of apartheid'. *Journal of Southern African Studies*, 42(4): 763–781.

Shear, K. 1998. 'Constituting a state in South Africa: The dialectics of policing, 1900–1939'. PhD dissertation, Northwestern University, Evanston.

Sibanda, S. 2011. 'Not purpose-made! Transformative constitutionalism, post-independence constitutionalism and the struggle to eradicate poverty'. *Stellenbosch Law Review/Stellenbosch Regstydskrif* 22(3): 482–500.

Sibanda, S. 2017. 'When do you call time on a compromise? The future of transformative constitutionalism in South Africa'. https://www.academia.edu/32424578/When_do_you_call_time_on_a_compromise_The_future_of_transformative_constitutionalism_in_South_Africa. (Accessed 5 August 2017).

Smith, RM. 1997. *Civic ideals: Conflicting visions of citizenship in American history*. New Haven: Yale University Press.

Smith, RM. 2001. 'Citizenship and the politics of people-building'. *Citizenship Studies*, 5(1): 73—96.

Steinmetz, G. 2014. 'The sociology of empires, colonies, and postcolonialism'. *Annual Review of Sociology*, 40(1): 77–103.

'The SACC Update on the Xenophobic Challenges in South Africa|The Methodist Church of Southern Africa'. https://www.methodist.org.za/news/04242015-0906. (Accessed 6 April 2017).

The Star (21 August 1928) (Chap 8).

Thompson, L. 1938. 'Indian immigration into Natal, 1860–1872'. Master's dissertation. University of South Africa, Pretoria.

Thompson, LM. 1960. *The unification of South Africa: 1902–1910*. Oxford: Clarendon Press.

Torpey, J. 2000. *The invention of the passport: Surveillance, citizenship and the state*. Cambridge: Cambridge University Press.

Trew, HF. 1938. *African man hunts*. Glasgow: Blackie & Son Ltd.

Van Onselen, C. 2001. *New Babylon, new Nineveh: Everyday life on the Witwatersrand, 1886–1914*. Johannesburg: Jonathan Ball.

Vigneswaran, D and Quirk, J. 2015. *Mobility makes states: Migration and power in Africa*. Philadelphia: University of Pennsylvania Press.

Wells, JC. 1993. *We now demand!: The history of women's resistance to pass laws in South Africa*. Johannesburg: Witwatersrand University Press.

Wilder, G. 1999. 'Practicing citizenship in imperial Paris', in *Civil society and the political imagination in Africa: Critical perspectives*, edited by J L Comaroff and J Comaroff. Chicago: University of Chicago Press: 44–71.

Yap, M and Leong Man, D. 1996. *Colour, confusion and concessions: The history of the Chinese in South Africa*. Hong Kong: Hong Kong University Press.

Index

This index is in letter-by-letter alphabetical order; spaces, hyphens and introductory words such as 'a', 'and', 'of' and 'in' are ignored. A page number followed by an 'n' (12n) indicates that the information is contained in a note on that page; a number following the 'n' (12n3) indicates the number of the note.

A

Africans
  internal boundaries 129–134
  labour recruitment 119–124, 168–169
  migration regulation from 1911-1927 118–135
  migration regulation post-1927 152–183, 201, 205–206
  mobility regulation pre-Union 32–39
  Mozambique Convention 66, 79–80, 120, 165, 168, 196
  Native Affairs Department (NAD) 45–46, 118–124, 152–182
  Native Labour Regulation Act 15 of 1911 65n3, 87, 119, 120–121
  Native Laws Amendment Act 46 of 1937 185–186, 201–202, 205n60, 205n61
  Natives Act 31 of 1917 161n19
  pass laws 15, 30–39, 85–87
  Portuguese East Africa Agreement 79–80, 119–120
  regulation of extra-Union Africans 119–128, 153–183
  urban mobility 129–134, 201–202, 205–208
Afropolitan denizenship 219–222, 222–228
Asians
  see also Chinese; Indians
  Asiatic Inquiry Commission 100
  Asiatic Law Amendment Act 2 of 1907 (Transvaal) 24–25, 27, 57–58
  Asiatics in the Northern Districts of Natal Act 33 of 1927 139–140
  Asiatics Registration Amendment Act 36 of 1908 (Transvaal) 26–27, 83, 138–139
  Commissioner for Asiatic Affairs 114–115, 145
  Commissioner for Immigration and Asiatic Affairs 95–96, 111–117, 136, 183
  economic restrictions 22, 24, 27–28
  A Law To Provide Against the Influx of Asiatics and for the Removal of White Criminals Entering This State from Elsewhere (1891) 27–28, 61–62
  mobility restriction 136–142
  nationalised population 142
  Registrar of Asiatics 21, 23, 26–27, 87–94, 96–97, 138
  Transvaal Asiatic Registration Certificate (TARC) 26, 27, 152–153, 201, 205–206
asylum-seekers and refugees 50, 219–222, 224, 228

B

border control 47, 90–92, 196–198
British subjects
  pre-Union 22, 28, 32, 51, 54, 62
  Union 54, 73, 75–76, 82–83, 188–190, 192–194, 200, 203–204

C

Cape Town Agreement 96, 114
Chinese
  see also Asians
  Act 7 of 1904 (Natal) 42–43, 42n107, 43n110
  Act 15 of 1906 29
  Chinese Exclusion Act 37 of 1904 (Cape) 28–30, 51, 143–151

Chinese labour importation scheme 15, 39–46
  immigrants 24, 28–30
  Indentured Labour Laws (Temporary Continuance) Act of 1907 45
  Proclamation 70 of 1904 42–43, 43n109
  Trinidad Immigration Ordinance of 1893 41–42
CIAA *see* Commissioner for Immigration and Asiatic Affairs (CIAA)
citizenship
  see also nationality
  and denizenship 210–228
  legal culture 8–11
  migration and mobility 5–8
  population building 3–5
  pre-Union 48, 60, 61
  and residency 219–222
  Social Assistance Act 59 of 1992 213n9
  South African Citizenship Act 44 of 1949 188
  Union 64–65, 73–77, 82–83, 113–114, 185–187
citizenship in post-apartheid South Africa 210–228
  contemporary policy 219–222
  contesting views 212–218
  South African Citizenship Act 88 of 1995 221
Commissioner for Asiatic Affairs 114–115, 145
Commissioner for Immigration and Asiatic Affairs (CIAA) 95–96, 111–117, 136, 143–151
  role in regulation of African migration 152–183, 201, 205–206
Constitution of the Republic of South Africa, 1996 1, 2, 213, 213n11, 217–218
Constitution of the Republic of South Africa, Act 200 of 1993 209, 211

D
denizenship 210–228
Department of Home Affairs on International Migration, March 2017 210, 219–222

deportation and repatriation 155–164, 170–183

E
education tests in migration regulation 68, 104–106, 110, 136–137

F
facially neutral 14, 16, 22, 42, 47–48, 51, 60, 75–78, 188, 195
FLD (Foreign Labour Department) 42, 45
franchise 68–71, 73–76, 193

G
Gandhi 23–24, 23n, 26–27
Godley Commission 130–131, 132
Green Paper on International Migration 210, 219–222

I
Immigrants Appeal Boards 106–110
Immigrants Selection Board 187, 195, 199, 200
immigration bureaucracy in the Union 95–116
  administrative justice 106–110
  Commissioner for Immigration and Asiatic Affairs (CIAA) 111–117
  Immigrants Appeal Boards 106–110
  relationship with courts 102–106
  rule of law 101–111
immigration legislation of Natal 50–54
  Immigrants Restriction Act 1 of 1897 (Natal) 11, 12, 52–52
  Immigration Law 1 of 1876 (Natal) 86
  Immigration Restriction Act 30 of 1903 (Natal) 52–53
immigration legislation of the Cape 48–51
  Act 22 of 1867 (Cape) 174
  Act 23 of 1879 (Cape) 32–33
  Act 30 of 1895 (Cape) 33
  Act 35 of 1888 (Cape) 51
  Act 40 of 1902 (Cape) 33
  Immigration Act 30 of 1906 (Cape) 48–51, 48n2, 77n41
  Immigration Act 47 of 1902 (Cape) 48n1

Index

immigration legislation of the Orange Free State 60–62
  Admission and Expulsion of Aliens To or From the Orange Free State Law 18 of 1899 (Free State) 60–62, 77n41
  Indemnity and Peace Preservation Ordinance 25 of 1902 (High Commissioner) 62
immigration legislation of the Republic
  Admission of Persons to the Union Regulation Amendment Act 60 of 1961 2
  Immigration Act 13 of 2002 221–222, 222n45
immigration legislation of the Union 75–87, 185–208
  Aliens Act 1 of 1937 185, 187–188, 195, 199–203
  Immigrants Regulation Act 22 of 1913 2, 7, 47, 64–65, 77–89, 92–94, 95, 96, 97, 98–101, 103–105, 107–110, 111, 119–121, 123, 131–132, 135, 136–137, 138, 139, 141, 149, 150, 179, 181–182, 185, 203–204
  Immigration (Amendment) Act 15 of 1931 19, 140–141, 140n16, 141n17, 141n19, 185, 197–198, 199
  Immigration (Amendment) Act 19 of 1933 (Union) 30, 150, 187, 200n47
  Immigration Amendment Act 27 of 1937 185–186, 202–204
  Immigration Quota Act 8 of 1930 140, 140n16, 149, 185, 187–188, 193–203, 196
immigration legislation of Transvaal 54–60
  Immigrants Restriction Act 15 of 1907 (Transvaal) 24–27, 55, 57–60, 70, 77
  Indemnity and Peace Preservation Ordinance 25 of 1902 (High Commissioner) 62
  Indemnity and Peace Preservation Ordinance 38 of 1902 55–56
  Peace Preservation Ordinance 5 of 1903 (High Commissioner) 55–56
immigration politics in contemporary South Africa 222–228
Indian Immigration Trust Board 18, 18–21

Indian populations 15, 16–28, 111–116
Indians
  see also Asians
  Act 2 of 1870 (Natal) 17
  Act 2 of 1903 (Natal) 84
  Act 17 of 1895 (Natal) 20, 84n63, 84n64
  Act 19 of 1898 (Natal) 20–21, 20n17
  Act 28 of 1897 (Natal) 20–21, 139, 149
  Act 39 of 1905 (Natal) 21, 84n66
  Coolie Law Consolidation Law of 1869 17
  Immigration and Indian Relief (Further Provision) Act 37 of 1927 137–138, 145, 147–148, 148n41
  indentured Indians 98–99
  Indian Immigration Act 25 of 1891 (Natal) 17–20, 99
  Indian Immigration Bureau 116, 138
  Indian Immigration Law 25 of 1891 (Natal) 99
  Indian Immigration Trust Board 18–21
  Indian Laws Amendment Act 68 of 1963 18
  Indian populations 16–28, 111–116
  Indian Relief Act 22 of 1914 79n46, 84, 136n1, 136n2, 145n32
  Indian Repatriation Commissioner 100
  inter-governmental negotiations 111–114
  Law 3 of 1885 (Transvaal) 21–24, 26–27, 55–56, 60
  migration regulation in Natal 16–21
  migration regulation in the Orange Free State 27–28
  migration regulation in Transvaal 21–27
  passenger Indians 17, 18, 20
  Protector of Indian Immigrants 17, 18–21, 115–116
  Solomon Commission 136, 136n2
  Transvaal Asiatic Registration Certificates (TARC) 26, 27, 138–139, 140–141
Indian-South African Conference 114
industrial pass system 31, 33, 34–36, 38, 66
influx control 27, 129–134
  see also pass laws
  urban mobility 201–201, 205–208
Intercolonial Conference 1908 67–68

241

Interdepartmental Committee on the Native Pass Laws 130–131, 132
internal boundaries 129–134
international migration in post-apartheid South Africa 219–222

J
Jewish immigrants 187–188

L
labour migration 35–36, 66
 Chinese 40–46
 Indians 98–99
 industrial pass system 31, 33, 34–36, 38, 66
 labour bureaus 124–125
 labour depots 161–163
 labour districts 35–36, 37, 39, 120
 Labour Importation Ordinance 1904 40–45
 mining industry 39–42, 179–180
 Mozambicans 36, 37, 40, 79–80, 165–169
 Mozambique Convention 66, 119–120
 recruitment 86–87, 119–124, 168–169, 179–180, 186
 tramping system 36–37
Lange Commission 100
legal culture of South Africa 8–11
literacy tests in migration regulation 48, 52, 57, 58, 61, 80

M
migration administration 95–117
 bureaucracy 101–111
 nationalisation 96–101
migration regulation
 see also immigration; mobility regulation
 Africans 118–135, 152–183, 201, 205–206
 Cape Colony 28–30, 32–33, 137
 Chinese 28–30, 39–46
 Indians 16–28
 Natal 16–21
 nationalisation of African migration regulation 152–183
 nationalisation of Asian migration regulation 139–142
 national registration 138–141

Orange Free State 27–28
 pre-Union 16–46
 Transvaal 21–27, 58, 138–139, 140–141
 Union 75–87
 and Union nationality 193–194
mining industry 32, 34–37
 Chinese mine labour scheme 39–42
 Gold Law 14 of 1894 (Transvaal) 35
 recruitment of labour 86–87, 119–124, 168–169, 179–180
 Witwatersrand Native Labour Association (WNLA) 40, 122, 123, 179–180
mobility regulation
 see also immigration; migration regulation
 Africans 30–39, 84–87, 118–135
 Asians 7–8, 16–30, 83–84, 136–142
 Chinese 39–46, 137
 deportation and repatriation 155–164, 170–183
 in development of citizenship 7–8
 early practices 14–46
 Europeans 83
 nationalised population 136–142
 pass laws 30–32, 85–87
 population registration 16–30
mobility studies 5–6
Mozambique Convention 66, 79–80, 120, 165, 168, 196

N
NAD (Native Affairs Department) 45–46, 118–124, 152–182
nationalisation
 of African migration regulation 152–183
 of Asian migration regulation 139–142
 migration administration 96–101
 Nationalization and Amnesty Act 14 of 1932 193n27
nationalised population 136–142
nationality
 see also citizenship
 British Nationality in the Union and Naturalization and Status of Aliens Act 18 of 1926 185, 189, 200
 and citizenship in the Transvaal 60
 and franchise 73–76, 193

laws in the Cape and Natal 51–54
  in the Union 73–75, 82–83, 188–194, 203–208
Native Affairs Department (NAD) 45–46, 118–124, 152–182
Native Recruiting Corporation (NRC) 122, 123
naturalisation 22, 64–65, 73–74, 75–76, 191–191
  Act 18 of 1905 (Natal) 54n29, 54n31
  Aliens Naturalisation Act 2 of 1883 (Cape) 51
  Law 8 of 1874 54n29
  Naturalization of Aliens (Amendment) Ordinance 10 of 1904 (High Commissioner) 60n55
  Naturalization of Aliens Ordinance 1 of 1903 (High Commissioner) 62
  Naturalization of Aliens Act 4 of 1910 64–65, 75–76
  South West Africa Naturalization of Aliens Act 30 of 1924 97n2
NRC (Native Recruiting Corporation) 122, 123

P
passenger Indians 17, 18, 20
pass laws 15, 30–32, 85–87
  Act 9 of 1908 (Transvaal) 38
  Act 18 of 1909 (Transvaal) 38
  Interdepartmental Committee on the Native Pass Laws 130–131, 132
  labour districts 35–36, 37, 39, 120
  Law 3 of 1872 (Transvaal) 34
  Law 22 of 1895 (Transvaal) 35–36
  Natal Act of 1888 134
  Orange Free State Ordinance 28 of 1903 39n95
  Ordinance 28 of 1902 (High Commissioner) 38
  Proclamation 18 of 1903 38
  Proclamation 19 of 1901 (High Commissioner) 38n90
  Proclamation 35 of 1901 (High Commissioner) 38
  Proclamation 37 of 1901 (High Commissioner) 38

people-building 3
population building 3–5
population registration 16–30
population regulation Acts of 1930-1931 194–199
population regulation Acts of 1937 199–208
population-specific migration laws 16–30
Portuguese East Africa Agreement 79–80, 119–120
prohibited immigrants 77–81
  exemptions 28, 48–50, 52, 58, 78–80
  grounds for exclusion 48–51, 57–58, 61, 78, 143–151, 196–197
  Immorality Ordinance 59–60
Protector of Indian Immigrants 17, 18–21

R
refugees and asylum-seekers 50, 219–222, 224, 228
Refugees Act 130 of 1998 50
Registrar of Asiatics 21, 23, 26–27, 87–94, 96–97, 138
repatriation and deportation 155–164, 170–183
residency 200–201, 202–204
  and citizenship 212–222
resistance to migration regulation 25, 27
rule of law and immigration bureaucracy 101–111

S
Solomon Commission 136, 136n2

T
TARC (Transvaal Asiatic Registration Certificate) 26, 27, 138–139, 140–141
territoriality 71–73, 196–199
  extra-territorial state duty 217–218
  pre-Union immigration laws 47–62
  in unification process 70–72
tramping system 36–37
Transvaal Native Congress 38, 181

U
unification 64–94
  franchise 68–71, 73–76

immigration laws 65, 75–87, 194–208
Intercolonial Conference 1908 67–68
nationality 65, 73–74, 192–193
naturalisation 64–65, 73–74, 75–76, 190–191
political and economic issues 65–75
South Africa Act, 1909 67–68, 71–75
Union nationality 75–87, 185–209
  and immigration laws 75–87
  laws defining status 188–194
  population regulation 194–208
  Union Nationality and Flags Act 40 of 1927 185, 189, 191–192, 204n57

urban mobility 201–202, 205–208
  see also pass laws
  influx control 129–134
  Natives Urban Areas Act 21 of 1923 132–134, 181, 185–186, 201–202, 205n61

W

WNLA (Witwatersrand Native Labour Association) 40, 122, 123, 179–180

X

xenophobia 7–8, 211, 226–227